GRANTA

GRANTA 69, SPRING 2000
www.granta.com

EDITOR   *Ian Jack*
DEPUTY EDITOR   *Liz Jobey*
MANAGING EDITOR   *Karen Whitfield*
EDITORIAL ASSISTANT   *Sophie Harrison*

CONTRIBUTING EDITORS   *Neil Belton, Pete de Bolla, Ursula Doyle,*
Will Hobson, Gail Lynch, Blake Morrison, Andrew O'Hagan, Lucretia Stewart

ASSOCIATE PUBLISHER   *Sally Lewis*
FINANCE   *Geoffrey Gordon*
SALES   *Claire Gardiner*
PUBLICITY   *Louisa Renton*
SUBSCRIPTIONS   *John Kirkby, Darryl Wilks, Pamela Rowe*
PUBLISHING ASSISTANT   *Mark Williams*
TO ADVERTISE CONTACT   *Jenny Shramenko* 0171 274 0600

PUBLISHER   *Rea S. Hederman*

Granta, 2-3 Hanover Yard, Noel Road, London N1 8BE
Tel 0171 704 9776 Fax 0171 704 0474
e-mail for editorial: editorial@grantamag.co.uk

Granta US, 1755 Broadway, 5th Floor, New York, NY 10019-3780, USA

TO SUBSCRIBE call 0171 704 0470 or e-mail subs@grantamag.co.uk
A one-year subscription (four issues) costs £24.95 (UK), £32.95 (rest of Europe) and £39.95 (rest
of the world).

Granta is printed in the United States of America. The paper used in this publication meets the
minimum requirements of American National Standard for Information Sciences — Permanence of
Paper for Printed Library Materials, ANSI Z39.48-1984. ∞

Granta is published by Granta Publications and distributed in the United Kingdom by Bloomsbury,
38 Soho Square, London W1V 5DF, and in the United States by Granta Direct Sales, 1755
Broadway, 5th Floor, New York, NY 10019-3780, USA.
This selection copyright © 2000 Granta Publications.

Design: The Senate
Cover photograph: Demitrios Tsafendas, Bailey's African History Archive;
back cover photographs by Kent Klich

ISBN 0 903141 34 5

The Abomination

Paul Golding

One of
the most
outstanding
literary
debuts of
recent years

PICADOR

www.picador.com

From a forest of fairy tales to a New world
of émigrés – a mesmerising debut

'Not only traverses time and geography, but sensibility as well...
a novel of great mythic weight' *Amazon.com*

JUDY BUDNITZ

If I Told You Once

GRANTA 69

The Assassin

HAMISH HAMILTON
SPRING 2000

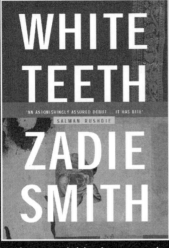

'An astonishingly assured
debut'
Salman Rushdie
27-01-00 • £12.99

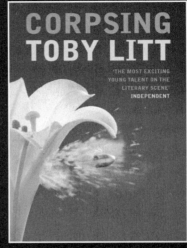

'The most exciting young talent
on the literary scene'
Independent
03-02-00 • £9.99

'Magnificently complex and
imaginatively satisfying...'
New Books in German
29-06-00 • £14.99

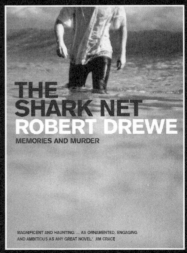

'As ornamented, engaging and
ambitious as any great novel'
Jim Crace
06-04-00 • £9.99

GRANTA

THE ASSASSIN
Henk van Woerden

Translated from the Dutch
by Dan Jacobson

Demitrios Tsafendas, circa 1922

LIZA KEY

1. The emigrants

On 11 February 1955 a man could be seen wandering about the streets of Hamburg. Sometimes he halted and stared up at the branches of trees. He wore a hat but no overcoat. Absorbed in conversation with himself, he crossed Langenhorner Chaussee. It was shortly after nine in the evening; the street was empty and ill-lit. A half-hour later he entered the main gate of the General Hospital and made his way to the emergency ward.

In broken German, speaking excitedly, he told his story to the porter. He had swallowed twenty sleeping pills, he said. Exactly twenty.

Damp snowflakes clung to his frizzy hair.

Dr Hans Nachtwey, the doctor on duty, thought the man must be either a Turk or a Syrian. He was big, with a swarthy complexion, a large nose and a double chin. His jacket was buttoned tightly across his stomach. He swayed back and forth on his chair, his arms clamped around himself. Nachtwey examined his reflexes and the pupils of his eyes. The contents of his stomach would have to be pumped out.

His father was African, his mother Greek. Or so the doctor understood him to say. This was noted down. Later in the evening Dr Nachtwey put down some other particulars about the patient. He carried a passport in the name of Demitrios Tsafendon. He was born in Lourenço Marques, the capital city of Portuguese East Africa, in 1918.

The man's agitation did not leave him. Sitting in his chair, he wept, clapped his hands to his ears, arched his back and uttered incomprehensible cries. Occasionally, without seeming to get any relief from them, he drew deep breaths into his chest. During calmer spells he let his body sink forward, as if his head had grown too heavy to hold upright. One of his hands remained on his stomach, forgotten; the other, thumb trapped inside his clenched fist, rested on the arm of the chair.

'Do you know anyone in the city?' Dr Nachtwey asked.

'I've got no problems,' the man answered hesitantly, in English.

Everything he had to say came out in fits and starts. What he would like to do, he said, was to go back to southern Africa. But it was too late now. Couldn't the doctor see how sick he was?

He opened his eyes wide: watery, amber-coloured eyes.

'It's been like this since 1937. I can't help myself. I can't defend myself. I'm always tired; always exhausted. It's eating me away. Can't you see? And no one believes what I say. I used to have muscles, now all I've got is flabby flesh. I'm not a man any more, just half a man.'

Suddenly he burst into a screech, followed by convulsive pants and moans. There was a snake in his stomach. For years he'd carried a worm or demon inside him. Yes, he'd been examined by the doctors, many times. But they'd found nothing. It had hidden itself too deeply inside him. In the early morning he could hear it talking to him. Sometimes during the day too. He could feel it struggling in his guts.

'I'm just half a man,' he said again. 'I'll never recover now.'

'The patient is thirty-seven years old, and appears to be in good physical condition,' the doctor wrote. And beneath that, in an almost illegible hand: 'Delusional psychosis.'

Delusional. Deeply confused. The initial diagnosis was left unchanged. Tsafendon—or Tsafendas, as he also called himself—was put into the closed wing of the hospital. Enquiries made at the Hamburg Hospital for Tropical Diseases revealed that he had been examined for an infestation of tapeworm a year previously, after making similar complaints to those now heard from him. That examination had shown the parasite tormenting him to be wholly imaginary.

The man did not smoke or drink; physically his constitution was sound. Dosed with opiates and tranquillizers, he nevertheless walked in his sleep. Sometimes, standing upright, he sank into trances so deep he would lose control of his bladder and bowels; then he did not even appear to notice what had just happened to him.

At the end of the month the medication was discontinued, though no improvement in his condition had been discerned. The patient refused to get out of bed and was always ill-tempered. He barely ate. Those who tried to talk to him sooner or later heard the story of the tapeworm. Nothing would rid him of it. Also, little hairy worms, he told a nurse, wriggled through his field of vision. They were like curly lines that would not disappear. Why did they never leave him alone? As for the dragon in his stomach—that had crawled into him many years before. Since then he had been its prisoner. It had taken possession of him.

'I've even drunk poison to get rid of it,' he said in confidential tones. 'Two metres of tape came out, into my underpants. But the head still remained inside. Look, they operated on me for it.' And he lifted up his pyjama jacket to show the scar of an appendix operation.

After another two weeks his condition appeared to deteriorate further. 'He urinated in the hall. He does not talk. He does not eat.' Several times the attendants had to restrain him physically. Finally it was decided to administer electric shock treatment to him.

Spring came. Hamburg thawed. With the change of season Tsafendas became calmer. Slowly but surely the storms in his head died down. He slept regularly and suddenly began to eat enough for two. His melancholy changed to a sort of nervous alertness. Even the imaginary beast in his belly retreated into the background of his consciousness. He was able to laugh, at times, with some of the hospital staff about his stupid imaginings. He winked at the nurses. He had an attractive glance under dark, caterpillar-like brows. When he felt like doing so he would tell stories, sailor's yarns, about his experiences. Stories of wild journeys, of Alexandria, Lourenço Marques, many crossings of the Atlantic and Indian Oceans. And about the Cape of Good Hope, 'Cabo da Bona Esperança' as he would call it, with an unusual, hissing emphasis. He would sing little songs the listeners could not understand but found charming nevertheless. They liked to hear him sing. They did not know what language he was singing in.

One morning he stood by the window, looking out. He held his head a little to the left, like a solemn ibis keeping watch over the gardens of the institution. When one of the nurses found him and asked him to come to the table for his meal, he continued to stand there. In his best German, he asked her to pardon him for his sickness. She responded with a reassuring pat on his plump shoulder.

Halfway through May he was moved to another part of the clinic where, in expectation of their discharge, patients were watched less closely. He offered to carry out small tasks for the staff. And he was allowed to go for walks through the park and the woods nearby. Now that the fever had died down, the nurses saw him as a conversable chap, a poor seaman who had touched bottom.

On the morning of 6 June 1955, Tsafendas bade a polite farewell to them. He was healed, out in the streets once more. The chestnut trees on both sides of Langenhorner Chaussee had already shed their flowers. He wore a faded, cinnamon-coloured suit. A taxi took him to the centre of town.

More than eleven years later, in Cape Town, in the chamber of the South African House of Assembly, he would kill Dr Hendrik Verwoerd, the country's Prime Minister, with four wild stabs of the knife in his right hand.

The sixth of September 1966 is inscribed sharply in my memory. At a few minutes before three in the afternoon the regular programmes of the state radio were interrupted by an urgent news item. An attack on the Prime Minister had taken place during a parliamentary sitting. It was not yet known whether or not Verwoerd had survived it.

I wandered through the botanical gardens towards the centre of Cape Town. Outside the parliament building, at the end of a long, shady avenue, there was no sign of anything unusual going on. The spring sunshine fell indifferently on the neoclassical pediment of the building. Squirrels skipped along the gutters. I went on further, heading towards a bookshop in Long Street. Here and there groups of people stood around radios. They spoke in low tones. An hour went by. Another thirty minutes. The stillness of the town was palpable. It was true: an entire country could hold its breath. Public life had come to a halt. An unfocused anxiety seemed to rustle through the streets.

Shortly after four o'clock it was made known that the father of the nation had passed away. The architect of apartheid was dead. The Verwoerd era was over. No one dared to rejoice openly. However, many did so secretly.

In the evening I attended a small party in the upper town, above District Six. The mood in the room was one of great elation. It did not occur to anyone to doubt that the murder was the expression of a deep dissatisfaction with everything that the Afrikaners and their

Nationalist Party stood for. Dissatisfaction—hatred, rather—was easy to feel. It went with being a student, in those days. Someone upstairs was keeping watch on the street below. Around the corner a black Austin had been seen with the silhouettes of two security policemen in it. A girl who had previously seemed perfectly sensible to me began to outline some instant plan of action for all of us to follow. Her voice was breaking with excitement.

I retreated to the little kitchen. The hectic tone of the company roused in me a kind of loathing. Perhaps it was the light-hearted glee with which they were speaking of their 'plans' that got me down. Perhaps jealousy also had something to do with how I felt. I looked askance at these students who had emerged from a comfortable, English-speaking milieu. They knew nothing of how life was lived in the impoverished, racially mixed suburbs in which I had grown up—on the wrong side of the tracks, as people said. They had never set foot in the Cape Flats.

In the week that followed, the assassin's motives were asserted to have been quite different from those the students had taken for granted. He was a madman; nothing else. Nothing more. In a few days Tsafendas's tapeworm had become famous nationwide. The illusory parasite was now known to have been the invisible giver of orders: part of a plot, indeed, but a plot for which no one was to blame. Whatever political elements there may have been in Tsafendas's statements to the police were not made known to the public. Barely any attention was given to the fact that he was of mixed parentage. The worm spoke more strongly to the imagination of the public. This suited the authorities well. Not the country but the unfortunate Greek was sick.

In October the judge presiding over the trial of Tsafendas declared that he was not fit to plead. He could not judge this man, the judge said, 'any more than I can judge a dog'. A dog? Demitrios Tsafendas was dispatched to the prison on Robben Island.

The attack on Verwoerd meant as much for South Africa as the death of Kennedy had done for the United States. It was seen as a break with the past, a loss of innocence, a giant word written on the wall. But what, actually, had taken place? Was it really just a chance event, the deed of a disturbed individual, a madman?

Nothing in South Africa is simple, however, or untouched by racial awareness and racial tensions: not even madness. Or so I came to think later. And there were other aspects of the events of that day in September which were to engrave themselves on my memory. First, there was the question of colour. In general Tsafendas was spoken of simply as a Greek, though he was half-African. The notes taken by the doctors in Hamburg had been careless in one respect only: it was his father who had been a Cretan and his mother a black Mozambiquer; not, as they had said, the other way around.

Tsafendas's victim, Hendrik Verwoerd, was also the son of an emigrant. He was an outsider in Africa, a half-baked Hollander, just like myself. The assault had been a confrontation between two immigrants. A half-Greek had murdered a half-Dutchman. The answer to many questions lay hidden in those discrepant 'halves'.

Hendrik Frensch Verwoerd was born in Amsterdam, in a house on Jacob van Lennep Quay. His mother was a Frisian, his father was from South Holland. In 1903, when Hendrik was just two years old, the family migrated to the Cape. The Anglo-Boer war had just ended. Wilhelm Verwoerd, the father, like many other Dutch people, had been much moved by the battle for their freedom fought by the Afrikaners, members of a 'brother-nation', Oom Paul Kruger's brave warriors who had been defeated and humiliated by the British. The fate of our Old Testament kinsfolk who had established themselves at the foot of the African continent would continue to attract emigrants from the Netherlands for generations. The elder Verwoerd was a carpenter by trade, but his ambition was to mount the pulpit as a dominee, a clergyman of the Dutch Reformed Church, though in the end he rose to be no more than a lay reader and a catechist. Driven into extreme poverty during the second decade of the century, Wilhelm became a hawker of Calvinistic texts and journals in the remoter districts of the Orange Free State.

His son Hendrik grew up with the High Dutch translation of the Bible, the *Statenbijbel*. He was much influenced by the anti-British sentiments of the circles in which the family moved. Until 1919, when he went to Stellenbosch University in the Cape, he spoke Dutch, not

Afrikaans, at home. In the course of his parliamentary career his origins would become something of a tender spot for him, something he preferred to play down. It was not only the opposition which grumbled that he was not a true South African; even among some of his own party, the Afrikaner Nationalists, he remained the 'Hollander'. Or worse still: the *'uitlander'*. The foreigner.

Young Verwoerd was exceptionally ambitious. He went to Stellenbosch to study theology and psychology. Soon, however, he was immersed in political questions, especially those involving white poverty and the 'race question'. Appointed a university lecturer in psychology before his twenty-third birthday, his prime concerns remained the future of the 'Volk' and the developing Afrikaner Nationalist movement. At that time Afrikaners from the *platteland*, from the backveld, were being driven into the Cape peninsula in a pauperized state; inevitably they were compelled to live in the closest proximity with the Cape Coloured population. To many Afrikaners, Verwoerd among them, that could only mean national degeneration. In the early 1920s he visited the mixed suburbs of Cape Town, places like District Six and Woodstock. Scandalized by what he had seen, he wrote in a university journal about this unhappy state of affairs: 'Often one finds Coloured and white families under one roof. No wonder that young Afrikaners see no objection to marrying with their former little playmates.'

Coloured or black little playmates, of course.

The migrant is an uncertain and incomplete man. He lives in an inveterate state of unease. The ultimate measure of his success is the extent to which he manages to adapt himself to the new circumstances in which he finds himself. But to what could those who are known as *'basters'*—half-castes, like Demitrios Tsafendas— adapt? Their colour was a mark they could not escape; an inheritance they could not leave behind. Why, I used to wonder as a schoolboy, were people of mixed racial origin always given names that sounded like an illness: *métique*, mulatto, half-blood, creole, bastard? To these terms was added the one always preferred by our then Prime Minister, that Dutch 'cheesehead' with a pig's nose, Verwoerd. To him they would always be Cape Coloureds. Henceforth all non-whites were condemned to live in a no-man's-land, even if it was just around the corner from ourselves. But to those who were the product of racial mixing there clung an especial sense of shame, of scandal, a measure of self-hatred, confusion and anxiety.

And Verwoerd?

His biographer says of him that he was 'the greatest gift which the Netherlands gave to South Africa in the twentieth century'. No success was denied to him in the course of his career. Academic, editor-in-chief of the Nationalist daily *Die Transvaler,* party leader, senator: always he aligned himself with well-spoken, upright, pious, respectable Afrikaners; and all this he did with an intensity that can only be explained in the light of his own background. The traditional system of racial discrimination which he took over, and which, in the 1950s and subsequently, was translated into the elaborate, ever more strictly enforced system of apartheid, had as its chief aim the separation of the whites of the poorer suburbs from their 'Coloured' and black fellow-countrymen. The aim was to establish an immovable fence between white poverty and black poverty.

One can easily see in all this the typical migrant's ambition to better himself and the condition of those like him: ex-European, ex-Dutch.

In 1950 Verwoerd was made Minister for 'Native Affairs' in the Nationalist administration. He was given unlimited power over the black population: in effect he became their dictator. No one reminded him any longer of his foreign roots, no matter how fond of pickled herring he secretly continued to be. In 1958 he became prime minister. Until his death eight years later he remained the Moses of the Afrikaner tribe.

Nobody questioned his leadership. Most Afrikaners felt that the gifted Verwoerd was in direct touch with both their forefathers and a transcendental realm above. He had brought his adopted people to their promised land. But did he really understand them? Enlightened members of the party complained in private that only a Hollander could have thought up his version of apartheid. His imagination was too hard in outlining policy, too inflexible and devoted to principle in putting it into effect. This immigrant's son had not 'grown up with the inheritance of his people'; or so the whisper went. He took too little account of history, or indeed of the Coloured people who, at one time, and in a half-hearted manner, had been offered the prospect of belonging to a 'brown Afrikanerdom'.

Emigration was an experience I too had undergone. My father left Leiden, in the Netherlands, for South Africa in 1956. Six months later—shortly after my ninth birthday—the rest of us followed him. The break with our country of origin was irreparable. Within a couple of years distant Holland became nothing more than a cliché. South Africa was now my home, yet it was a country in which no one appeared to feel at home.

In the early 1960s the racially mixed suburb of Cape Town in which we lived was, in effect, done away with. Our Cape Coloured neighbours disappeared. I was about thirteen years old when it happened. They had gone against their will: everyone knew that. Everyone remained silent. The neighbourhood bar was closed, then knocked down. I could no longer go with my sketchbook to draw the drunks who made a racket on the stoep of the bar or stretched themselves out to sleep on a patch of empty ground nearby. The local mosque was left standing—it was consecrated ground—but the believers, the people whose mosque it had been, were removed from our district. It all happened very quietly. I cannot remember their departure, only a vague feeling of unease and the question: where have they gone? Not long afterwards the answer became clear. 'They' had been taken to the Cape Flats, many miles away. Our neighbourhood held its peace.

How many South Africans were chased out of their cities during those years? Three million? Four million, others say—between twelve and fifteen per cent, anyway, of the entire population of the country. And for what reason? The differences between the 'poor white' Afrikaners and the Coloureds, especially, were not all that easy to make out, on either side of the colour line. Both groups spoke the same language and felt the same longing for a recognition of the wrongs done to them in the past. But what a child could not understand was this: that the war between races was always fought most fiercely when the differences between them were least apparent.

'Borderline cases', my mother used to say. And of the awful fate that had just befallen such 'cases' she added, with a sense of shock and compassion that made a deep impression on me (and all the more so because my father did not share her sentiments): 'No wonder there's already been so many suicides and murders among them.'

It is difficult to convey how deep was this sense of mutual estrangement. Differences of language, faith or race were never more than the most obvious indicators of a chronic, irremediable lack of civil cohesion within the country as a whole. Little effort was made by most urban whites to cultivate any sense of common human decency. They had no idea that the social attitudes they took for granted had been learned: painstakingly inculcated and acquired. It is a mistake to imagine that they were brought up merely to discriminate against others on grounds of colour. The repulsion they felt was more profound. They had been taught to hate: a hate that gnawed at them like the hunger of an animal waiting to be fed.

I felt it too; but my own repugnance focused on everything that was white. During my final year at school I seldom went to a pub or party where my classmates would be found. All they ever did was bullshit about rugby matches or boast about their feats in the surf. Beachboys in the making. As soon as I was old enough to go about on my own, my inclinations drew me towards the inner city. There I found quite a different Africa from the one we were told about in the seclusion of the classroom. In the Muslim Upper Cape, on the slopes immediately above the downtown area, and in District Six, far from the teeny-boppers and the petit-bourgeois claustrophobia of the lily-white southern suburbs, there remained a world outside the crazy racial exclusions that bound our lives elsewhere.

At the age of eighteen I moved to Woodstock, close to District Six, a notoriously rundown area. For that very reason it felt freer than elsewhere; it was still the amorphous melting-pot which Verwoerd had felt so threatened by in 1920. Racial integration had gone further here, and was more difficult to undo, than anywhere else. That it was a slum, a filthy and violent place, went without saying.

During the nineteenth century the population of District Six had consisted chiefly of liberated slaves, or their descendants, transported to the Cape from Java, Malaya and elsewhere by the Dutch East India Company. By the turn of the century they had been joined by immigrants and refugees from Europe, including about 7,000 Jews from the Baltic provinces of the Russian empire, British soldiers discharged at the end of the Anglo-Boer War, Boers bankrupted by that same war, black migrant labourers from the colony's eastern frontier. Ten or fifteen years later the district was regarded as a kind of transit zone: by which I mean that those who had succeeded moved away from it. The whites established themselves in the suburbs to the south of Table Mountain and along the coastline of Sea Point. The people who were left behind, within walking distance of the city centre, were dependent on employment in the harbour area and the factories around it. They were paid by the hour or day. When Verwoerd came to power the overwhelming majority of them were Coloured, a warning (to him) of the racial mixing that white poverty inevitably brought in its wake.

Alas, this area too was to be destroyed by the state. District Six was regarded by the Nationalist Party as a 'black spot' (their term) disfiguring the fair forehead of the city. On 11 February 1966, the Minister for Community Affairs (their term, again) announced the end of District Six. There was to be no going back. It was to be completely flattened. The inhabitants would be driven en masse to the Cape Flats. They would have to manage there as best they could, far from their work, from the shelter of Table Mountain, and from the streets once familiar to them. Dumped in a region tormented by dust and wind, they were left to their fate.

In the summer of 1966, after the murdered Verwoerd had been succeeded by a much-feared former Minister of Justice named Balthazar Vorster, Demitrios Tsafendas was transferred from Robben Island to Pretoria Central Prison. He was placed in a cell next to death row and forgotten. Those who had hoped that the murder of Verwoerd might be followed by a popular revolt, or that such an event might shake the Afrikaners from their slumber, were shown to have been deceiving themselves. Dreamers all. Within their narrow coterie, the whites clung to each other more closely than ever before. Any attempt at intercourse with the people with whom I had always felt myself most at ease—the Cape Coloureds—was automatically suspect in their own eyes. I was frozen out, as were others like me.

If only I had been born black! What was left for me to look for, as a white?

Six months after the assassination I went into the consulate of the Netherlands, in Strand Street, and asked—in English—for a passport. They barely lifted their heads to look at me. Nor did they take notice of the fact that officially I had no existence in South Africa: in order to escape compulsory military service, I had never registered for an identity document. I wandered around as best I could, paid no tax, and carried no 'white pass'. The passport was issued forthwith.

I arrived in Europe in the spring of 1968. I had burned my boats behind me. I felt optimistic, wholly unprepared for the great thirst that awaited me, the nostalgia I would feel for the future I had left behind.

2. The bastard

Born in 1918, Demitrios Tsafendas could remember nothing of the first house and garden he had lived in, on the Rua Andrade Corvo in Lourenço Marques (now Maputo). He spent no more than a year there.

His father, Michaelis Tsafandakis, who was Cretan by birth, had migrated from the Egyptian port of Alexandria to the highveld city of Pretoria in the Transvaal. Early in 1916 he moved to Mozambique to take a job with an Italian firm of marine engineers. He was a striking young man with a heavy moustache and a lengthy stride; like an ostrich's, some said. He soon won a reputation as a hard-working but excitable man. The Africans who worked under him looked on him with some fear. Within the local Greek community he was respected for his independence of mind. People put his brusque, inflammable temperament down to his Cretan origins. That he employed two black maids in his house on Rua Andrade aroused no particular comment. With one of them—the seventeen-year-old Amelia Williams—he shared his bed. She was a girl of mixed European and African descent. In the tropics it was more or less the order of the day for a single man to keep a concubine. Everyone assumed that Michaelis would eventually marry a fellow Greek.

The house was semi-detached. The neighbours saw Amelia going about her chores and working in the garden. She watered and fed the chickens, humming with a strange intensity as she did so. She went barefoot and wore a multicoloured cotton skirt like that worn by the women in neighbouring Swaziland. Over her shoulders she wore a light shawl. The rumour was that Michaelis had his hands full keeping her under control.

In 1917 she fell pregnant. She spent some time with her family in Namaacha, a district on the border between Mozambique and Swaziland. She returned in midsummer. In January she gave birth to a boy.

Michaelis was confronted by a dilemma. The child was his first-born son, but marriage with Amelia was out of the question. He allowed the child to be registered in his name in the office of the local Administração Civil. The entry reads: 'Demitrios, 14 January 1918, son of Amelia Williams and Miguel Tsafandakis.' Some months later an Orthodox priest was brought down from Johannesburg to baptize Demitrios. His godfather—Michaelis's good friend Perandonakis, also a Cretan—bore the costs of the ceremony. Amelia did not attend it. By then relations between her and Michaelis had been severed.

The house next door was occupied by Anthony Maw who later became honorary consul for Greece in Lourenço Marques. After Amelia Williams's departure Maw and his wife wondered how their neighbour would cope. The baby was unmistakably a half-blood. For the young English couple this meant that he was bound to become a shackle around his father's legs; but they kept their opinion to themselves. In effect the baby was being brought up by the servant girl.

One day in spring Maw leaned over the hedge that divided the two gardens. He could see the maid sitting among the bougainvillea with the baby on her lap. The father stood nearby. Tsafandakis— who had always been on the sturdy side—had grown stout. The two men fell into conversation. Michaelis spoke English only hesitantly. In three months' time he would turn thirty-five, he confided to his neighbour. His family, which still lived in Crete and in Egypt, was in the process of seriously searching for a bride for him. Maw remarked that a young European wife would not find it agreeable to be burdened with an illegitimate child of that kind. After some roundabout palaver Michaelis confessed that he wanted to send his little son to Alexandria. There he could be brought up by Michaelis's mother. The problem was that he did not know anyone who would be able to accompany the weanling to Egypt.

By this time Maw's wife had joined in the conversation. It so happened that she knew someone who would shortly be going to Athens. By steam ship, through the Suez Canal. She promised to find out about it.

Among the Greeks this was quite a common way of dealing with such matters. Many grandparents brought up their grandchildren.

The widow Katerina Tsafandakis fetched her grandson Demitrios from the boat in Port Said. He was to spend his next six years in Alexandria. That is to say his earliest memories were of the cosmopolitan cultural life of the eastern Mediterranean. At home he spoke Greek; in the street, Arabic. His first impressions were coloured by Mediterranean light, a confusion of warehouses and bazaars, the heat and crowds of the small lanes near the docks. The great commercial city looked at the same time east and west; though one window was open on the unstable world of the Levant, the city still lay within the British sphere of influence, and its closely knit Greek colony dated back to ancient times.

Katerina lived on the top storey of a house on Rue Toussoum Pasha, not far from the pale red building of the Banco di Roma. Around the corner was Place Mohammed Ali, the biggest square in the town centre, where the colonial court-buildings and the cotton exchange were to be found. Towards evening the noisy chatter of the Alexandrian sparrows could be heard from the trees. The sparrows, which landed in great numbers on the terrace of the house, fascinated Demitrios from an early age. During the hot summers he slept on the terrace and closed his eyes to the rustle of the birds. In the mornings, at first light, he was woken by the voice of the imam, carried from the mosque all over the suburb.

Grandmother Tsafandakis gave him the pet name 'Mimis'. She took him with her to the market, to the Anglican church in the Place Mohammed Ali and the cathedral of Saint Saba, the seat of the Orthodox patriarch. Later she took him to the English puppet theatre in the city, which was particularly popular among Greek children. For the rest he would spend the whole day dressed in a trailing djellaba, playing at being a little Arab boy.

From his grandmother the little boy learned to identify the electric trams which ran in an elaborate network all over the city. Mimis surprised her by the quickness with which he learned to recognize the different services. He pointed out to her their symbols: the green lozenge which marked the tramline to the south, the red half-moon of the Ragheb Pasha line, the white star, red circle and green leaf of the other lines.

Sometimes Katerina worried over her grandson. He was seldom ill-behaved but often she thought him too withdrawn. He was uneasy with children of his own age and kept to himself. She stuffed him with sultanas, raisins and dates, which he loved.

His father visited Egypt a few times. The sea route along the coast of east Africa was well used and Michaelis's contacts with Greek ship owners made such journeys easy to arrange. Mimis looked forward to these visits, though they were too irregular for him really to get to know his father. The little presents he received from him he found strange: wood carvings of an unfamiliar kind, a little hand-held thumb piano, made out of a gourd, and keys of bent steel.

By this time Michaelis was a married man. His wife Marika, who had come to him from the Greek community in Port Said, accompanied him on these journeys. As Demitrios grew up, he began to look on Marika as his mother: a mother at a distance. In remote Lourenço Marques he eventually acquired from her a little sister and brother— Evangelina and Victor. But they remained mere names to him and Lourenço Marques was a phantom, a dream town found only in stories.

Mimis had to go on living with Katerina.

When he could not fall asleep she would recite to him long passages from the *Erotokritas*, an epic that she knew by heart, just as the Muslim youngsters could recite from the Koran for an hour at a time. They lay together on the sofa next to the open window. The evenings were smoky and restless. The Cretan verses comforted him like candy.

But Demitrios had the feeling that something was being kept from him. For reasons he could not understand he was at a disadvantage. The circumstances of his birth remained unspoken-about, unknown to him.

By the time he was seven years old he was a quiet but outwardly contented boy. He was free to wander as he wished through the town. He rambled about the docks, attracted by their hubbub and by the ships on their way to Tripoli or Heraklion. He spent the midday hours on the Corniche, the broad road along the coast from which you could see the fort on Qayt Bay. It was the only trace of the ancient lighthouse still standing, or so Katerina had once told him. In the Greek quarter of the town, behind St Saba Cathedral, Mimis was a well-known figure. Only Ras el Tin, the Turkish district near the Cape of Figs, was forbidden territory. Disorder was brewing there.

The uprising of the Arabs against the British regime made a great impression on him. All the doors of the house were bolted. There were riots in his street. The nationalists set fire to the covered market where he used to buy his sherbets. From the terrace of his house he looked down on the English and Australian troops as they formed up and suddenly opened fire. With salvo upon salvo they drove the rebels out of the district. When his grandmother saw him sitting there she dragged him roughly indoors. It was the only time he could remember hearing her curse.

By 1925 Katerina had grown too frail to look after him. Mimis had become too much of a handful for her. In the course of that year his father arrived. The plan was that he would take the boy south, back to the promised land of Lourenço Marques. Mimis had grown into a slender youngster, with a narrow face surmounted by an uncontrollable bush of crinkled hair.

Things had gone well with Michaelis, whose family, for some time resident in the Britannia Hotel, was now living in an apartment on the top storey of a large, whitewashed building in a pleasant part of town, on 24 July Avenue. In it there would be enough room for them all: for Marika, Michaelis and their two children, Evangelina and Victor. Another girl, Helena, soon followed. Michaelis wished to do his best for Mimis, too. He had to go to school and learn the local languages. Marika had objected to his arrival, but she had been overborne. The domestic staff was expanded to include an extra maid. For the eight-year-old Demitrios it was difficult at first to accept the change from a Mediterranean to an African style of life. He could understand nobody outside the family. He missed the familiar sounds and the comfortable neighbourhood of his grandmother's house. He was sent to school in a Portuguese mission in the city and was placed among the children in the lowest grade. The white children spoke in a harsh, bitten-off manner, as if giving orders. The blacks shouted. Even nature and natural events seemed loud and abrupt here. In the evenings it looked as if the sun died in a single moment behind the hills. In the mornings it stood up as if with a clap above the horizon. There was no sense of intermediacy, no dawn or dusk.

This absence of nuance was visible everywhere. In Alexandria the Greeks were a respected minority, protected by the British, even after Egypt had declared itself independent in 1922. Here, beneath the equator, prejudices were much sharper. The Anglo-Saxon and Portuguese way of doing things emphasized distinctions within the colony. Race and class reinforced each other. The Greek merchants, tobacco planters and manual workers were looked down on, along with 'coolies and local savages'. The Greeks in Mozambique clung together in their own community, seeking to preserve what they could of the culture of their motherland. Michaelis Tsafandakis knew less about local politics than he did about developments in Athens. And in general he was less well informed and educated than his wife.

Demitrios was not a part of his father's milieu, but then where did he really belong? In his new surroundings he missed the intimacy, warmth and mutual trust which he had enjoyed with Katerina. Whether or not he would ever be able to fit in would depend largely on Marika.

She was an intelligent woman, born to a worldly family in Port Said. Next to the corpulent Michaelis, she looked small, with an athletic figure and an urgent way of going about things. She had a pockmarked but agreeable face. A thick plait hung down almost to her waist. She spoke French and a little Italian and had rapidly learned Portuguese and English. At the time of Demitrios's arrival she was just twenty-three years old, seventeen years younger than her husband.

In her heart she looked on Michaelis's love child as an intruder and feared that his father would favour him above her own children. Nevertheless she had decided to treat him no differently from the others. It was clear to her that Demitrios had to be taken in hand.

He could not read or write, he knew nothing of Greek history. He seemed to have been left to his own devices in Egypt.

Mimis soon came to admire his new mother. Even if she remained rather distant in manner, she gave him treats from her kitchen and was good at telling stories. She told him about De Lesseps and the building of the Suez Canal, about the Acropolis and the Orthodox saints. After dinner she would bring thick books to the table and read to the children. She had a gramophone on which she played European records. And what perhaps impressed him most about her was that she had set up a small shrine in an alcove near the bedrooms. (There was no Greek Orthodox church in Lourenço Marques.) The family paid a formal visit to that confined, darkened space last thing at night, every night. Little oil-lamps she had brought with her from Port Said remained alight twenty-four hours a day.

The flames threw a wonderful scintillation over the icons. It kept alive in Demitrios's mind the places he used to visit with his grandmother in his Alexandrian days. Evening after evening the chilly golden saints and fathers of the church stared flickeringly down at him. It was as if the air itself was aflame, while preserving an eternal coolness of its own.

Outside, the heat was overwhelming. For six months or longer Marika stood by her resolution not to make a distinction between her children and the newcomer; then, all at once, it shattered. It was clear to her that Michaelis had become greatly attached to the boy; even more so than she had feared. He gave much less of his attention to the younger children. And then there was the climate! She complained that her head of hair was much too heavy to bear. She wanted to cut it short, because she suffered from severe, recurring headaches, especially now, in the summer. It was as if her skull was being constantly pulled at. But Michaelis forbade her to cut her hair. Sometimes he could behave like a tyrant towards her.

'Your son has been messing about with your things,' she would call out maliciously to him. *Your* son.

Mimis was a nuisance, a burden to her. He disrupted the harmonious life of the family. Evangelina and little Victor, especially, suffered under his teasing and changes of mood. Punishing him did not help. When Michaelis rebuked him he would sit in the kitchen and stare silently in front of him. Or he would fall into a rage. Outside the house he was treated like some kind of primitive. And he behaved like one too: unpredictable and threatening.

The rows between him and Marika became a daily occurrence. Michaelis found their quarrelling insufferable. When Mimis turned nine he was sent to a boarding school for white, English-speaking children in the Union of South Africa. Many children from middle-class families of continental European background went to such places and managed well enough. The educational system in the Transvaal was more developed than anything to be found in the Portuguese colony. His command of English would no doubt soon improve.

So, for the first time in his life, Mimis found himself living far from the coast and the smell of the sea. The bleak little Transvaal town of Middelburg lay 400 kilometres west of Lourenço Marques and about a hundred kilometres east of Pretoria.

He was placed in Nelson House Hostel, a large, elongated, colonial-style building with a shady veranda and a neglected garden in front of it. The pupils in this hostel came almost exclusively from Greek and Portuguese families, a group that was kept together partly but not entirely because of their backwardness in English. On their arrival, all students of foreign background were put back a year or two in class. Stimulated by the differences in lifestyle between themselves and the other boys, they developed a camaraderie of their own. They also had the advantage of being able to speak in secret tongues, and they generally did well in all subjects other than English and Afrikaans. For this they were duly persecuted by the other boys. The prejudices of the English-speaking townsfolk ran no less deeply than those of the local Afrikaners. The Portuguese were called 'sea-kaffirs'; the Greeks were notorious for being untrustworthy. The whites whispered among themselves about the dark practices that went on in the hostel.

'We all knew,' one of the Afrikaans-speaking boys from another hostel later recalled, 'that sodomy was a common habit in that tightly knit group.'

Demitrios was in the same position as the others from Mozambique, and this created a bond between them and himself. If he was noticed at all in this group, initially, it was because of his seriousness. He was strikingly earnest for a boy of his age. Evidently he believed himself to be out of the ordinary. He would speak in a joking, offhand manner to one of the women teachers about his life in Egypt. Later his feelings about the school grew darker. British ways were stricter and more heavy-handed than those he had known before, either from his father or his grandmother. He was compelled to take part in sports like cricket and athletics of which he understood nothing. He frequently suffered feverish attacks; perhaps—nobody asked—their origin was malarial. If he felt homesick it was not so much for his parents as for his racially mixed companions at the mission school in Lourenço Marques. He missed particularly the voices of the black children. He missed Marika's kitchen maid. The food in the hostel was unpalatable to him: sausages, kippers, oatmeal with too little sugar, mealie-meal porridge.

His greatest pleasure was to go to the automatic sweets-machine outside Cleggs Café in the dorp's main street. Each time he was given his pocket money by Mr Martindale, the warden of the hostel, he went straight to Cleggs. He fed the machine with the giant, British-style copper pennies then in use, with the date of their minting stamped on them: 1921, 1899, 1909. Then the candies came out and he rolled them in his hand.

'Very good. Remarkably good.'

That was how he felt then, with his mouth full of chocolate. That was how, a lifetime later—after asking me if I happened to have any chocolate with me—he chose to describe the taste to me.

At the age of twelve or thirteen, after a couple of terms in the Transvaal, Mimis was familiar with five languages, but he could speak none of them correctly. His Arabic lay in the past. The same was true of Shangaan, the local African language, which he had learned from the mission-school children. He disliked Afrikaans (South African Dutch) which struck him as a language appropriate to the country: one of naked, stony sounds. In Middelburg he dreamed in Greek and woke in English. His command of English was still limited, but he could speak it freely enough.

By the time he reached the fifth grade in the school he had become the clown of his peer group, more because of his wild gesticulations than because of anything he said. When he sang Cretan songs at school concerts, he had the excited, laughing, applauding audience eating out of his hand. Yet his gesturing and general appearance also provoked the other boys to tease and bully him. He was plagued especially by a boy named Benjamin Levy, whose father was the manager of the Savoy Hotel in Lourenço Marques. On one occasion the fat Benny, together with friend Sammy Schmahmann, kicked him on the shins in the wasteland beyond the playing fields. Mimis struck back at them vainly, and came away with a bloody nose.

This was the first time that he heard the expression 'Coloured' being flung at him.

'You're nothing but a lousy Coloured!' shouted the fat boy. 'A lousy bloody Coloured.'

He at once felt ashamed and humiliated, though he did not know why. Boer, Briton, Jew, Coloured—these distinctions had largely passed him by. His parents were Greek: could there be anything surprising, then, if his skin was darker than that of the pale, English-speaking ghosts of the highveld? Nor was Mimis the only boy with crinkly hair in Middelburg Primary School. But there was no one else whose words were so twisted and strange. His boasts were always exposed, his fantasies convinced nobody. Whenever he told lies or tried to cheat at games the others saw through him at once. Only in eating and in singing did he distinguish himself.

In the hills outside the little town he had discovered some caves. It was a primitive and isolated place, surrounded by strangely formed boulders, some the work of nature, some of men's hands. He spent hours in these caves. Alone. With a candle. Though no icons were to be found there, the place was his shrine.

Twice a year, during the school holidays, he went home by train: for a couple of weeks in the winter and for almost two months in the summer. Marika was happier to see him go than to see him come. In September 1928 she had had another girl, who was baptized Katerina, in honour of the child's grandmother in Alexandria. In addition to the three girls, Marika had her son Victor, who was often unwell, to look after. Each time her stepson appeared she became more and more convinced that there was something abnormal about him. He was always acting, putting on a performance the whole time. When he thought no one was watching him he would pull crazy faces. The full story of Amelia was still hidden from Demitrios, but Marika was not surprised to hear that the boys at his school called him a Coloured. It would have been better for him, she thought, if he had remained in Egypt. In Egypt he would have 'passed' more easily.

Demitrios spent much of his time in the kitchen. He had no real relationship with the other children, Evangelina aside. She was three years younger than him, and he would sometimes go into her bedroom. He called her Betty Boop, after the little girl in the American strip cartoon. He explained to Betty Boop how gunpowder worked, and told her he was going to make skyrockets with it. Evangelina understood little of what he was saying, but she enjoyed listening to him. Her brother used words that were strange to her. He spoke of 'tuck' when he meant sweets and crisps; he called bananas 'lady's fingers', and brought a bunch of small bananas from the kitchen to show her what a good name this was for them.

His father, too, was unhappy with the boy's appearance and demeanour. He asked himself why Demitrios was so timid and turned-in on himself; so chicken-breasted, skinny, weedy. He had round, girlish shoulders, and showed no interest in the activities that kept the other youngsters busy in the neighbourhood. At home he was under everyone's feet; when Michaelis took him to his workplace, at the firm of Vucellato, he usually just followed his father about. He would watch the welders at work and then lose interest. He collected strips of metal from the lathes, played with grindstones and moulds.

Michaelis discussed the boy with an old acquaintance, Guilliema Conte, who had set up a gym in the city. Senōr Conte offered to take the youngster under his wing during the summer months. Demitrios, he said, should learn to box. Then at least he would be able to defend himself if anyone ever called him a 'blackie' back in Middelburg. In subsequent years Mimis went fairly often to the gymnasium set up by Conte and his brother; at first in order to oblige his father, later because he became interested in the sport.

Jack Dempsey was soon one of his greatest heroes. The other was Buster Keaton.

At the beginning of the 1930s the worldwide depression dominated life in southern Africa. Michaelis did not know if he would be able to survive in Mozambique, or how he would be able to pay Mimis's fees at the boarding school in Middelburg. Shipping had dwindled. The firm for which he worked was going downhill. Many immigrants in Portuguese East Africa were leaving for the Transvaal, where conditions were a little better. In 1931 Michaelis applied to the South African Department of Immigration and Asiatic Affairs (*sic*) for permission for the children, at least, to be registered as members of the Greek community in Pretoria.

That summer Demitrios returned once again to the family residence in 24 July Avenue. After four years, his time in Middelburg was over. He went back to the Portuguese mission school.

For the most part he simply played truant; he spent his days wherever his fancy took him. At night he rummaged around the house. Marika found it hard to cope with his appetite. He ate as much as he could, whenever he could; yet he remained as thin as ever. Was that usual for a boy of his age? She did not know. The only thing he really cared for was the gramophone. He said he wanted to learn the piano, but there was no money to buy such a thing for him. He sat with red-rimmed eyes in the front room of the house, doing nothing. She went to her brother, who had been living in the neighbourhood for the last few years, for advice. He told her that Demitrios was a loafer; the trouble with him was that he had never been properly disciplined. Marika's sister, Anna, who had married a Greek wrestler and also settled in Lourenço Marques, said the exact opposite. They should let the youngster alone.

In his own haphazard fashion Demitrios explored the various quarters of Lourenço Marques, the docks, the outlying slums to the north. He liked to visit Gregoris, who supplied the whole town with ice cream. The cold storage abutted on a house with many rooms. In one of them he got to know Cora, a woman who wore nail varnish of a different colour every time he visited her; she was a Portuguese or possibly a Coloured. He also liked to hang about in the Akropolis, the large, modern department store in the centre of town, where everything was spread out for inspection. In the evenings he visited the Contes' gym, where they called him 'Skinny'. He boxed featherweight, flailing his arms wildly in the ring. No one took him seriously as a contender. He didn't have it in him.

One afternoon he lay in bed with Betty Boop. No one else was at home. The two of them had taken off nearly all their clothes, but it was not clear to him who had taken the initiative in doing this. Mimis stroked her shoulder.

After the murder of Verwoerd, Tsafendas was questioned for days at a time by the security police. Several times they went over the story of his life. On a Monday morning, 12 September 1966, he said that he had forgotten to tell them something important the previous night. What he then declared threw a startlingly different light on the unhappy relations within the family between 1925 and 1927, when he had first been sent away to school—and indeed subsequently. His stepmother, he said, had abused him. Because he was heir to his father's property, Marika had turned the whole family against him. She was determined to destroy his 'masculine qualities'. Having used that unusual phrase, Demitrios followed it with another. She began, he said, 'to corrupt me'. He felt that he had been spoiled and defiled. Even before his departure for Middelburg she had persuaded her brother to rape him.

'My uncle dragged me into a room and committed an unnatural deed with me. I got very scared. I was just a child.'

It sounded as if he had grabbed the story out of thin air. It appeared to have been put together out of tales from the experiences of others, or from events that had happened earlier or later in his life. Demitrios looked at his past as if through a kaleidoscope—depending on need or desire, he would give it a quarter-turn this way or that.

He regarded the period 1934–35, after he left the school in Middelburg and was living again in Lourenço Marques, as the most painful he ever went through. In retrospect he felt it was then that he had been most vulnerable to what he called 'corruption'. It was then, he insisted, that his view of himself and of the world at large had darkened and hardened irrevocably.

Of the hiding given to him by his father, when he came home and found Mimis and Betty Boop in bed together, Demitrios could remember little, except that he had lost consciousness: or rather, that he had come round while the Portuguese doctor was attending to him. His aunt Anna was trying to calm Marika. For many days afterwards she would not address a single word to him. During this time Michaelis simply stayed away from the house. Demitrios could not understand why his father had attacked him so violently. Evangelina and he often lay on top of one another, in the garden too—tickling each other, playing leapfrog, carrying on like crazy people. Sometimes they pretended that her bed was a boat. Betty Boop was by far his best friend in the family.

He was kept out of school; not as a punishment but because after that episode he began to be overcome by attacks of uncontrollable rage. His parents were afraid of what he might do to the other pupils. He refused to eat for a week and they could do nothing but again call the doctor to come and see him. He was left with a bottle of tonic of which he was to drink a tablespoon a day until he felt better. The doctor recommended exposure to sunlight too. Every day he was to spend such and such a period in the sun. After a month of this treatment he was almost as dark as an African. He refused to go back to the mission school, even when he himself declared that he now felt much better. Finally they arrived at a compromise. Mimis would now go to evening classes at an English-language institution in the town.

Michaelis Tsafandakis eventually came to the decision that he no longer had a future in Mozambique. The family should move to Pretoria as soon as possible. He would go ahead, to find a job and a place for the family to live in. Marika would follow with the three children. And Demitrios? The ambitions that Michaelis had once nourished for him were by now much moderated; his erratic behaviour forbade them. It was clear that he would never become an engineer of any kind, like his father. Given the state of race relations in South Africa it would probably be better for him to remain in Lourenço Marques. Talking to the Greek owner of the Akropolis, Mr Sideris, Michaelis suggested that a place might be found for the boy in the store—possibly in the kiosk selling books and magazines.

Mimis saw little of his father in the months before the departure of the family. Nothing Michaelis said to him assuaged his conviction that he was being abandoned. Even his stepmother suddenly seemed more concerned about how he would manage in the future than Michaelis, the man who had previously been the most important figure in his life.

In the late summer of 1935 Marika saw to it that a medicine against tapeworms, prescribed by the Portuguese doctor, was administered to Mimis. A day or so later, to Marika's surprise and relief, a worm two or three feet long was found in his stools. That was the explanation, presumably, of his underfed appearance.

Mimis wanted to take the entire stool to the doctor, so that it could be investigated. Had he not promised he would do so? He also wanted to be certain that the head of the creature did not remain in his bowels. But, ignoring his protests, Marika washed the entire mess down the lavatory. Too late, she realized how much importance he had attached to it. On hearing what she had done he rushed into the kitchen and began hammering on the dresser with his fist— hammering and hammering. When he paused for a moment Marika gave him money and told him to buy an ice cream with it. He turned around and threw the coins out of the window. What did she think he was—a child?

Mimis felt as if a door in front of him had been slammed shut. Left behind in Lourenço Marques, he no longer had any obligations to the family and could do whatever he wished. He regarded Marika's assurance that he would always be welcome in Pretoria as nothing more than hypocrisy. They were glad to be rid of him. In August 1935, aged seventeen, he asked for permission from the South African Interior Ministry to enter the country. It would be a formality, he thought. Five months later he received a note telling him that his application had been refused.

Mimis was bitterly disappointed—and suspicious. The South African consulate in Lourenço Marques would not discuss the matter further. Also: why was he suddenly held in such disregard by the local Greek community? His step-uncle, Marika's brother, would have nothing to do with him. In any case this uncle was on the point of leaving for Rhodesia, where he planned to become a tobacco farmer. Mr Sideris, for whom Mimis now sorted newspapers, arranged the books in the kiosk and helped with the cash sales, allowed him to take back to his little flat each day a free copy of the *Lourenço Marques Guardian*. But it was clear that Mrs Sideris did not want him to come near her house. Was she afraid for her daughters? He was a head taller than her husband, taller than his own father.

Mimis could not let the matter rest. The Sideris girls were pretty, like pictures. With their pale, oval faces and black hair they reminded him—or so he liked to believe—of the girls of Alexandria.

He did not know his place. When he made an unannounced visit to the Sideris house and, omitting the usual greetings in Greek, went straight to the gramophone, Mrs Sideris spoke sharply to him.

'You're just like your mother,' she shouted at him.

He gazed at her in astonishment.

'Your mother, your real mother, was a black, a Coloured woman. A mulatto,' she repeated, in Portuguese.

He heard her, all right; but he regarded what she had said as just another of the many obscure insults or accusations he had shaken off before. He was a Greek, the son of a Greek, the grandson of a Greek. He left the house without replying to her. The following day, however, he went to the office of the Administração Civil. He looked up the records there, and for the first time in his life read the name of his mother: Amelia Williams. She had died nine years previously, in one of the 'native' areas of Lourenço Marques: on 12 January 1927, two days before his ninth birthday. Someone in the office confirmed for him that she was a Coloured, of part-Swazi origins.

Suddenly he had to think of himself in two parts, as a kind of double: one half this, the other that; half *non-white,* the other half... acceptable. In South Africa 'White' and 'Swazi' were written with capital letters, as if they referred to nations; 'mulatto' and 'bastard' with small letters, for such people were without consequence; they had come from nowhere and would amount to nothing. He listened to the sound of the fan going round and round in his room. Who then were his grandparents?

He returned to the Administração Civil, and went from office to office seeking information which might be relevant to him, but came out with nothing. One file said that Amelia Williams had a German father; another that her father was English. No one could tell him where she was buried.

For the eighteen-year-old Tsafendas everything he had always felt to be suspect or ominous about himself now fell into place. His close-packed, curly hair. His skin colour—which he had previously thought of as Mediterranean. Grandmother Tsafandakis's vagueness whenever he asked her about his mother. The resentment and hostility of Marika and the contempt towards him shown by his uncle. The teasing at school. The negative reply from the South African immigration service. The tentative, curious glances constantly thrown at him; the indefinable hesitation with which people greeted him.

In one blow he had become other to himself. He now knew himself to be literally and figuratively the black sheep of the family. And the authorities in the neighbouring country, South Africa, knew all about him, too.

However, he did not abandon his hopes of joining his family there. By this time Michaelis was working as a welder for the state-owned Iron and Steel Corporation (ISCOR). Again Mimis applied for permission to enter the country; again the consulate in Lourenço Marques reported that it would not be granted to him.

He consoled himself as best he could with Cora, the woman with painted nails, who lived in the house of many rooms.

3. Adrift without anchor

Of all foods Demitrios most loved lobster. He told me so, with much emphasis, when I visited him for the first time in the psychiatric institution in the Transvaal in which he had long been incarcerated. The giant crabs which his stepmother had served up in Lourenço Marques were splendid. But nothing could beat lobster or langoustine.

'The best food I ever ate, lobster.'

The attendant in the ward, a hefty man in a white coat who happened to be passing at that moment, turned to us with a grimace. 'Lobster? What's lobster?' and before we could answer let the door to the kitchen bang shut behind him.

People in the interior of the country are often suspicious of seafood. Creatures that live in their shells are thought to be disgusting: impure somehow.

As a schoolboy Demitrios had made the journey between Mozambique and the Transvaal at least a dozen times, travelling uncomfortably in the steam train that connected the coastline on the Indian Ocean with the great plateau, 2,000 metres higher, which is the heartland of South Africa. In 1936 he decided that he would follow his family to Pretoria, despite the refusal of the authorities to give him a visa to enter the country. He knew the borders were porous and poorly controlled. In the autumn of that year he concealed himself among some machinery packed in a railway goods-wagon, and crossed the border at Komatipoort with no difficulty. Then on to Pretoria.

For some time after his arrival he worked in the Fountains Café, not far from the railway station. He scrubbed tables and ran about the streets on errands, often with a tray in his hand. For the first but not for the last time in his career he was living as an illegal immigrant, someone who had slipped through officialdom's nets. On the Witwatersrand—the sprawling metropolis of Johannesburg and its surroundings—there were many thousands of others in the same position. The depression of the previous few years had coincided with a severe drought on the highveld. Needy farmers, both white and black, as well as poverty-stricken families from the neighbouring Portuguese and British colonies, streamed towards the city. Most of them would never return to the rural areas from which they had come. The struggle for existence among these newcomers was inevitably fought out on racial lines, and hence on unequal terms. The whites had the vote; and their representatives in parliament passed law after law to protect their constituents against competition from the blacks.

Demitrios had not been warmly received by his family in Pretoria. With Marika's encouragement, his brother Victor now regarded himself as the oldest son. Within two months Demitrios had moved to Hillbrow, a suburb of Johannesburg not far from the centre of the city. There he went from one petty job to another, most of them in the catering trade. From the City Tearoom to the Elgin Café in Jeppe Street and from there to the Cosmopolitan Restaurant.

He was almost nineteen years old. His employers found him friendly enough, though sometimes touchy. Those who got to know him better thought him talkative, intelligent, given to daydreaming.

While on his own in Lourenço Marques he had changed, turned some kind of a corner. The introverted, hollow-chested pubescent had become a rough, loquacious young man who was proud of the languages he spoke and of the ideas he could express in all of them. He read the newspapers and kept abreast of political issues: the strikes in the gold mines, the behaviour of the police—who would go hunting the streets for blacks without 'passes'—and the agitation to revise the electoral laws and strike off the rolls that tiny minority of 'non-Europeans' who still retained the right to vote. (One per cent of the electorate.)

Spokesmen for the government of Generals Smuts and Hertzog declared that a shared vote would lead directly to shared beds and bastardization.

Demitrios allowed himself to be taken by some acquaintances to meetings held by the Communist Party, a noisy but ineffective little groupuscule. Films from the Soviet Union were shown in one of the city's cinemas. Small private gatherings were also addressed by the party's intellectuals. What he saw and heard during these meetings he guilelessly tried to pass on to the clients of the restaurants he worked in. Perhaps more provocatively still, he occasionally distributed pamphlets on behalf of the Party.

It is not known who finally gave his name to police headquarters in Marshall Square, or if he drew attention to himself by applying for legal right of residence. In the winter he was picked up and deported to Mozambique.

From then on he was kept under surveillance by the authorities in both Mozambique and the Union of South Africa. In Lourenço Marques he attempted to enlist in the Portuguese army, but on principle the recruiting office turned away people of mixed racial origin. Subsequently he went back to his old job at the magazine kiosk in the Akropolis department store. Within a few weeks his incessant chatter had turned his colleagues against him. He was put out on the street.

A time of great anxiety followed. He slept badly. He suffered from severe indigestion. In the early mornings he would wake to a turbulence in his stomach.

He lived hand-to-mouth, sometimes working as a porter in the docks, sometimes hanging about the city's Catholic mission or its Anglican church, where many members of the Greek community attended the Sunday service. He relaxed in the company of blacks, among whom he could even play the hero, or the boss, like his father. But the more he felt himself to be going downhill socially, the less he could understand or control what he was becoming.

To his own surprise he was given a job, in the winter of 1937, by the British state airline, Imperial Airways. A new airport was being built in the most northerly province of Mozambique, on the marshy, malarial coast near Quelimane, and the firm needed a translator in Portuguese and Shangaan—though the second was a language he had to struggle to master. Out in the swamps and bushveld no one cared what exactly his status was or who his antecedents had been. He could make his own way there. He learned to drive and chauffeured his superiors around.

His leisure hours he spent studying the few technical books he could get hold of in that isolated corner of the world. Sometimes he browsed through an English translation of the Bible that the previous occupant of his quarters had left behind. During this period he made friends with a mechanical engineer from Scotland who went by the name of 'Scotty'. The man was an extrovert and a reprobate who was not much interested in Mimis's tales. He organized hunting parties that went out into the marshes not far from the mouth of the Zambezi. Plenty of game was to be found there. The employees of Imperial Airways earned pocket money by exporting buffalo meat to Rhodesia and Nyasaland.

Scotty lived with a black woman from a neighbouring tribe.

'How can you go with someone like that?' Mimis once asked.

She was terrific in bed, Scotty answered. He laughed loudly. 'She can take the skin off your dick.'

Mimis said to himself: 'Never mind.'

Alone at night in his little room, he would fantasize about his fate. His real mother must have been an exceptional woman. Just as black and no less fierce than Scotty's friend. What had actually happened between her and his father? Could it be that she had brought into being some kind of new, separate tribe? Where that particular idea had come from he did not know. Perhaps she had not died, but had left his father for her own reasons, and somewhere, in a secret corner of Africa, she was ruling over a group of rebellious women of mixed race. Sometimes these thoughts took forms more grotesque still. His own imaginings pursued him. They were out of control.

Overcome by severe stomach pains, Demitrios was admitted into the nearest clinic, where a local doctor removed his appendix. The anaesthetic seemed to remain in his system and continued to affect his daydreams for weeks after. He fell silent; stood motionless for minutes on end, unable to utter a sound; moved tentatively, like a partially sighted person. The operation seemed to him to have cut him off from his own being. His body had become what the locals called *dungeka*: obscure, husk-like, set apart.

Scotty could no longer understand him. Demitrios found it hard to explain to him how he felt. In the evening, as he was about to enter his cabin, he would hear through the half-open door the cry of a muezzin, becoming one with a sound that came from the stars. At other times he heard the hissing of a snake. He would find himself in an underground vault where he would be compelled to stand and listen to the snake. It made a horrible, urgent, muddy, incomprehensible sound.

These anxiety attacks went on for three or four weeks. He was hardly able to keep himself going. Such things were not uncommon in Quelimane, among both the half-crazy expatriates and the mocking, malignant indigenes. After about a month the feeling that he was under constant threat began to recede slowly. Mimis was able at last to speculate about other things. Like travel. Air travel especially. Though he had yet to set foot in an aeroplane, the idea of it roused his enthusiasm.

In January 1938 he went to the South African consulate in Lourenço Marques and asked again for permission to enter the country. This time he made sure that the translation of the Portuguese birth certificate presented to the consul showed Marika (who was registered as 'white' in the records) and not Amelia Williams as his natural mother. This manoeuvre did not help him. In July he applied to the consulate for a tourist visa. That, too, was denied him. Not even as a tourist was he welcome in South Africa. He managed to get into the country, nevertheless.

He was determined that this time no one would know where he was going or what he was doing.

Then—silence. More than a year was to elapse before his name once again surfaces in the official South African files. This time it is because he has meticulously gone to register himself at police headquarters in Marshall Square, Johannesburg. For the following three months he attends the Progress College in the same city. He studies electrical welding, metal-cutting with an oxyacetylene burner and how to work a lathe. The moment he is given his certificate by the college, he signs on as a member of a trade union, the Boiler Makers and Welders Union.

These are feverish times. The South African economy is expanding rapidly; the Second World War is about to break out and skilled labour is in short supply. At the beginning of May he finds work with the British Mining Supply Company in Faraday Street. The firm has recently switched to the production of armoured vehicles; his speciality becomes the production of filters and pump-cowlings.

Demitrios invests in a tailor-made suit and crocodile-leather shoes. His work turns out to be not too arduous. Whenever he doesn't want to work, or when he feels too weak to do so, he stays in bed. No one is going to make a fuss about it. He soon gets in touch with the Communists once more. He pays his monthly subscription of two shillings and sixpence to the Party and goes up and down Loveday Street distributing leaflets. Every now and then he attends meetings on the City Hall steps or in various community centres. What he most enjoys, however, is his visits to the local library. He spends hours there, bent over the latest technical and scientific journals. He is now interested in technology, maritime architecture, astronomy and metallurgy.

These journals make him long for 'overseas', those lands where everything is more modern, moves more rapidly and is less provincial than in South Africa. Would it not be a great thing to stand one day in London's famous Trafalgar Square? Or among the skyscrapers of New York?

According to the files, Demitrios had voluntarily registered his presence in Johannesburg at the police headquarters in Marshall Square. Twenty months later, however, some anonymous official scrutinized the Tsafendas dossier and found that not everything in it was as it should be. He had committed an offence against the Aliens Act, and on 6 August 1940 he was summoned to appear before a judge, who sentenced him either to pay a fine of twelve pounds, ten shillings or to spend a month in prison. Demitrios was relieved. His employers, British Mining, had presented to the court a statement from which nothing suspicious or untoward about him could be elicited. It had been decided that he was not to be expelled from the country. He paid the fine immediately and temporary papers were issued to him, on the grounds of his claim that he was performing 'essential war service'.

But another zealous pen-licker in the Department of Immigration and Asiatic Affairs was not satisfied. He wanted to know why the case of Tsafendas had been dealt with so leniently—not according to the book. This official's head of department was persuaded to send a note to the Commissioner of Police informing him of the following damaging facts: the man was a half-caste, a Coloured; and a Communist too. Further: 'The above is passed to you in order that the activities of Tsafendakis [sic] may be watched, and I shall be glad if you will advise me in due course should anything to his detriment become known.'

Was it for this reason that six months later Demitrios left his 'war job' with the British Mining Company? At the beginning of 1942 he applied at the consulate in Johannesburg for a Portuguese passport. The document issued to him was valid for one year only. The Greek consulate, to which he had also applied for a passport, issued him with a document which, like the other, was valid for just a single year. He knew that he would not be left undisturbed for much longer; the security services were watching his comings and goings. In May he left for Cape Town, intending to sign on with a ship sailing for Britain or the United States. The Greek consul in Cape Town helped him to get a berth on the cargo ship *Eugenie Livanos*. Its destination was the east coast of Canada.

On the day of his departure Mimis climbed up Table Mountain. The view over South Africa's mother city and the bay was spectacular.

To the left were the white horses of the Atlantic Ocean. To the right, in the distance, he could see the mother-of-pearl peaks of the Hottentots Holland mountains. The wind hissed among the rocks and slopes around him; the noise of the city below was barely audible. It was as if he looked at it all through a tinted wall of glass.

Many jumbled thoughts passed through his mind. He was leaving the region of his birth to prove to himself that he was a man at home in the wide world; that he was no bastard but a cosmopolitan. After a while he broke off the tapering silver leaf of a shrub—which he could not name—and put it inside his pocket Bible. Then he wandered slowly down to the docks.

It is hard for us today to imagine the expectations that Cape Town harbour once aroused in the breasts of all who passed through it, whether arriving at the quasi-mythical foot of Africa, or departing from it certain only of one thing: the difficulty, perhaps the impossibility, of ever returning. The vacancy between two landfalls, the void that the ocean used to represent to those crossing it, its tedium and formlessness which engendered a longing for the shore, for any shore—all that has been lost. The difference between the Cape and the 'real world' once amounted to 7,000 nautical miles; at sea it was experienced as an apparently interminable period of suspension, a yawning hiatus in the lives of all who were on board.

On 12 June 1942 Demitrios Tsafendas, now aged twenty-four, sailed northwards, not knowing that twenty years were to pass before he would return to the city.

The crew of the *Eugenie Livanos* were Greeks; they spoke his father's language; Demitrios felt that he knew their ways. But after some time he took against the hothouse atmosphere of the boat, the mutual dependence of the sailors on one another, the isolated, hierarchical nature of their closed society. In it he occupied the lowliest rank of all. He had the title of 'mess boy' and served the others: kneading dough in the kitchen, pulling loaves out of the oven. At first he was teased by being sent about the ship on long, pointless errands. When he complained to the officers they shrugged their shoulders and laughed.

He was on board because he had wanted to get out of South

Africa. Now he found himself among rejects—some of them flamboyant, dope-smoking, foul-mouthed brandishers of knives. And it was wartime. The further north they sailed the more his unease grew. Panic overtook him when he realized that his flight might be doomed at its outset. Once they had crossed the equator, and the *Eugenie Livanos* entered the war zone of the North Atlantic—where German U-boats prowled—Demitrios withdrew into himself and fell sick. He pined for landfall long before they finally entered Canadian waters.

No sooner had the boat berthed in St John's on the island of Newfoundland than he packed his few things together and fled.

It was autumn in America. He was picked up by the police near Montreal. He begged the Canadian authorities not to send him back to the *Livanos*. He spent months under informal arrest in Halifax, Nova Scotia. The Canadians were not sure what to do with him.

In the winter of 1942 he escaped, together with two other sailors who had jumped ship. After a journey of 500 kilometres they reached the border of the United States. On foot and in daunting conditions Demitrios crossed the frozen St Croix River. Three weeks later he was picked up in Bangor, Maine, and arrested for entering the United States illegally. On his arrest he started babbling nonsense, gibberish; with some deliberateness, in all likelihood, he presented himself to his captors as a man who was deeply disturbed. These were the circumstances of his first admission to a psychiatric institution. It was attached to a hospital in Boston. He did his best there to convince the doctors that he heard voices, that horrible voices spoke to him out of the hospital's central heating system. After a while he no longer needed to exaggerate the state he was in; it seemed that the long ocean voyage had indeed unhinged him.

Any hope of getting permission to reside in the United States, which had been his original aim, was now ruled out. Demitrios's next four years were spent either in detention or serving aboard the so-called 'Liberty Ships'—cheaply and hastily built freighters which sailed the Atlantic in convoys to supply the Allies in Europe with food and arms. He was taken into institutions six times during this period, with complaints that sometimes seem to have been serious, sometimes trifling. Each time he was discharged he was sent straight back to sea. When he was not in hospital he was on board ship—always against his will.

The spring of 1945 found him on another Greek vessel, the *Marina Nicolao*. From there he wrote a letter to President Roosevelt complaining that over the last few years he had spent no more than twenty-nine days ashore and at liberty. Now that Nazi Germany was on the point of capitulating, could his 'war service' not be taken into account, and permission for him to reside legally in the United States finally be granted?

From March 1946 onwards he spent eighteen months on land, in the North Grafton State Hospital, Massachusetts. The prognosis, according to the doctors, was poor. Demitrios hallucinated: he dreamed of a girl who was waiting for him somewhere in southern Africa; at the same time he was convinced that all his progeny would be black. In January 1947 his condition was described as 'hebephrenic schizophrenia'. Hebephrenia is another term for congenital retardation. Six months later he was declared cured and discharged. The doctors wanted him to be repatriated, but in the meantime details of his previous life had filtered through to the authorities. The fact that he had been a member of the Communist Party was regarded as even more sinister in post-war America than it had been in the Transvaal some years earlier.

The officials who knitted their brows over Demitrios's future had to determine who he was and to what country he belonged. No simple answer could be expected to either question, for they were dealing with someone who had as many names as personalities.

Was he the illegitimate son of a lathe operator now living in Pretoria? A Mozambican agitator? A South African *métique* with a Greek background? A deranged sailor? 'Retarded' he plainly was not. Apart from fluent Greek, English and Portuguese, he spoke Shangaan, Arabic and a little Afrikaans. His Greek and Portuguese passports had long since expired. He possessed the papers of an American seaman, but these were of doubtful value. South Africa offered no solution to the problem: from the authorities there came a clear indication that he would not be welcome. They confirmed that they had refused him a visa several times already and would do so again if he should seek one.

Somewhere in those offices, with their bakelite telephones and packed filing cabinets, the knot was finally severed. Demitrios Tsafandakis, it was declared, was *definitely* Greek.

In August a deportation order was issued. A month later, under police escort, he was put aboard the SS *Marine Jumbo*. The ship was about to sail to the Mediterranean and to call at Piraeus, the port for the city of Athens.

Piraeus in the sunset light of 1947. The harbour a random assemblage of fortified, bomb-battered structures. Hawkers and barrows swarming on the pavements. The cafés filled with men, men only, most of them moustached and unemployed. The daily papers under strict censorship. Streets reeking of petrol and sesame. Turkish hubble-bubbles for hire. On every corner rousing gramophone music of the kind Demitrios can remember from his parents' house in Lourenço Marques. He is at last free, ashore legally, done with the fear of being followed.

Not that all was well. A civil war was in progress. German occupation and years of starvation had been succeeded by guerrilla fighting; now an outright war was being fought between the Left and Right. Demitrios had arrived in a country with an empty stomach and darkness at its heart. Yet he was about to enjoy a period that was free of the attacks that had been tormenting him since leaving Cape Town. It was as if in Greece he had at last found some of the stoic fatalism which the Greeks think of as peculiarly their own. Like many another macho Greek, he also learned to boast and complain. He talked himself into a job with the American Reconstruction Mission, a subsection of the Marshall Plan. He worked first as a translator, subsequently in the section dealing with the delivery of supplies to American and British troops. He had status again, he used his languages, he bought a hat.

Nevertheless he applied more than once for a visa to reside in South Africa, or at least to visit the country, and in the letters accompanying these applications he did his best to deny that he actually 'belonged' to Europe. A hectoring tone began to enter into his correspondence with both the South African Department of External

Affairs and the American authorities. 'I was sent to Greece, a country I have never seen before... It is not a small mistake. The difference is between the North Pole and the South Pole.' He insisted that South Africa was the country in which he had been educated and that it was 'the country of my mother, Amelia Williams'. Just as he had done previously in the United States, he told the story about the anonymous woman who had remained faithful to him for so long. 'Will you please permit me to go home again, and to return to the girl with whom I grew up, whom I want to marry, and with whom I have so much in common.' And in conclusion: 'I am here a man without a country... I have a lot more to mention but cannot put it into writing.'

This letter ends with the words, 'Remain Yours, James Demitrios Tsafandakis.'

He had acquired the name James in Piraeus. In all likelihood this was the consequence of his having become a member of a group of young men and women who kept in touch with what they called, simply enough, The Christian Church. They used to meet occasionally in one of the suburbs of Athens in order to study the Scriptures. The chief language of the group was English. It was not exactly a church; nor was it a sect or cult; rather a vague, pleasant fellowship of faith with worldwide contacts. Its doctrines, so far as there were any, emphasized the equality of all races, a not-very-strictly observed abstinence from alcohol, and a peace-loving, almost American kind of optimism. His conversion to the faith had been confirmed by baptism in the sea, along with his new name. Shortly after his dismissal from the Reconstruction Mission, the thirty-year-old but already corpulent James, wearing only his underpants, had been ritually immersed in the waves near Piraeus. After the ceremony he was joyfully applauded and thrown on the sandy beach.

He lived in Greece for almost two years—that is, for about as long a period as he had spent on the Witwatersrand. Then restlessness and chronic anxiety struck at him again. In the late summer of 1949 he worked for some time on a Greek cruise ship, the *Corinthia*, which went from port to port around the Mediterranean. In Marseilles he left the ship and travelled to Paris, where he applied for a visa to Spain. On 8 November he arrived at a Portuguese border post, Barca d'Alva, only to be arrested by the guards on duty.

He spent a month under arrest in Oporto, while the Policia Internaçional e de Defesa do Estado (President Salazar's notorious secret police) examined his baptismal certificate. The refugee passport given to him in Athens revealed that he had been deported several times from the United States. His putative Portuguese citizenship was investigated and confirmed from Lourenço Marques. But in that case why had he never been called up for military service? Immediately he was declared to be a deserter and locked up. Three months later he appeared before a military tribunal in Lisbon. The PIDE reported that the Mozambique administrators had described him as an unwanted person of alien descent who would not be permitted to re-enter the province. The report also acknowledged, however, that he was not wholly accountable for his own actions. He was a rogue *que tem una vida sempre instável e de aventuras*—'constantly drawn to an unstable and adventurous way of life'.

The rogue was set free, given temporary papers, and allowed to remain in Portugal.

From there he wrote letters to his family in Pretoria. They did not respond. They had no intention of helping him; such feelings of affection as they might once have had were now dead.

For the next year or so he could be seen wandering about the banks of the Tagus, earning his keep by hawking assorted goods of the cheapest kind: little combs, sunglasses, plastic whirligigs. He liked to go aboard ships in the harbour and gossip with their crews. He also made himself as agreeable as he could around the offices of the Companhia Naçional de Navigaçâo. Through his connections there he eventually succeeded in getting a job at sea once more. Destination: Mozambique.

October 1951: the cargo steamer *Save* makes its way through the Straits of Gibraltar, sails east and passes along the Suez Canal. Within a couple of weeks it enters Delagoa Bay and ties up in the harbour of Lourenço Marques. Demitrios leans over the railing. What he sees is too beautiful to be believed: the busy quay, and, beyond the warehouses, the city of his birth.

Once ashore, however, he is held by passport control. 'Dimitrie

Tsafandakis' is known to them as a Communist, a draft dodger, a troublemaker. His papers may be in order but he is not allowed to proceed further. He puts up a protest against this treatment, before returning unwillingly to his ship. At noon he reports to its sickbay, doubled over with stomach pains, barely able to keep on his feet. He appears to be suffering from an acute attack of appendicitis. A decision is taken to admit him urgently to a hospital in the city.

No sooner is he off the ship than his condition improves remarkably. He has no time to lose. An hour or two later he sneaks out of the hospital and makes his way to the honorary Greek consul. He needs a Greek passport to enable him to travel from Lourenço Marques to Pretoria. Surely that is little enough to request?

The consul for Greece was Tony Maw—that same Tony Maw who had been a neighbour of Michaelis Tsafandakis many years before, in the Rua Andrade Corvo. He remembered Mimis both as the little half-breed who had been sent to his grandmother in Alexandria and as a schoolboy. Now he was back in Maw's office after all this time, not lost forever in the wilderness of the world: a strong, suntanned, loutish fellow, beefy but well spoken, complaining about his treatment at the hands of the Portuguese.

For his part Demitrios was confident that he had come to the right place. He was dealing with a friend of his father's, after all. He hadn't seen his family for ten years, he said; he had been blocked and frustrated everywhere, and especially so by the PIDE and the South Africans. It was time that he visited Michaelis, who was now sixty-six years old and who, according to Demitrios, was waiting impatiently to see his long-lost, firstborn son.

Though it would have been little enough trouble for Maw to issue him with a travel document, he was not inclined to oblige. Demitrios had arrived in the office out of the blue. He was not even a Greek citizen, formally speaking. Demitrios's father was indeed known to Maw, but it now transpired that Tsafandakis had never taken the trouble to register the birth of his illegitimate child with the consulate. Let him plead as much as he liked; the consul was determined to stick to the letter of the law. All else aside, Demitrios had feigned illness in order to get ashore. He was an illegal immigrant.

What could he have been thinking of? Nothing could be simpler, the Englishman said threateningly, than for him to phone the police. He'd be deported immediately.

'Do you know anything about my natural mother?' Demitrios asked, more in an attempt to distract Maw than in hope of rousing his compassion. 'I spent years looking for her grave. To tell the truth I'm not even sure that she is actually dead.'

The consul was not impressed. He had never known Amelia, he said curtly. According to reports, she was not someone who was fit to have been a lifetime's companion for the good-hearted Michaelis. She was black, 'a native'.

Demitrios hesitantly took his hat off his head. His legs began to tremble. He did not know what to say. A few minutes later Maw told the eccentric seaman to clear off.

'Just remember that one day I won't want a Greek Orthodox funeral,' Demitrios shouted weakly, from outside the office.

Not long after this episode the authorities returned him to Lisbon. He was trapped like an eel in a basket, it seemed, and would never escape. His old ailments duly reappeared. In the Hospital do Ultramar a diagnosis was made: *'parasitose intestinal; psicose maníaco-depressiva'*. However, on this occasion the parasites in his intestines and brain apparently responded rapidly to treatment, for he was discharged from the hospital after a mere three weeks.

The PIDE was convinced that he was up to no good. He was arrested trying to cross the border into Spain; for this he spent the next eleven months in jail. Initially he was kept in the 'Aljube', where political prisoners were interrogated; later in one of the cells in Fort Calxias. In both places he was manhandled as never before. Nothing in his previous experience had prepared him for it. A couple of times he feared for his life. No cock would have crowed if he had been put up against a wall: in the Portugal of the dictator Salazar anything was possible. But the interrogations yielded nothing and towards the end of April 1953 he was set free.

He found himself in the Albergue de Mendicidade de Mitra, a shelter for the homeless which was run by an order of mendicant friars in Lisbon. He became a pedlar once again. Along the quays and avenues of the capital he carried his wares: lacework, this time, and local embroidery, along with various other gewgaws.

During the two decades Tsafendas spent outside South Africa the sea was the only constant presence in his life. He remained almost exclusively on the coastline of the countries he lived in, in cities where the docks beckoned him and where the sounds of winches, seagulls and engines rose above the hiss and roar of the ocean. Piraeus, Oporto, Lisbon, Marseilles, London, Hamburg—he was most himself amid the restless, provisional lives of people who did not know where they might be the next day or the day after it. It was as if an unspoken judgement had been passed on him, once he had reached a certain age and had gone a certain distance: he had to serve out his days within earshot of the sombre clamour of waves and spray.

From 1951 onwards his name appears on the official list of those banned from entering South Africa—the so-called blacklist. In Portugal the PIDE would always be suspicious of him. From the United States he had been permanently excluded. A period in Germany had ended with Dr Nachtwey in the Ochsenzoll Clinic; after his discharge he was despatched to Lisbon, where he again plied his trade as a hawker along the Tagus and in the city's parks. Two years later he attended the Brussels trade-fair, optimistically bringing with him a stock of Portuguese embroidery. For the failure of this particular venture he later blamed 'the Chinese competition'. In the spring of 1959, after a further spell in Germany, he decided (in his own words) 'to leave western Europe and try my luck in England'.

The move did nothing to change his luck. As a foreigner, the holder of a Portuguese passport, he was denied an official work permit. Casual jobs were hard to come by, and he found the place and the people unfriendly. Nevertheless he managed to keep himself going until the autumn. Always a lover of public debate, he was fascinated by Speaker's Corner in Hyde Park and went to meetings of the Labour Party at Caxton Hall, and gatherings of the nascent anti-apartheid movement. One such group used the North Middlesex Cricket Club—of all improbable venues—as its meeting place. A member of it, a South African, recalled 'Tsafandakis' explicitly introducing himself as a Cape Coloured. He was eager, he said, 'to create resistance to the regime', though he had no plausible suggestions about how this might be done. While in London he made a further attempt to gain entry papers for South Africa; this approach, like all those that had preceded it, was firmly rebuffed by the authorities.

Early in his stay he was admitted to University College Hospital and to the Hospital for Tropical Diseases; on both occasions he came in complaining of stomach disorders. Once again the doctors were unable to help him. He did not blame them for their failure; to him it was evidence of how difficult and special his case was. Later his condition deteriorated and he was admitted to the St Pancras Hospital in a psychotic state. The episode was a brief one, but it was followed by a more protracted collapse which led to two months' confinement in the Whitecroft Hospital on the Isle of Wight. On his release the authorities gave him a choice: he could be sent back either to Germany or to Portugal. Staying on in the United Kingdom was out of the question. Demitrios chose Germany. From there he made yet another attempt to reach southern Africa.

Overland, this time.

On 30 June 1960 Demitrios left by train from Munich for the Balkans. After a short stop in Piraeus he travelled to Alexandria, the city of his childhood. Arriving there in October, he was arrested almost immediately. Towards the end of that year he was helped by the Red Cross to get a passage on a boat going to Beirut. Some weeks later his presence in East Jerusalem was noted. He made an effort to enter Israel, carrying a small suitcase in each hand. He was absolutely penniless and he could not convince the officials at the Mandelbaum Gate of his good intentions. 'Is there no place here for a mendicant monk?' he demanded of them. An investigator was summoned and after a short conversation he was sent back to the Jordanian sector of the city. A note was taken of the interview and thus Tsafendas's name was entered into the dossiers of Mossad, too.

For months Mimis went back and forth across the two sides of the Jordan River. The little Arabic he spoke, so far from helping him, was a source of unease to the people he encountered. On at least one occasion it led to an ugly misunderstanding, after which he had to be treated by a Jerusalem doctor—Dr Theodore Phylactopoulos—for a broken nose. Claiming to be a political refugee, he also visited the Spanish embassy in East Jerusalem. But the Spaniards were not prepared to help him get a visa to Israel. Finally he left Jordan on a bus which was bound for Beirut via Damascus.

He was unable to find work in Lebanon. He set out once more by bus, this time heading towards Tripoli, and subsequently to Aleppo, in Syria. From Aleppo it was possible to reach Adana, in Turkey. A difficult trek through the snow-covered passes of the Toros mountains brought him to Ankara. Demitrios—the Wandering Greek—had in the meantime grown a beard. His upper jaw was inflamed. His teeth were in a bad state, some of them had crumbled away, and he suffered constantly from pain in his gums.

After a month in Ankara he had picked up some Turkish, a language which his father had been able to speak. There were several things here which reminded him of Michaelis: Turkish cuisine, the songs he heard in the teahouses. Even the physical appearance of the men, and a certain pride or boldness in their gaze, as well as their habit of sharing the pleasures of a hubble-bubble pipe on the pavement, seemed reminiscent to him, like a vague echo of the lives of the Cretan forebears he had never known. The same was true of Istanbul. The look of the streets struck him as somehow familiar too, and he himself went about unnoticed through them. With his beard and his belly he could easily be taken for a down-and-out Muslim.

For want of anything better he sold his blood regularly to the Istanbul blood transfusion service. Most of the money he earned in this way—for each pint he was paid about an average week's wages in Turkey—he spent on the dentist. His upper teeth were ground, the incisors filed down, and a gold bridge fitted. Over it was spread a silver layer. At the age of thirty-five Demitrios had acquired a steely smile.

Later he got a job in the Tarhaban College. He taught English, and for a while lived with a Turkish woman working in the same institution as himself. She did what she could for him, and with a word here and a word there managed to get a residence permit for him. In winter the relationship between them deteriorated; when he left the city—this time on the way to Lisbon via Rome—he carried in his wallet a reference from the college. In it he was described as a teacher of English phonetics.

After seaman, translator, lathe operator, hawker and pilgrim, he now described himself, when the opportunity arose, as 'Professor of English'.

Then the unexpected happened. For the first time Marika answered one of his letters. A full year after the event he learned that his father had died. Mimis wrote back to Marika to let her know that he was still unable to get a visa to enter South Africa, but nevertheless he expected to receive his share of the inheritance. By this time he was back in Lisbon. Soon after receiving her letter he went to the South African embassy and applied for a visa. The young woman at the desk told him in a loud voice that the request was pointless. He had been blacklisted by the Ministry of External Affairs, and instead of wasting his money in trying to get a visa, he would do better to spend it on something useful. A clean shirt, for instance. Demitrios fell into a rage. He tore up the application form he had been completing and threw the scraps in her face. Then, still enraged, he left the building.

His next stop was the shelter for the homeless run by the mendicant friars of Mitra, in which he had taken refuge during his previous stay in Lisbon. But he soon got on the wrong side of his benefactors there. They said he made trouble among the other inmates. They were tired of listening to his lectures about Palestine, the Bible, and the bad state of affairs in Portugal's colonies. The friars wrote letters to Pretoria: could the man's family not take care of him? He was lonely and longed for a home. They even got in touch with the PIDE. Why could Demitrios not go back to the country of his birth? He was now forty-five; the whole issue of his conscription had in effect been resolved by the passage of time.

It is hard to know who, if anyone, might have been pulling the strings behind the scenes. In August 1963 Demitrios heard that the colonial administration of Mozambique, after thirteen years of hostility, had granted him a sort of amnesty. The brothers of the Albergue de Mendicidade de Mitra paid for his passage on a ship called the *Princippi Perfecto*.

Early in October the *Princippi Perfecto* steamed into Delagoa Bay. Once ashore in Lourenço Marques, Demitrios went to stay with his aunt Anna, Marika's sister, who in earlier years had occasionally protected him against the wrath of the family. At Anna's request Marika arrived from Pretoria a few days later. She told him straight out that Michaelis had left nothing to his oldest son. The family had never been well off: that was something he must understand once and for all. The little properties Michaelis had owned he had left to his daughters, as their dowry. There had never been anything else.

He was deeply disappointed. Could she, he asked, at least arrange for him to stay under her roof in the Transvaal? For a while? Marika phoned her brother in Pretoria. He owned a motor car. It was agreed that Victor would come and fetch them.

On Saturday morning, 2 November, Demitrios went to the South African consulate in Lourenço Marques and asked for a permit that would allow him a period of temporary residence in the Republic of South Africa. A Mr J. van der Berg, the official responsible, made a cursory search for the name of Tsafendas on the 'Stop List', and failed to find it. As far as J. van der Berg was concerned, the man was in possession of a valid Portuguese passport, in which he was described as resident in Mozambique. He was accompanied by members of a family with South African identity papers. Besides, van der Berg was sure that had there been anything suspect about this Tsafendas, he would certainly have heard of it from the PIDE.

On Monday 4 November, the family—Demitrios, Marika, Victor and Anna—passed into South Africa via the customs post at Komatipoort.

The South Africa that Demitrios was entering was in most respects the same country as the one he had left two decades before—only worse. The Afrikaner Nationalist Party, under Verwoerd, was still in the saddle and ruling as relentlessly as ever. Segregation was enforced even more strictly than before: laws against mixed marriages and sexual acts between the different races were in effect, as were draconian pass laws ('movement control' was their stated aim). Forcible clearances of black and mixed-race areas in larger and smaller cities took place on a regular basis. After the Sharpeville rebellion of 1960 the Prime Minister had adumbrated an ideology of so-called 'separate development', which involved the delineation of Bantustans for the blacks. The resounding logic of the programme—white tribalism fortified, deepened, aggrandized—astonished even his own supporters. In practice it meant little more than large-scale deportations of blacks to various remote, impoverished corners of the country.

Mimis stepped eagerly into his brother's house. As far as he was concerned he had come home an older and wiser person. He bought a bicycle.

4. A dangerous Communist

It did not take long, after his return to Pretoria in 1963, for things to go badly between Mimis and his family. Initially he boarded with his half-brother Victor. After just a few days Victor had had enough of this arrangement. Demitrios was an eccentric, restless, troubling person to have in the house. He got up at five in the morning and stood next to his bed with his Bible open in his hand. He was convinced that his travels abroad had given him a wisdom that the provincials around him lacked. He would give instructions to anyone he came across and made a habit of interfering in other people's business. That, at any rate, was his half-brother's view of him.

His stepmother and half-sister Evangelina also found him a handful. He would hold forth to them about his travels and about The Christian Church, with whose members in the Transvaal he had managed to make contact. It was difficult to get any sense out of much of what he said. Marika regretted bringing him back with her from Lourenço Marques. He could not accept the fact that he had not come into an inheritance of any kind. At meals he stuffed himself shamelessly. Marika's grandchildren laughed at the way he ate. They thought of him as a kind of hippopotamus, a hippo who carried them on his back, barked like a dog, and sometimes rode on his bike with them in the city parks. He was a remarkable sight on his bicycle. People stared after him. He was oversized and wore a stetson hat.

A week after his arrival he was caught going through Marika's desks and cupboards in search of his father's effects. Marika and Victor gave him some money and told him to be on his way.

For the next six months Demitrios worked as a welder and an odd-job man in Pretoria. He paid regular visits to his brother-in-law,

Nikos Vlachopoulos, who, with Demitrios's younger half-sister, Helena, managed the Proclamation Hill Café. He would spend hours there, reading the newspapers and receiving acquaintances as if he were holding audience with them. At the beginning of July his current employers, F. A. Poole (Pty.) Ltd., moved from Carl Street to an industrial area outside Pretoria. This move involved a stocktaking, in the course of which Demitrios fell out with the foreman. Some days later he was fired. That same day he applied to the Department of External Affairs for an exit visa.

Demitrios felt optimistic about his future. His papers were in order, he could go where he liked, he could even think of himself as a kind of tourist in southern Africa. In July 1964 he crossed the border into Rhodesia. He had fifty pounds in his pocket. In Marandellas, near Salisbury, he visited his sister Katerina, now Mrs Pnevma. Her husband was unpleasantly surprised by the arrival of this new-found half-brother, whom Katerina barely remembered: a man who had been rejected by the family and who brought with him an unpleasant reputation. An hour's conversation between them was enough. Demitrios was told to move on.

So he went to Nyasaland. From the capital, Blantyre, he travelled to Lake Nyasa in the company of a fish trader. Failing to find work there he returned to Salisbury. At the end of August the British South Africa Police deported him on the grounds that his entry permit had expired. He used his Portuguese passport to return to Mozambique. The end of the year found him living in the town of Gondola and working for the Hume Pipelaying Company.

At weekends he would drink a few glasses of beer with members of the local Greek community. They were impressed by his travels and his command of languages, but they also thought that he talked a lot of nonsense, especially about Portugal's colonies. Sometimes he declaimed biblical texts at them. An orthodox priest who visited Gondola from Umtali, in Rhodesia, spread the rumour that he was actually not a Greek but a Turk.

On one occasion he admitted to people he met at an hotel in Gondola that he was the black sheep of his family. When they appeared not to understand him, Demitrios took off his hat and showed them the greying, tight-packed curls of his hair. 'That's why they won't have me near them,' he said. He declared that one day a complete mingling of the races would finally take place in Africa. Everyone then would be a bastard. They would all come together in bed; and God would find it good.

One member of his audience angrily banged his glass down on the table; the others burst out laughing.

On another occasion Demitrios was standing at the bar with a group of black employees of the Hume Company. He was in high spirits—speaking to them in their own language and, it seemed to others present, instructing them as though they were his disciples.

'This isn't going to last long,' he shouted out suddenly, in Portuguese. 'This country isn't called Portugal; it's called the United States of Mozambique.'

All the whites in the room pricked up their ears.

The following day he was arrested by agents of the PIDE. He was taken to the port of Beira, and handed over to the local commandant, Captain Luis Tavara. Subsequently he was interrogated by another officer, Inspector Horacio Ferreira.

Ferreira was determined to find out if this troublemaker had made contact with the terrorists of Frelimo (the Mozambique Liberation Front). Demitrios was kept in preventive detention through the last months of 1963 and into 1964; ten weeks in all. He asked for some of his books to be sent over from Pretoria, so that he would have something to read and would be able to keep in touch with the members of The Christian Church in Durban and Cape Town.

By mid-January the investigation had led nowhere. The mendicant monks had been consulted; the headquarters of the PIDE in Lisbon had also turned in a report. The conclusions drawn about Tsafendas were no different from those that had been minuted in 1950, 1953 and 1962. Many years had passed since he had last been admitted into a psychiatric ward, but he was once again declared to be 'fundamentally a psychopath'. Ultimately Inspector Ferreira found the ever-lengthening tale of his wanderings around the world pointless and bewildering. At the end of January he closed the dossier and let Demitrios go.

On 5 March 1964 he boarded the Indian passenger liner, the *Karanja*. The journey from Beira to Durban took just two days. On the morning of the eighth he was admitted to the Republic of South Africa. He came ashore with two suitcases and some cooking utensils in a cardboard box. He never left the country again.

He rented a room in the central area of Durban and went to look for the Cuban Hat Tearoom, near north beach. The owner of the tearoom, Kyriakos Skordis, had been recommended to him. Skordis had no work for him, but told him he could use the place as a postal address. A few days later Demitrios called by to say that he had been registered at the local court as a translator in Greek and Portuguese. When he next visited the tearoom it was to say that he had got a job with the South African Railways. As he was obviously broke, the railways' personnel department advanced him some money and admitted him to a hostel for its employees. The work was tedious: he had to couple and uncouple the vacuum hoses connecting one carriage to another and do minor electrical repairs. After three weeks he had had enough of it. A week later he left his depressing room in the hostel. He took from it the Gideon Bible he had found in its chest of drawers. By then he had already managed to get himself a new position. This was in the little trading town of Mandini, a hundred kilometres north of Durban. He was going to work there as a fitter for the firm of Fraser & Chalmers Ltd.

In May Demitrios was admitted to the hospital in Mandini with a severe stab-wound in his left arm. He and a colleague, a fellow Greek by the name of Nikos Vergas, had had an argument in the Fraser & Chalmers canteen. In the course of it Demitrios knocked Vergas off his feet. Vergas came back at him with a knife he had drawn from his back pocket. The wound on Demitrios's arm was fourteen centimetres long. He laid a charge against his opponent and both men appeared before the local magistrate a few days later. As the quarrel between them had been conducted in Greek throughout, none of the witnesses could say what it had been about. Demitrios volunteered to act as translator, but since he was a party to the case his offer was not accepted.

Case dismissed.

'Communist bastard,' Vergas shouted after him, out in the street.

Some time after this incident Father Hanno Probst of the Roman Catholic mission to Zululand drove into Mandini. He called at the post office, as he always did, and at the local general dealers in the main street. Leaving the store, he noticed a middle-aged man sitting in the sun on a bench. His left arm was swathed in a bandage. He was reading a newspaper. Probst was struck by his dejected expression.

The priest was from southern Germany originally. During the many years he had spent in South Africa he had acquired a sharp eye for the physical characteristics which distinguished the races from one another: subtle gradations in pigmentation and bone structure, differences in the shape of the nose and the curls of the hair. He was proud of his refined powers of observation in this regard, especially as such indicators were considered to be of life-and-death significance in those days. To his eye the man with the injured arm was plainly a Coloured. He was convinced of it immediately. But he was sure, too, that he was not a South African.

'If you don't mind my asking, are you a Mozambican?'

The man looked up morosely.

'You're far from home, aren't you?'

'How do you know I come from there?'

'Oh, I've been around a lot. It's a hobby of mine, to guess where people come from.'

The Mozambican moved up on the bench. He too had travelled a great deal, he said. Soon he was boasting in front of the stranger. Apart from English, he said, he knew seven languages. Probst tried him in Spanish and Italian. To his surprise the man spoke both languages fairly well; his Portuguese, not surprisingly, was fluent. Then there was his German: spoken, after some hesitation, with an unmistakable Bavarian accent. Probst was astonished. What was a man with a command of these languages up to in this remote corner of Zululand?

'You must have had very good teachers in Moscow,' the priest said suddenly, to throw the other off balance.

'And you in Rome,' the man answered after a short silence, and with an odd turn in his voice.

Hanno Probst, who was in mufti, admitted that he was indeed

a Roman Catholic priest, and that he lived on the mission station in the Mangete reserve, not far from a place called Mtunzini. They did a lot of good work there.

Suddenly excited, the man burst out: 'You Catholics are all the same. Profiteers. Exploiters. Look at Salazar. Those little nuns in Mozambique—you know what they do? They pump insulin into the blacks. They think there are too many of them, so they just do away with them. And the Portuguese know all about it.'

'You're a Communist,' Probst cried out.

The Communist folded up his newspaper and casually strolled towards the filling station nearby.

The meeting left Probst nonplussed. Was he indeed a *métique*, he wondered, or a European? In any case, someone ought to be warned about him. The next morning he once again drove fifty kilometres along the coast road, from his mission station to Mandini. The little town did not have a police station, so he went instead to the security office of the biggest local factory, SA Pulp and Paper Industries on the Tugela River. The officials there listened attentively to his story. They assured the priest they would pass the information he had given them on to the police at Nyoni. Clearly the man was dangerous. One Nikos Vergas had been in to see them not long before, bearing much the same kind of information.

Demitrios picked up his post at the Cuban Hat Tearoom towards the end of August. Among the items waiting for him was a little note from a certain Helen Daniels, a member of The Christian Church. She was a pious, single, Coloured woman from Cape Town. She wrote that she was eager to get to know him, as she had heard much about him from others. The possibility of marriage was not excluded.

That night he packed his bags once again.

In one big case he put the following: a brown suit, jerseys and a raincoat, two cream-coloured jackets, underpants, socks, four handkerchiefs and twelve neckties, a pillowslip, two green sheets, a blue blanket, two hats, and various items of dirty laundry. Mixed up with these items were his books and papers, including: *Poems Old and New*, *The Concise Oxford English Dictionary*, *A Hebrew Grammar*, an *Afrikaans Exercise Book*, *Ogretmen not defteri* (property of the Tarhaban College, Istanbul), *An die Freunde des Practical English, Compêndio da Gramátika Francesca, Gramática de Xisonga*, a map of Athens, the Gideon Bible he had taken from the railwaymen's hostel, and a medical manual about intestinal disorders and acute stomach ulcers.

The other case contained: a carpenter's square, two bolts, a tin-opener, needles, eleven keys, two rolls of cotton, a saw, two combs, a pair of welder's goggles, a pair of reading glasses, a little tin containing buttons, a pair of swimming trunks, a dishcloth, hairbrushes, two saucepans with lids, one saucepan without a lid, a toaster, a hammer, a file, a spirit level, two pairs of shoes, a plastic helmet, a spoon, a fork, two pairs of striped pyjamas, a little pot of glue, a mirror and a bar of soap.

He set off the next day. Having arranged a lift as far as Port Elizabeth with a commercial traveller, he loaded all his gear into the boot of a Ford sedan. From Port Elizabeth he continued his journey by rail. After a journey of two days his train halted under the elaborate Victorian iron roof of Cape Town's main railway station. He was back in the city he had left in 1942. He felt that there was something not quite right inside him. It was as if he had a slight fever. Or as if a hunger of an unfamiliar kind was gnawing at him.

5. The man with steel teeth

Sometimes one cannot help wishing that everything, for centuries past, had been captured on film. In Technicolor. With each individual life no more than a small segment of the entire show.

Who, in such a case, would turn his gaze away from Demitrios Tsafendas, newly arrived at the main Cape Town railway station, carrying with him two suitcases containing a bundle of dirty linen and a collection of pots, pans and cutlery.

But were one truly in a position to play this game, what moments from any life would one actually choose to witness? In the context of Tsafendas's tormented career, his murderous assault in the House of Assembly—which took place exactly one year and nine days after his arrival in Cape Town—might appear, bizarrely enough, as an almost inconsequential or marginal event. Why should one choose to witness a thirty-year-old murder if one might instead hear again the long-vanished shuffle on linoleum of two pairs of shoes, in a nondescript house in the suburb of Bellville South? It was there, in the front room of the house, in the midst of the Cape winter, that Tsafendas met for the first time the woman who had indicated to him that she wished to become his wife. Her name was Helen Daniels. She was thirty-five years old. How did they greet each other? What did they say next?

Her father and brother had gone in their car to the station, where they had picked him up. Helen knew nothing about him, other than that he had travelled the world and that he was a member of the fellowship, The Christian Church, to which she and her family belonged. She had written two or three letters to him earlier in the winter, and had also sent a snapshot of herself, asking him to do the same for her. But that request had been ignored. In the end she knew only his handwriting. Demitrios wrote his letters with a fountain pen, in a strikingly elegant, self-assured, un-South African hand. From what he had actually put down little had emerged.

When he made a flesh-and-blood appearance at the gate to the front garden, and then advanced towards the door of her parents' home, she took somewhat against him. He had a double chin. She had imagined him to be thinner. He was unshaven; there were holes in his jersey; and his bags—those battered suitcases, those pots and pans—made him look like some kind of hawker carrying his goods from door to door. Still, this out-of-luck pedlar (which was what he reminded her of) had good manners. Demitrios took a seat. He drank his tea and began to tell his tales. He had served in American warships and had once been torpedoed. He knew Europe like the back of his hand. He had been in Palestine and visited the holy places and wandered along the banks of the Jordan. That he spilled some of his tea in his saucer, Helen felt, should not be held against him.

When her father began to pray and sing hymns, after they had drunk their tea, Demitrios joined in fervently. Obviously there was nothing amiss with his faith. He was shown the little room which had been set aside for him. It was agreed he would lodge temporarily with them in Sans Souci Street. They knew that on his identity document their lodger was registered as a white, and that they as

Coloureds were therefore breaking the law in letting him stay under their roof.

Helen was left feeling ill at ease about her suitor. Her distrustful glances had not escaped him, though his stories about the Middle East, about his Greek father and his natural mother, had softened the first, rather unfavourable impression he had made on her. He had let it be understood between them that henceforth he planned to live his life as a Coloured. He wanted to get a new identity document: one without the 'W' before and after his name and number, which indicated that he had been accepted as a member of the 'white population-group' (as it was officially referred to). He was determined to see to the matter immediately.

The word 'marriage' was uttered by neither of them. Both felt embarrassed about it.

The following day he went to the Population Registration Office and handed over his identity document. He wanted to be registered as a Coloured, he said. In order to achieve this end he had to make a formal declaration, as stipulated under the Population Registration Act. The declaration was drafted in the usual terms: Demitrios Tsafendas regarded himself as a Coloured, lived in a Coloured residential area, had the intention of entering into marriage with a woman of mixed racial origins.

The bureaucratic mills were to grind slowly over this request. At that time applications were flooding in from Coloureds who wanted to be classified as whites. Applications to change status in the other direction were rare indeed. Demitrios was one of the exceedingly small number of people who were volunteering to disadvantage themselves by crossing in this particular direction the mad, artificially imposed boundaries between races.

For six weeks he remained with the Daniels family. During that time he heard nothing from the Population Registration Office. He wondered why his reclassification was taking so long. In the meantime he had managed to get a job as a fitter in a local power station. Perhaps, Mr Daniels then suggested, he might make a contribution to the costs of the household, as their means were so limited. Demitrios now began to complain of stomach pains. At meal times, grimacing, he would withdraw from the table and head for his room.

Still nothing had been said about the putative marriage. At forty-seven he was twelve years older than Helen. In the end, relieved that he kept silent on the subject, she decided to let the prospect of marriage between them quietly evaporate. He was a charming man, she thought, and she enjoyed listening to his opinions on various subjects, but his manners increasingly struck her as odd. At nights he would go into the kitchen and hunt around for something to eat. She had once found him on his bed with his shoes on.

'He was just lying there with his feet on the bedspread,' Helen complained. It was a fluffy, rose-coloured bedspread made of combed cotton.

During September and October of that year Demitrios went regularly to meetings of The Christian Church. These meetings took place in various houses all over the Cape Peninsula. In the whole western Cape there were about 800 people in the group. Their 'church' did not have a building of its own, gave out no reading matter, and did not hold collections during its services. The gospel was presented in an informal, friendly manner; the transforming power of Christ's presence was proclaimed; tea or a light supper was shared after the service. The community abided strictly by the law. In the words of one of its leaders: 'Our faith caters for European and non-European races. We are not multi-racial, but we do gather with Coloured members of The Christian Church during our annual conferences. We, however, obey the apartheid laws. By this I mean that the members of different races eat and sleep separately.'

It made no difference to Demitrios whether the services he attended took place in Coloured areas or in the better-off neighbourhoods of the whites. He went back and forth between them as the spirit took him. His white fellow-believers formed the impression that he came to the services chiefly for the food. He appeared devout, but was ignorant of the texts. He sat with his hands on his knees. Sometimes his legs could be seen trembling. And he called for the discussion of strange questions. How, for instance, could Jesus have been active in heaven before appearing in Mary's womb? He sang hymns with the enthusiasm of a child; this went down better among the Coloureds than among the whites.

One day, after a Bible reading, he was taken aside by James Johnson, a white elder of the community. This was the second time that the man had questioned him. What exactly was the colour of his skin, Johnson wanted to know. As determined from the official point of view, of course. Was he a Greek or a 'non-white'? Demitrios began to explain his circumstances. Johnson interrupted him. As long as his racial classification was officially white ('European')—surely this must be clear to him?—he should no longer go to prayer meetings in the houses of Coloureds. Nothing but trouble would come of it.

Towards the beginning of summer Demitrios left Bellville South. He wandered from one hired room to another in the city centre, and finally found himself in the southern suburbs, in Lansdowne, where a family by the name of O'Ryan offered him shelter. Patrick O'Ryan, who he had met at one of the meetings of The Christian Church, was a teacher at the Bishop Lavis High School. He took pity on this homeless Greek. He shared with him not only his bread and his belief, but also a mixed background. It was apparent to him that Demitrios had only a limited understanding of the Bible, but for the rest he found him easy to get on with.

Demitrios remained unemployed for several weeks. He applied for a job as a concierge at the French embassy, in vain; and for a clerkship at the Groote Schuur Hospital, with the same result. Soon after the New Year he tried for a job as a conductor on the City tramways, but had no success there either—he was too plump to run all day up and down the narrow stairs of a double-decker. Then he applied to the Marine Diamond Corporation, a company with its headquarters at the harbour. On 13 January 1966 he successfully underwent a medical examination. Two weeks later he was at work.

The company dredged for diamonds on the Atlantic coast. He sailed on a supply ship for a site 600 miles north of Table Bay, at the mouth of the Orange River. He and the other workmen on board spent a night getting there; then they were transferred to a dinghy with an outboard motor. A strong south-easter was blowing. With difficulty the dinghy reached the giant pontoon on which the dredging machine was mounted. While the others were still vomiting over the railings, or taking to their bunks below, Demitrios, exhausted though he was, went to the bathroom and made his early morning toilet.

The foreman at once decided that this man 'knew the sea'. The crew took it in turns to work in shifts of twelve hours apiece, for twenty days at a time; then they were sent away for ten days' leave in Cape Town. At first he fitted in well. Though lazy, he was seldom sick; he ate like an ox and generally slept about three hours less when off-shift than the rest of the men. Together with John Hulse, a student earning money during his vacation, and an older American crewman, he maintained the pumps which sucked up the mud from the sea bottom and passed it into giant bins.

Demitrios talked non-stop while on the job; it was as if being back on the ocean, even in these circumstances, had loosened his tongue. In no time at all everyone knew all about his *Wanderjahre* and his contempt for the South African regime. He was proud of having spent time living among Malays and Coloureds. You could get on with such people, he announced; at least they had some sense. The Nationalist Party was crap; nor was it going to last long. As for the Immorality Act—which forbade love between the races—it was the Act itself that was immoral, not what it tried to prevent.

The head of security on board—a certain Keith Martincich—warned Demitrios to put more distance between himself and the black riggers and unskilled workers on board the dredger; also to keep away from the filters through which the mud was sieved. Quite apart from mud and diamonds, the pumps sucked up quantities of red lobsters. Demitrios, the seafood lover, could not keep away from such a bonanza. At free moments during the night-shift he would fish about in the bins, and then, in the mornings, bring his harvest into the kitchen.

Martincich was a slightly built man of twenty-three. He decided to watch this odd fellow, and crept after him whenever he took himself to some deserted corner of the deck. To his surprise he heard the man, at these times, talking loudly to himself. It was a long monologue—or was it a dialogue? Demitrios spoke of himself as a man who had dived into the sea to rescue drowning men. He acted out the story of the Cape hero, Wolraad Woltemade, who rode on horseback to bring shipwrecked sailors ashore.

In his mind he was listening attentively once again to the English mistress at his school in Middelburg. Lost in these reveries, he clapped his hands and cried out loudly. Then he would fall silent and stare at the strip of land visible in the distance. He felt an inexplicable sadness. He longed for Mozambique, for Cora in her house of many rooms. And still further back too, for Alexandria and his grandmother Katerina, who had always treated him so kindly. The sun went down. The mud from the broad mouth of the Orange River streamed out to sea, turning the sea water blood-brown.

Two months later Demitrios appeared in the office of Gillian Liebermann, head of personnel for the Marine Diamond Corporation. The noise and vibration on board the great dredger had damaged his hearing, he told her. His nose was troubling him too; this was an after-effect of having had it broken six years before, in a fight in a Jerusalem slum. In Liebermann's opinion his clothing and physical appearance were not those of the average employee of the Marine Diamond Corporation. His hat and his European-style suit helped to make him something of an exception, an oddity. He struck her as a unique and imaginative person. She questioned him, listened to his stories, and found herself drawn into a prolonged conversation with him. The upshot of their meeting was an appointment with the firm's medical officer.

At the beginning of April he took two weeks' leave and was admitted into the Groote Schuur Hospital. Dr Leon Goldmann, an ear, nose and throat specialist, operated on his left nostril. Three days later he was discharged. A social worker took him from the hospital to a boarding house run by an ex-nurse in the suburb of Observatory.

Demitrios shared his room with an Afrikaans-speaking bus-driver and a German backpacker. When, at the end of one of the meals they took together, he politely thanked the black serving-maid who had served at their table, he saw the Afrikaner scowl. This led to a heated argument between them about Verwoerd, the blacks, and the Bantustans supposedly being developed for them. The tension between Demitrios and his room-mate deepened over the next few days. Demitrios refused to put out his bedside lamp at night; he insisted on reading into the small hours. He slept with his money and papers hidden under his pillow. On the last day of May he told the owner of the boarding house, to her face, that the Afrikaners were a backward people. She responded by telling him to go and look for lodgings elsewhere.

He must have felt particularly hopeless during the winter of 1966. Again he went from rented room to room, in that flat stretch of the city which lies just below Devil's Peak. He applied for one menial job after another, never with any success. Now and then he went back to the Population Registration Office, to record his changes of address, so that he could be informed if his application to change his racial status had been granted. The papers, he was told, had been sent to the Ministry of the Interior in Pretoria, where they were being carefully studied. Continuous headaches and dizziness led him to seek help from a neurologist, but nothing emerged from the examination he went through. He was told that he was suffering from a form of migraine, and that he was overweight: nothing else. The doctor sent him away with some codeine tablets and a pamphlet on slimming. Because of his gross appetite and table manners he had become notorious in the rundown café where he usually took his lunch, on the edge of District Six. The people working there had given him a nickname: 'The Pig'.

During one of his many visits to the labour bureau he fell into conversation with a retired railwayman. The railwayman told him that casual jobs could often be found in the Senate and House of Assembly. As the South African government migrated seasonally between Cape Town and Pretoria—spending summer on the coast, winter on the highveld—the officials who ran the day-to-day business of parliament were always looking for temporary messengers and suchlike. The pay was poor—such jobs should have been filled by Coloureds, really, but the dignity of parliament demanded otherwise. A temporary position there would be better than nothing, anyhow.

On Monday 18 July Demitrios appeared for a short interview in the parliament buildings. He had cut his hair for the occasion and shaved himself with especial care. He wore a grey suit. He was received in an impressive panelled office by the Chief Messenger, Mr Burger, who was accompanied by two Senior Messengers, Schuin and Wiehahn.

First of all, they told him, he must not expect to get a permanent appointment. This was for reasons he already knew. The work itself was not onerous: for the most part it consisted of sorting post and delivering messages, documents and newspapers. If he were to be appointed, he would have to be obedient to his superiors. At the end of the Cape session, in three months' time, he would be discharged. Schuin lit a cigarette. Wiehahn stirred his coffee. Burger asked him if he understood the position.

Demitrios answered that he did indeed. A number of formal questions were then rapidly put to him. Was he a South African? Could he prove that he was classified as a white? What grade had he reached at school? Who were his previous employers? When had he been discharged from their employ?

The officials examined the certificate of attendance he had received from the Middelburg School, as well as the registration card issued by the labour bureau, on which his identity-card number (with its 'W' for white) also appeared. They listened to his account of the time he had spent working for the Marine Diamond Corporation, and did not question the reason he gave for resigning from it. ('On account of age.') Demitrios added that he had also worked at one time as a court translator in Natal.

'Did you really translate from Greek and Portuguese in front of a magistrate?' Wiehahn asked, after he had listed his languages for them. Burger, who had been watching him closely, said in Afrikaans to the other two, 'I don't think we can use someone like this as a messenger.'

Demitrios turned towards him. 'I understand what you're saying, sir. But I'm hungry. I'm desperate. I need the job.'

'You should be looking for something better,' the Chief Messenger told him. 'We have trouble with people like you.'

Burger had a poor opinion of most of those who came to his door in search of a job. A spineless lot: unemployed youngsters, sacked railwaymen, marginal types. The law compelled him to appoint to these positions whites only. But what kind of whites would choose such a 'career'? Rubbish, the sweepings of the slums. Or else older and better educated men who would take off at the first opportunity. As far as he was concerned it was the latter category to which Tsafendas belonged.

'Yes, we do have trouble with people like you,' Schuin joined in. 'You're here for a day or two and then you're gone.'

Demitrios promised that he would stay for the full three-month period.

Schuin and Wiehahn nodded politely in the direction of the door. Tsafendas took the hint. Other applicants were waiting in the ante-room. He would be informed by post whether he had got the job or not.

Just three days later the Greek oil-tanker, *Eleni*, en route to the Persian Gulf, lost a section of its rudder. It wallowed helplessly in the Atlantic Ocean, to the south-east of the Cape of Good Hope, until a Portuguese trawler responded to Captain Michaelis Fountatos's call for help. The *Eleni* was towed into Table Bay and moored at the Duncan Dock on Sunday evening, 24 July.

Demitrios always followed carefully the column in the newspaper devoted to the comings and goings of shipping in and out of the port. On Monday evening he went on board the *Eleni*. He spent a couple of hours with the ship's cook and others, introducing himself to them as a fellow-seaman. Later that evening they offered him a place at their mess table.

The entire crew of the *Eleni* was Greek. The boat would have to spend weeks in dry dock, while its rudder was being repaired. Any diversion was welcome. Demitrios told his new-found friends about the shows in town. If they wanted to buy clothes or anything else he knew where to take them.

Thereafter he appeared on the *Eleni* for lunch every day. After all, he was a Greek among fellow Greeks once again. He accompanied members of the crew when they went ashore and introduced them to Mike Augustides, of Mike's Outfitters, who was eager to do business with them. He also took them to a bar in Woodstock, where the booze was cheap, and then to the little lanes in District Six and Walmer, where the whores plied their trade. A number of the men had visited the Cape previously, and had fond memories of the high quality of its *dagga* and the good looks of its Coloured women. But Mimis warned them to be careful. Some of the police might wink an eye at what went on, but in general magistrates dealt harshly with people brought up before them. For a white man to have sex with a Coloured woman could lead to a month or more in jail. His friends shrugged their shoulders at this. What was forbidden by day was hidden at night. Besides, one of them said, everybody knew that this Verwoerd was himself married to a Coloured woman. She had 'passed', or her mother had 'passed'. So now she was white.

The watchman on the *Eleni* was an Afrikaner by the name of Stollenkamp. He was on the qui vive even during the small hours of the night, when the seamen would try to smuggle their women up the gangway. 'No Coloureds on board,' he insisted fiercely.

On 1 August Demitrios took up his duties as a parliamentary messenger. Schuin and Wiehahn gave him his instructions. He was attached to the press and information division of the House. A blue uniform was issued to him, along with a set of khaki overalls and a locker in which to keep his belongings. Most of his time was passed in a basement lobby. It was there that the messengers waited. They were summoned to different rooms in the buildings by lights going on in a panel fixed to the wall. He had to take tea or coffee to members of parliament and visiting journalists and to carry bundles of papers from one place or person to another.

Thus, to his own bewilderment, Demitrios Tsafendas found himself, day after day, close to some of the most powerful people in the country: ministers, parliamentary representatives from near and far, the bigwigs of the governing Nationalist Party and the opposition. In the poorer quarters of the city anyone who was acquainted with him knew how much he detested Verwoerd and his Nationalists. Yet, through some freakish mischance, here he was, at the very centre of the country's political life. Among them. Surrounded by them. Yet as if invisible to them.

The irony of his holding a position just there, at that place and at that particular moment, was even greater than he could have known. His request to be re-registered under the Population Registration Act as a Coloured—a request he had initiated exactly eleven months previously—had been passed from office to office in the Ministry of the Interior in Pretoria until, some time in July 1966, it had been discovered that the name of the applicant actually appeared on the blacklist of those forbidden to enter South Africa. On 8 August the Secretary of the Interior submitted to his Minister a deportation order against Demitrios. The order was signed by the Minister the next day and dispatched to Cape Town. On Friday 2 September, a low-ranking official in Cape Town finally got round to typing a letter informing Tsafendas that he was to be deported. The letter remained in the official's out tray until the day of the murder.

Who can tell when Demitrios decided that he would one day have to carry out an action which would heal, or make whole, his past? Was it in Durban? Or when that Catholic priest in Mandini had accosted him?

He was sick with shame and nostalgia. Nostalgia for he knew not what. Between the women of his mind and the women he met there was a gulf that nothing could bridge. He had worn out the soles of his shoes on the streets of Cape Town, looking for companionship; but no sooner did he find anyone to talk to than another face, a face from the past, would come between himself and his interlocutor. Everything he remembered melted into everything else. It was as if someone else was walking alongside him, but always just out of step with him. Sometimes he seemed to be ahead of his companion, sometimes behind. Even the thoughts he had, his own thoughts, actually seemed to well up inside this other person. Always he felt himself to be on a journey from one place to another, or from one place which strangely substituted itself for another. Now his imaginings ran together, unstoppably, violently, indiscriminately, filling him with shame; now they put before him, with a shameless reality far stronger than anything before his eyes, precise, changeless moments from his past.

During the weekends of August he could no longer bear to go out of his room. The lavatory was at the end of a corridor, but it was impossible for him to negotiate even that distance. When he was sure his landlady was not around he peed into cola bottles and threw them out of the window, into the garden. He ate Cadbury's chocolate bars incessantly, one after the other, a whole bar at a time. His room was littered with their silver wrappings.

When he finally understood what he was going to do, what he

had to do, when the deed he was going to commit finally made itself known to him, he felt a kind of relief. It was as if all the turmoil in his mind was suddenly stilled. In its place there came an emptiness. It was impossible for him to know whether it was agreeable or not.

What could be easier, now that he had a job in parliament? Everything was at hand. He had long believed that a firearm was the most efficient weapon a man could use to kill another. A revolver or pistol had the great advantage of striking from a distance, and of therefore allowing the assailant to escape. Previously he had had no idea what 'escape' might mean, but now that the *Eleni* lay in harbour the answer seemed clear to him. Once you were inside the parliament buildings, he knew, security was very lax. He would come on the man in one of the corridors, shoot him down, escape in the confusion that would be bound to follow, and run like hell towards the docks.

But time was getting short: it was now or never. The *Eleni* was due to sail within a few days. He had become very thick with some members of the crew. They often complained to him about the stupidity of South African laws. He allowed himself to drop some vague hints of what he had in mind and they encouraged him to go ahead; or so it seemed to him. He even gave himself a definite date on which he would carry out his plan: 2 September. Manolis, the tall bosun on the *Eleni*, had told him that he had a Beretta which he would part with for eighty dollars.

On 1 September Demitrios went to the Adderley Street branch of Barclays Bank. He produced his passport and bought as many American dollars as he needed. Then he took a taxi to the docks. He greeted the man on day-watch and went below. But now that Manolis realized Demitrios was in earnest, he suddenly got cold feet. The two men began to shout at one another. Manolis took him into the kitchen, knowing that the cook's assistant, a seventeen-year-old called Nikolas Mavronas, had a small pistol he had been wanting to dispose of. He brought it out for them to look at: a black weapon with a white butt and the inscription on it: BREVETTATA .22 MADE IN ITALY. Mavronas did not have any ammunition for it. Mimis finally counted out thirty dollars and left the boat with the gun in his pocket.

Manolis saw him off the side and told the watchman not to let him on board again; the man was crazy. The watchman did not take this instruction seriously. The fat fellow had been coming and going all month long, without doing any harm, and was obviously on good terms with some of the men on board.

That evening, in his room in Aldor Apartments, Rondebosch, Mimis discovered that the gun was little more than a toy. It was a small calibre gas pistol; barely a firearm at all. He swallowed his anger as best he could. He consulted his Bible but got no guidance from it.

The following day he carried out in a distracted fashion the jobs he was given to do. Sent into town to dispatch a message for one of the parliamentary correspondents, he came back with the wrong change. That evening the press corps gave its annual party for members of both the Senate and the House of Assembly. Demitrios was asked to help out as a waiter. One of the guests at the party was John Hulse, a member of the Students Representative Council at Cape Town University, who was a friend of an opposition MP. He recognized Demitrios and greeted him warmly. They'd worked together on that dredger: didn't he remember? Demitrios gave him an evasive answer.

On Saturday 3 September he went on board the *Eleni* for the last time. He wanted to get back his thirty dollars. Either that or another gun. Or even a proper knife. Manolis and the cook's assistant told him that they'd spent the money and it was too late now to ask for it back.

'Piss off,' the bosun said. 'What do you think we are, a couple of cowboys?'

Nevertheless Demitrios ate in the galley with them and some others. At three o'clock he went on to the bridge, where Michaelis Fountatos was preparing for the boat's departure. He complained to the captain that he'd been swindled; but the captain simply hustled him off the bridge. He should settle his own accounts with the men below.

At six o'clock that evening the ropes that moored the *Eleni* to the quay were cast off.

At a quarter to seven on the morning of Tuesday 6 September— it was a clear spring day—Demitrios took up his position in the lobby of the House of Assembly. He was expected on duty only an hour later, and he occupied himself with the morning newspapers. During the weekend Verwoerd had had a meeting with Chief Leaboa Jonathan, the leader of Basutoland, a former British Protectorate. Today, at two, the Prime Minister was expected to report on this meeting, and to make an important statement on the future of the Bantustans. Parliament would be full, Mimis knew. Almost all the members would want to be present, not to speak of members of the public seeking admission to the gallery.

But there was no way back for him.

He left for the city centre before nine. In one shop, William Rawbone's, he bought a dagger. Five minutes later, in City Guns, Hout Street, he bought another, larger knife. The owner of City Guns took him to be a fisherman or a sailor and asked no questions of him. He wandered over to Greenmarket Square and fifteen minutes later returned to his post in the messengers' waiting room. No one had noticed his absence. By the time he resumed his usual place, he had deposited the knives in his locker. He had tied their scabbards to a belt which he concealed under his blue uniform jacket. Then he served tea to the reporters, in their room on the first floor.

By two o'clock, just before the bell rang for the sitting to begin, the crowd that had gathered under the portico of the building was even bigger than he had expected it to be. Some 400 people were heading for the House of Assembly, among them the final-year students of the Afrikaans medium school, Du Preez Hoërskool, in the city's northern suburbs. Mimis went downstairs to pick up his knives and secrete them under his jacket.

At ten past two Verwoerd made his appearance. He was accompanied by his personal bodyguard, Lieutenant Colonel Buytendag, and his private secretary. Demitrios stood among the crowd in the entrance, fumbling with his jacket as Verwoerd passed by. He followed the crowd into the House of Assembly. Buytendag turned and went up into the gallery. In a moment the Prime Minister would take his seat on the benches.

Demitrios approached him. He had finally managed to free one of his knives from its scabbard. He leaned forward. People assumed that he had a message to give to Verwoerd. Then he struck. His entire weight went into the blow. The blade disappeared in Verwoerd's chest; it had been buried right up to the hilt. The premier's upper body rose; it was a reflex response merely, not a defensive movement. Demitrios remained motionless for a moment, leaning over. He pulled the knife out. It could now be seen by the people around him. He stabbed the man in front of him yet again, three more times, before he was overpowered by the bystanders.

Everyone was screaming. A group of men had thrown the murderer on the floor. He was dragged over the benches, struck, stamped on, kicked.

Dr Matthys Venter, a dominee of the Dutch Reformed Church and the MP for Kimberley District, was holding Demitrios's right arm. The knife was still clenched in his fist. With something more than a clergyman's strength, Venter managed to force his fingers open and took the weapon from him. While others struggled to hold the assassin, he carefully laid the knife on the Speaker's table.

Verwoerd's lifeless body was removed to the Groote Schuur Hospital. An autopsy would have to be held in order formally to establish the cause of death. To all intents and purposes the Prime Minister had died at the moment of attack. He had stab wounds in his right shoulder, his right upper arm and between the ribs; one of the thrusts had pierced his lung to a depth of thirteen centimetres and entered the right chamber of his heart.

Tsafendas was taken in a police van directly to the police station in Caledon Square, around the corner from the parliament buildings.

At a quarter to three, and at the request of the police, he was examined by the District Surgeon, Dr R. Kossew. Demitrios had sustained bruised ribs and a cut along his eyebrow and the bridge of his nose. His shirt was covered with blood. Looking at him more closely, the doctor realized that his nose was broken; also that he had seen this man before. Two months previously Demitrios had come to see him in connection with an application for a war pension. He had then thought him to be in a manifestly unstable state. Indeed, though he was not a psychiatrist, Kossew had jotted down the word 'schizophrenic' in his notes.

Eventually Demitrios followed the Prime Minister's corpse to Groote Schuur. The wound on his brow was stitched up and his nose was put in plaster. He was also given an anti-tetanus injection.

Four hours after the attack he was taken into the office of Dr Sakinofsky, the hospital's head of psychiatry.

There were just three people in the room, Dr Sakinofsky, his assistant, and Demitrios. Sakinofsky asked him to lie down and to try to relax.

Could he remember what had happened? Was it true that he had killed the Prime Minister?

Demitrios looked at him with an air of surprise. 'I don't remember what happened afterwards; but yes, I did stab him right through.'

'What made you do a thing like that?'

'I didn't agree with the policy...'

Demitrios sat up. He put his face in his hands and broke into tears. He cried for some time. A flood of words, of broken sentences, followed. The doctor could make sense of few of them.

'Why are you crying?' he asked at one point.

'I don't know.'

'Aren't you pleased with what you've done?'

'Yes. I'm glad to speak to you...someone better class. I'm always among the poorer class of people.'

Sakinofsky asked him about his background. He listened attentively to the story Demitrios began to tell him.

'Why have you never married?'

Demitrios looked embarrassed; he even blushed. 'I was working in a defence plant in Johannesburg when the war broke out. Then I joined an allied convoy. I was very weak. I broke down after three months at sea. I didn't know then that I was troubled in my nerves... I see things, because of high blood pressure, coils and springs in front of my eyes. I hear no voices.'

'Does God speak to you sometimes?'

Demitrios shook his head.

'Not personally. Only when I am in bed, fast asleep. Then I feel something that passes me by.'

'Are your thoughts normal?'

'They are too rapid. In Portugal they brainwashed me and put alternating current in my head. Since then I have lost my faculties.'

'Who are you against now?'

'I'm against Verwoerd. He's a foreigner... He is a Nationalist and he hasn't got the people behind him. I see no progress for the African people. There is something spiritual in me... I thought this thing had gone too far, they have made an ideology of it. The sexual part of it too—the Immorality Act, telling you who you can't marry... The only girl who wanted to marry me did not have the right identity card. I could not keep changing my identity card.'

Then, after a short pause, 'What do they actually say over the radio about the Prime Minister?'

'That he was stabbed to death in parliament.'

'I remember stabbing him.'

Sakinofsky noted that Demitrios answered his questions spontaneously. He seemed to look at what had happened from a distance; as if astonished that he had done something that had created such an uproar.

'What did you feel when you committed the murder?'

'Nothing. I just went blank.'

Epilogue

Demitrios Tsafendas spent the remaining thirty-three years of his life under detention in South Africa, at first in prison and then in the closed section of the Sterkfontein Hospital near Krugersdorp, a gold-mining town about fifty kilometres west of Johannesburg. He died there on 7 October 1999. Two days later a funeral service was conducted by a Greek Orthodox priest in Krugersdorp, and he was buried in an unmarked grave in the cemetery adjacent to the hospital.

□

GRANTA

HONOLULU
HOTEL STORIES
Paul Theroux

Hearts of Palm

The Christmas carols in Waikiki were being sung in Japanese. On the second floor lanai which contained the overspill from our Paradise Lost Lounge, Buddy Hamstra began reminiscing to me about last year, when the Japanese man in the Kodama next door signed all the company Christmas cards and then jumped out of the window, landing messily on the edge of the swimming pool.

'He thought he was being a good employee. Funny thing is, they had to send new cards.'

'That sort of thing happens at this time of year,' I said.

'Because Christmas is always a rat fuck,' Buddy said. Buddy was the bartender. 'God, I hate those carols.'

'I don't mind that one.' Even sung in Japanese it was clearly 'Rudolph the Red-Nosed Reindeer.' I said, 'Something like "In the bleak mid-winter" never fails to undo me.'

We could see the tops of the palm trees that fringed the beach two streets and a row of hotels away. The light was beautiful. No Old Masters existed in our museums but outside we had Turner sunsets and Titian heavens and I remarked that at least the world's clouds have not changed in the planet's history—sometimes I imagined our skies as Renaissance ceilings.

When I pointed to the sky, Buddy muttered something about a new Ramada hotel going up near Fort DeRussy. He was a big bulky man who whenever he was idle was always leaning on something. His elbows rested on the railing and his hands cradled his cheeks.

'I love looking at the sultry fulguration of these skies,' I said, just to try out the sound. But it didn't register. Just a noise I was making.

'Oh, yeah,' Buddy said. 'Hey, look at them palms.'

I often stared at them too, thinking: South Seas dream, where the golden apples grow, balmy Paradiso, under the hula moon.

'Some good eating there.'

I thought he meant the sushi bar with the tall vertical sign on Kalakaua but he was still talking about the palm trees. Having seen them yanked down and their feather-fronds battered by hurricane winds—they were never uprooted and stood gracefully upright again as soon as the wind eased—I'd come to regard palms as indestructible.

'You basically lop off the trunk and tear open the core. Chop it up. Pickle it in brine. It's awesome in salad. I had palms in my yard in Waimanalo. It looked clear-cut when I moved out. I basically ate the whole yard.'

He was a fat man with lovely teeth and the memory of feasting on these tasty trees made his mouth juicy with saliva.

'Any palms in England?'

'No palms. Just qualms.'

He queried me by squinting and opening his mouth.

'What's the book?'

'This is Céline. *Journey to the End of the Night.*' I read a passage aloud: 'The human race is never free from worry, and since the Last Judgement will take place in the street, it's obvious that in a hotel you won't have so far to go. Let the trumpeting angels come, we hotel dwellers will be the first to get there.'

'That babe knows what she's talking about. I love to read,' Buddy said. 'Ever read *The Prophet*? Kahlil Gibran?'

'I honestly have not.'

'You should. Stella and I used one of his poems in our wedding service. Some of his stuff really makes you think. Maybe I should read one of your books one of these days.'

'Not necessary.'

I was a little sensitive on this point. The week before, Sweetie had told one of the hotel guests I was a writer. I had specifically warned her about this. 'Say, hotel manager.' It had the virtue of being true and was less of a minefield.

'Your wife tells me you're a writer.'

I smiled, dreading what was to come.

'Do you write under your own name?'

'Yes.'

My name rang no bells; and yet, keen to demonstrate his love of reading, he recommended several bulky books I saw in the hands of sunbathers whenever I strolled along the beach at Waikiki.

Some guests, seeing posters for *The Nutcracker*, said to me, 'There's opera here?'

'Indeed there is. Also ballet and the Honolulu Symphony.'

'We love shit like that,' one guest declared.

I said, 'Just because you see palm trees and barefoot residents tossing beer cans out of their car windows doesn't mean there's no cultural life.'

But give me the barefoot beer-drinkers, I thought. I hated talk of books. I hated the mimicky opera. It embarrassed me when Buddy, who boasted of his barbarism, talked about books. I needed to talk to the chef, Peewee, about bread recipes. I liked hearing Buddy tell me something I didn't know about hearts of palm and how he ate a half-acre of them.

Sweetie considered herself an intellectual because she listened to audiobooks while she rollerbladed, pushing our daughter Rose in the jogging stroller.

Peewee said, 'You must miss the big city.'

I said no, truthfully. That I hated the foul air. That I was just one of the big mob, in my little slot, feeling tiny and hemmed in by huge buildings. That in big cities it was never dark and never silent.

'But the culture,' he said. 'Shows and concerts, like we only have at Christmas, and they're not even the real thing.'

'You can carry it with you. Your recipes are culture, Peewee,' I said. 'And you know language is culture.'

Peewee's girlfriend Nani said, 'I got my own language. Pidgin.'

Nani said some words of it, and Tonga, washing windows, smiled, comprehending as clearly as if he was hearing music. But it was a sort of fractured music, a debased and highly colloquial form of English composed of moody-sounding grunts and utterances and wilful mispronunciations.

Everyone called it 'pidgin', they said it was a language, just like Portuguese or Greek—it wasn't English, they said; though it was, just slovenly and ungrammatical and never written, without the verb to be, usually in the present tense. In their squinting ignorance people were used to translating what someone said on the basis of sound alone.

Nani said, 'Why he heah. He huhu? Or udda ting. Dis lolo he kolohe. But he keeds more bettah. Like dat.'

I said, 'Would you say there are any verbs in this language?'

She looked insulted. 'You fucking with me.'

'In that sentence "fucking" is a verb. In this one, "is" is a verb.'

'Peewee, man, this haole fucking with me,' she said. 'So you pretty smart.'

'What do you think?'

'Try wait.'

Peewee said, 'I told some people I knew you. They were like "Hey, he's famous." They want to meet you.'

But I declined. So, on Christmas Eve, I was left with Buddy, and Peewee, and Nani, and my pretty wife and daughter, at our annual party, on the second floor lanai outside Paradise Lost Lounge.

I said, 'I am through with books. Some are just junk and I get sad when I see them.'

'Books are good,' Peewee said.

'It's Christmas,' I said. 'I would rather talk about birds. Or turtles. Or the sea. I saw a whale last year from the roof.'

Peewee said, 'Nani saw some dolphins yesterday.'

Nani heard her name and said, 'We got so many birds we don't know all their names.'

I liked that. I told myself that an ignoramus was preferable to a pseudo-intellectual. Some hotel guests spent hours telling me the plots of books they liked. Some returned ostentatiously overdressed from the local production of *The Nutcracker*, lording it over the tourists gaping at our Happy Hour hula.

'I wanted to call her "Taylor" but my husband said no,' Sweetie was telling one of the Christmas party guests.

'Taylor means tailor,' I said. 'It seems inauspicious. Like calling her Cobbler.'

'That's a kind of drink,' Nani said.

'Logan is a real nice name,' Sweetie said. 'Or Shannon. Next kid maybe. We're waiting on one.'

'Shannon is Irish,' I said.

'I got some Irish in me,' Buddy said. He was peeling the foil from a platter of salad. 'The crazy side. Also the strong side. Go ahead, have some.'

'You know what's really incredulous?' Peewee said, picking up a white disc from the salad and eating it. 'The way the government treats prisoners. Hey, they should put them destructive guys in mailbags and line them up in Aloha Stadium one morning and get big fat Samoan women to beat the bags with baseball bats. If a guy woulda lost his life they'd take it more serious.'

'Them trees are making him hungry and driving him nuts,' Buddy said.

He was not looking at Peewee but rather at the tops of the palms that lined the beach, two streets away.

'Don't laugh, you'll be joining me.' Sniffing the pine boughs Peewee burst into tears. 'That's the smell of my childhood,' he said. 'We were real poor.'

No one was listening. Sweetie was laughing. She said, 'Sometimes I see him writing. I go, "What are you doing?" He goes, "Nothing."'

She had not said this to me before in the five years I had known her. She could only say it in front of other people; she felt protected by them. They were witnesses, and her people. Unlike our daughter, Sweetie was afraid of me.

'I never know what's going on in his head.'

I was looking west, towards the beach. I said, 'I bought some Christmas lights for the palm tree out front.'

Buddy said, 'I put that palm tree in this salad.'

Shtrong. Morneen. Makeen. Driveen. Joineen. Dee-shtructive. If he woulda lost his life.

Mr and Mrs Sun

People in the hotel said, 'They hold hands,' and always smiled because Mr and Mrs Sun were in their late forties and rather plain and well past the hand-holding stage of marriage. Even some of our honeymooners didn't do it. Chubby hands like gloves made the hand-holding noticeable. I liked saying, 'So what?' The hugging and clasping was less interesting to me than the Irish names of their children, Kevin and Ryan, very skinny kids, a different physical type altogether. Plump parents usually had plump kids. This seemed to be breaking some fundamental family rule. The other thing was, their kids were famous brats.

The first year—my first year, their fifth or more—they came without their children. While the parents were model guests, their two boys had a history at the hotel and a reputation for trouble. One was destructive, the other a thief. 'Attention-seeking' was one of the kinder explanations. I liked the hand-holding Suns, without in the least bit understanding their children. They were from San Francisco,

Chinese-Americans. Their name was so attractive.

Soon after I arrived in Hawaii I had reflected on how the sunlight here was so dazzling as to give us the conceit that we were virtuous and pure and better than other people; that we took personal credit for the sunshine and expected gratitude from strangers for sharing it with them. It was the Hawaiian heresy, and a dangerous one for making us complacent about the damage we did to these little crumbly islands. We were so smug about our sunshine we were blind to everything else, as though we had been staring at the sun too long.

So much for the sun, yet I still found Sun a lovely bright open-faced name. More American than Chinese, Jerry and Amelia were quiet people, and I had not paid much attention my first year because I had mistaken them for middle-aged lovers, surprised by their mutual attraction, delighted and grateful, for whom no one else existed. On their visit my second year I still saw them as distant, inward, happy, compliant, practically magnetized lovers, but also realized they were the parents of two disruptive teenaged boys.

In spite of the staff warning the boys all week, one night they had thrown furniture into the hotel pool.

I was checking to see that the chairs and tables had been fished out when I found a soggy book lying on the tiles. It had been badly splashed, an early edition of Michener's Hawaii, and although the inked inscription was blotchy with water the handwriting was so upright and enthusiastic I could easily read it:

'To my dear husband, to commemorate ten years of the greatest happiness I have ever known. May the future shine as brightly upon us and let our joy be endless! Your adoring wife, A.' And a date.

Apart from the old-fashioned and impossible-to-mock romantic gusto, and the date—five years before—I was struck by the joyous penmanship, the exclamation mark as bold and expressive as a Chinese brush-stroke. The book was nothing special but the inscription made it a trophy.

'That thing down there with legs is a table,' Kona said. 'Something like an occasional table.'

He meant the dark object at the deep end that the young fools had thrown in with the chairs and ashtrays and cushions.

'What did you say, Kona?'

I loved hearing him repeat it, the unexpected precision of occasional. It was wooden, now split and ruined, from a guest room.

'Them Sun kids again,' Peewee said. 'I know what I'd do with them.'

We had the weird vitality of spectators at a disaster, and stood marvelling at the wreckage, watching the junk being hoisted, hoping there were no corpses.

'Burlap sacks,' Peewee said. 'Samoan women. Baseball bats.' I went upstairs to the Suns' room and knocked. I heard a soft voice, I'll get it, darling.

Mrs Sun answered the door. Her husband was in a chair across the room holding a book. Another chair had been drawn next to it. Lovers mostly were the habitual rearrangers of furniture, pushed chairs together like this, or—also like the Suns—deleted the night-stand and pushed the twin beds cheek to cheek.

'Yes?'

I never spoke to the Suns without feeling I was intruding on their intimacy and perfect peace.

'We've had another complaint about your boys.'

Mrs Sun looked so sorrowful I found myself apologizing and eager to get away, suddenly finding the vandalism trivial compared to my disturbing the happiness of this wonderful couple. Mr Sun put his book down. They both looked abject. How many times had they been put in the position of having to be sorry and make amends?

Mrs Sun said, 'I'll ask my husband to speak to them. Of course we will pay for any damage.'

'The patio furniture isn't a problem. There was some breakage though,' I said. 'And a guest-room table will have to be replaced or refinished. It ties up Maintenance when these things happen.'

'I know it has happened before because of our boys,' Mrs Sun said, something I had planned to say.

'Are they around?'

'Across the hall.'

She knocked: no answer. I knocked, then used my master key. But by then Mr Sun had called to her with affection and concern and she was now back in their room with the door shut.

The boys were out but judging from the condition of the room,

Maintenance and Housekeeping would have some work to do: broken mirror, broken blinds, spills on the carpet, footprints on the wall—on the wall?—and that was only what I saw from the doorway, peering in.

'That's nothing,' Trey said. 'A few years ago they trashed the bar. Buddy went ballistic.'

One boy was a drunk, the other smoked dope, he said, but Trey admitted he did not know which was which. It did not matter. They were a year apart, fourteen and fifteen. In the second week of their vacation the older one was caught stealing from an ABC store and the younger one was picked up for vandalizing a public telephone. Because of their ages, no charges were filed. The boys were put into the custody of their parents, which was odd because I never saw the four Suns together. The children were seldom around. I saw Mr and Mrs Sun at the Academy of Arts. They never did tourist things. On another day they volunteered the information that they were just returning from St Andrew's, the church in which they had been married. Their visits to Hawaii were always planned around their wedding anniversary.

They were, as always, holding hands. Mr Sun tugged his wife's hand with such affection that I was moved.

'I can see that the romance hasn't gone out of your marriage,' I said.

'It never will,' Mr Sun said.

Is a marriage a family? Mr and Mrs Sun were inseparable, utterly devoted to each other, quiet, and kind, their love creating a magnetic field of orderly flowing energy between these two people. The flow did not exclude anyone else; it neither attracted nor repelled. No one else mattered.

They left, all of them. The following Christmas on a sunny afternoon one boy shot himself in a motel in Great Falls, Montana. The other boy moved to Seattle. Still I did not know which boy did which.

The Limping Waiters

People, thinking it was remarkable, whispered that our two waiters who were friends had the same distinctive disability, each a foreshortened leg, Wilnice's left, Fishlow's right. They wobbled and bobbed, bumping shoulders, but it was no coincidence. They had met in a hospital ward where there were many others like them, and been room-mates there in the Hip Unit, and made friends in rehab. Their common disability helped their friendship, formed a crude basis for mutual understanding, like a racial trait, but was not their bond. No one except me knew their bond was much odder, a disability of a profounder kind, nothing like the leg.

Our busy season at the hotel, November to March, and the Japanese frenzy of Golden Week, meant we had to hire more wait staff—and for this from their home in Texas, where the slack season was winter, I hired these two men in their forties, Eddie Wilnice and Ben Fishlow, who came as a pair rather than a couple. They came pedalling and pumping at you. They were through with the Waikiki Pearl, our neighbour hotel, where they'd worked the previous season; they said they would tell me why, providing I never asked for references. I understood this to mean that the story itself would define them, as sometimes when someone wishes to express something forceful they say, 'Let me tell you a story.'

Wilnice had been waiting on a young Japanese woman. You noticed their big floppy hats, which with their skinny stem-like bodies gave them the aspect of decorative flowers. This one had said shyly but in a formula, like a sentence she had practised, 'Please you can deliver this to my room,' and handed over a small purse. Wilnice did so after work, she met him at the door. He was surprised to see her— what was the point of the delivery?—then he knew everything. She was dressed—undressed, rather—wearing a robe, a happi coat, which was undone, loose at the front, unbuttoned—no, the buttons were her nipples, this young woman was naked. 'Like one of those pictures,' Wilnice said. I think he meant those over-precise Japanese erotic prints called *shunga*, which depict egg-faced women exposing themselves improbably, the proper woman made wanton. This young woman mimicked a courtesan, tempting Wilnice by seeming meek.

'Please you come in.' And yet she cowered. Her bad grammar made her more innocent and helpless.

Wilnice stepped backwards, bobbing on his bad leg, and went away, hike-hop, hike-hop.

Telling Fishlow about it later, seeing his friend smile, Wilnice had no idea that his shock, his puritanism, his disapproval had made him remember every detail of the fleeting encounter—the button business, her slightly bow legs, the hollows of her inner thighs, her red thick-soled clogs, her black-painted nails and black lipstick. And he repeated the story, answered questions ('It was a junior suite... Yes, she was alone'), believing Fishlow was also shocked.

The next day, Fishlow sought out the young woman, went out of his way to serve her. She seemed to notice his leg, the way he walked, how he surged towards her, bumping people as he passed them.

She asked for tea. Fishlow brought it solemnly to her table. She offered him the purse that Wilnice had described and repeated the formula, 'Please you can deliver this to my room?'

Attempting a bow Japanese fashion Fishlow bent himself crookedly, lifting his arms for balance, and at four when he knocked off work he went up in the service elevator to the woman's room. She answered the door, it was all as Wilnice had said, like a promise kept: the loose happi coat, the nakedness, skin like silk, hairless, smooth, without a mark, pigeon-toed in the red clogs; she invited him inside.

'You sit here?' she said tentatively, patting the sofa next to her.

Fishlow obliged. Without any preliminaries—Wilnice had supplied those—he kissed her. She clung to him, groped him through his clothes, but thoughtfully, as though she was squeezing a fruit, testing it for ripeness. Her small almost pressureless gestures chafed him and roused him.

She suddenly got up and went to the window, peered through the blinds, turning her back on him. If she heard the drawer open and shut she did not show it.

Holding the Gideon Bible, Fishlow came bobbing and swaying behind her, hiked up her happi coat, moved her feet wider apart and as she canted forward to receive him, Fishlow chucked the Bible to the floor, pushed his short leg on it, and thus braced he entered, lifting her. Then she reacted, as though lifted on to a peg.

'No! No!' she cried out, which terrified him. He stopped, fearing that her plea might carry even through the closed window; but in a softer voice she implored him to continue. All the while, she remained turned away from him; said nothing more, did not appear to see him balancing on one leg to hoist his pants before pedalling out of the room.

Recklessly, against all hotel rules, he met her again. He could not help himself. It was a feature of their love-making that Fishlow never saw her face, that somehow she always contrived to hide it; and they were always upright, and so the Gideon Bible was another feature. And 'No! No!' And her reaching behind and clawing him like a cat. Like lovers on Sundays who sleepwalk through museums as a break from bed, they went to a movie and once to a sushi bar—perfunctory, almost meaningless, she had almost no English. But her body spoke. Her body said: For the sake of my modesty, I must pretend that it is rape but don't be fooled—look closely and you will see it is rapture.

'Rapture?' Wilnice said, and looked so wounded that Fishlow said nothing more.

Still they worked, waiting on tables. Fishlow's intensity bordered on obsession, he had no words to describe it, he was possessed. What he wanted to say was insane: I understand cannibalism. What was that supposed to mean? Then, six days from the day he met her, the woman left, her holiday at an end, Golden Week over.

Sneaking her name from the hotel register, Fishlow wrote to her.

Her address was a whole incomprehensible paragraph of short words and long numbers. There was no reply. Fishlow called her telephone number. Now he could not remember whether she had ever spoken to him in English. He got someone shrieking in Japanese, a sexless squawk-box, to his pleading questions.

Wilnice did not know what to do with Fishlow during his crying jags. He did not know how the little doll-woman had swept over his friend, nearly destroying him. Fishlow had been so happy, so hungry, she had made him into a willing dog, and now she was gone and he was still a dog but desperate. That was the worst of love. Fishlow's only solution was to seek help from his limping friend Wilnice, who had seen the woman first. So he told him one day when they were out walking—bobbing and bumping, as usual.

Fishlow's story was so sorrowful that it had the precision of regret, of guilt and blame, every incriminating detail noted: the back of her head and her neck as she turned away, the manner in which he had snatched the Gideon Bible and thrown it down, his mounting her from behind, her body full of chicken bones, the way she had pretended to resist. He was specific and self-mocking because he was wounded.

'What do you mean "at the window"?' Wilnice said, his mouth agape.

Guessing that he could have been the man she wanted, that the young Japanese woman could not tell them apart; how their staggering and limping made them equal in her eyes—Wilnice was envious and the envy was corrosive, making him sick with sorrow for having backed away from the woman's door. He took a ghastly delight in Fishlow's descriptions of the woman's hunger. Like a cat! From behind! Like squeezing a fruit! Tottering on her clogs! And Wilnice moaned to himself, I have always lacked conviction.

But Fishlow envied Wilnice's self-possession, the way in which he had simply backed off from the woman and gone home. This woman who burdened Fishlow's memory—more than that, infected him with regret, a humiliation, a casual demon. Just as Wilnice could not rid his mind of the details Fishlow had related, Fishlow continually saw Wilnice in the little apartment, taking his shoes off, one shoe thicker-soled than the other, microwaving some chilli and eating it out of the can with a plastic spoon, all this innocent economy, sitting like a child in front of the television set, while he stood lopsided in spite of the Bible, naked in the naked woman's room, the naked woman crying out, 'No! No!' and averting her face.

Fishlow envied him and thought: I have always been too impulsive—it will shorten my life; and Wilnice thought: I am afraid, I don't know how to live.

Each man was consumed by regret, the one from having rejected the woman, the other from having made love to her. Each man believed he had failed, and the way they walked was like emphasis, as though trying to rid themselves of the memory of the woman.

Human Remains

For years, Lionberg drove from the North Shore once a week to have a hamburger, and then he began to come almost every night, and drink instead of eat, and so it was obvious that something had changed. He always asked for me. This man who had been secretive and subtle was now expansive and blunt. He would turn to a woman wearing heavy mascara at the bar and say, 'You look like a raccoon!' And not in jest but angrily, as if—even if it were true—she had no right.

In the way a drinker at a bar becomes Chairman of the Board, Lionberg engaged in lengthy monologues instead of conversing—monologues that with modest expansion could have been worked into short stories. I was tempted but I had abandoned the awful business and anyway I liked the bare bones of his stories, and the telegraphic way he told them: 'The Shutter Sisters. Famous twins. All sorts of celebrity as a double act. Merle died, and so Beryl could not be famous any more. She kills herself.'

In another, a man named Doughtry—they always had names—indulged himself in sexual fantasies on the phone with his high school sweetheart, Lamia, whom he had not seen for years. It was beyond phone-sex. It was a phone-relationship, which included the wildest sex. Unable to stand it any longer, they met, had a solemn, awkward cup of coffee and parted. Afterwards, there were no more calls. The relationship was over; they had met.

'Andy Vukovitch was a very good friend of mine,' Lionberg said.

Whenever a man mentions how close the friend is you prepare yourself for the worst.

This Andy loved his wife Lorraine but was at his most passionate and demonstrative when he was having an affair, being unfaithful to her and feeling guilty. In the course of a long affair with his mistress, Nina, he was glimpsed by Nina being tender towards his wife. Nina dumped him and, without a secret life, Andy became demanding and hypercritical. He seldom went out—why should he? He was doggedly faithful to Lorraine who, at last, could not stand his constant scrutiny, and left him.

'Maybe it was doomed to happen,' Lionberg said. 'There is a point in life, if you live long enough, when everything that happens is just repetition. You have done this before in precisely the same way. You have met this person already. You already own one of these contraptions. It is the nightmare of the eternal return—nothing is new. You see in this repetition that your life is over—nothing to look forward to. You are able to anticipate what the man or woman will say and you want to scream.'

Lionberg himself was full of plans.

'I bought myself a treadmill,' he said.

'A treadmill is somehow not a declaration that you are going places.'

He didn't laugh, he probably hadn't heard, but monologuers have no humour. He was smaller, paler, more intense as a drinker than he had been as an eater. He took on the face and posture of a small burrowing animal as he announced his plans—cruising the inside passage off the Alaskan coast, his great seats for the Michael Jackson Millennium Concert at Aloha Stadium one year hence, a slot in a timeshare in St Barts, a trip in a limited-edition battery-operated electric car. All his plans involved considerable expense.

The socialite Mrs Bunny Arkle stopped in one night to see Buddy.

Lionberg said, 'She's a fine woman. I knew two of her husbands. I should marry her, I really should.'

Mrs Bunny Arkle heard this through Buddy and began showing up when Lionberg was around.

Lionberg ignored her and yet he still said to me, 'We'd make a great couple. What does it matter that I have no sex drive? She's probably past it, too, though women of sixty think of nothing but sex.'

Finally, Mrs Bunny Arkle gave up on him, saying that the worst of Lionberg was that these days she could not tell whether he was drunk or sober. Lionberg just shrugged. He asked me out of the blue whether I got sick of doing the same thing every day. I was too insulted to give him a reply.

'No more composing,' he said. He knew that I had been a writer.

'Now I'm decomposing.'

'Don't say that!' he said with his chairman's anger.

The saddest task for the ironist is having to tell the listener that it's a joke, because of course it is never a joke.

'I want to see the Taj Mahal. The pyramids. The Panama Canal. The Shwe Dagon Pagoda.' He was off again, not listening, not even looking. 'Make a great trip around the world, see everything at once. They have these tours.'

And even when he was not around he was in the hotel talk.

Buddy said, 'You've been to Africa, right?'

'Yes.'

'Lionberg's going there.'

Manu told me that Lionberg had asked him to build an orchid house—very elaborate, with a triple pitched roof and sprinklers and its own climate control.

'I heard about your orchid house,' I said, the next time I saw Lionberg.

He said, staring and lifting his drink, 'You get these rich Japanese who kill themselves by slamming the door of their Mercedes on their silk Hermès tie and getting strangled at the side of the road.'

It was odd and exhausting that he showed up so much, after his quiet weekly visits of the past. He had the energy and that air of exclusion of the man possessed with plans. He was moving back to the Mainland, buying a winery in Napa. Investing in semiconductors. Living on a yacht in Marina del Rey. Ranching in Montana.

Maybe these were empty dreams, but his spending was a reality. He was so preoccupied with it that he could not do it on foot—he sat at his desk, and sometimes at the Hotel Honolulu bar, phoning his mail orders: Zegna suits, Ferragamo shoes, shiny gizmos and trinkets from The Sharper Image. He developed a commitment to anything made of titanium. 'It'll survive a nuclear winter. They use it on jet fighters.' He bought a titanium Omega watch, titanium sunglasses, titanium golf clubs, a titanium bicycle. 'They're indestructible.'

Why tell me?

Perhaps he could read the question on my face, because as I was thinking this, Lionberg said, 'I want to write a book. What's it like?'

'Awful when you're doing it. Worse when you're not.'

'I'd do it in Mexico. Get a little place in San Miguel de Allende. Learn Spanish at the same time. Do some painting. Take my bike for exercise.'

A cooking course in Italy was also among his plans. A visit to the Hermitage museum in St Petersburg. Learning to tap-dance and play the piano. Register for a six-credit course in astronomy at Cal Tech.

'Do you see love in your future?' I asked.

He heard that. 'I've known so many beautiful women. All my

wives have been beautiful,' he said. 'But no one is uglier, more witch-like, than a beautiful woman after she's hurt you or done something bad. Yes, she still has the right bones and contours but there's a definite stink. Did you know that girl Rain?'

'Buddy mentioned her.'

'She's getting married. I'm delighted. She's going to have a child.' He sounded pleased and paternal. 'I have a wonderful present for her.'

Another plan, the wonderful wedding present, along with doing some skydiving, collecting Sepik River masks and adding to his collection of netsukes, learning to windsurf. 'I'm not too old. Go to the Columbia River gorge—world's best windsurfing. Find a windsurfing partner.'

'Sure, look at me,' Buddy said. 'Pinky's twenty-three. Best sex I've ever had. She's sick!'

At that, Lionberg laughed, because Buddy was drunker than he was.

It was tiring to be around Lionberg in this making-plans mood. His plans required me to be attentive, to see him in Mexico riding a bike and learning Spanish, to imagine him harvesting grapes or hot-air ballooning. He gave the governor money for his next campaign and then he prevailed on him to listen to his plans, some of which were plans for the state of Hawaii. He was at the bar almost every night, and we watched him closely, as you do someone who is mapping out a future and making predictions.

Then his chair was empty for two days straight. That seemed serious. Another day passed. Something had happened. We reported him missing, as perhaps he suspected we would, and he was found in the garage of his big house on the North Shore, dead in his car, with the engine running. No note.   □

GRANTA

GOODBYE, MOTHER
Hanif Kureishi

If you think the living are difficult to deal with, the dead can be worse.

This is what Harry's friend Gerald had said.

The remark returned repeatedly to Harry, particularly that morning when he had so wearily and reluctantly got out of bed. It was the anniversary of his father's death.

Whether it was seven or eight years, Harry didn't want to worry. He was to take Mother to visit Father's grave.

Harry wondered if his children, accompanied perhaps by his wife Alexandra, would visit his grave. What would they do with him in their minds; what would he become for them? He would never leave them alone, he had learned that. Unlike the living, the dead you couldn't get rid of.

Harry's mother was not dead but she haunted him in two guises: from the past, and in the present. He talked to her several times a day, in his mind.

This morning it was as a living creature that he had to deal with her.

He had been at home on his own for a week. Alexandra was in Thailand attending 'workshops'.

When they weren't running away, the two children, a boy and a girl, were at boarding school.

The previous night had been strange.

Mother was waiting for him in her overcoat at the door of the house he had been brought up in.

'You're late,' she almost shouted, in a humorous voice.

He knew she would say this.

He tapped his watch. 'I'm on time.'

'Late, late!'

'No, look.' He thrust his watch under her face.

For Mother, he was always late. He was never there at the right time, and he never brought her what she wanted, and so he brought her nothing.

He didn't like to touch her but he made himself bend down to kiss her. What a small woman she was. For years she had been bigger than him, of course; bigger than everything else. She had remained big in his mind, pushing too many other things aside.

If she had a musty, slightly foul, bitter smell, it was not only that of an old woman, but a general notification, perhaps, of inner dereliction.

'Shall we set off?' he said.

'Wait.'

She wanted to go to the toilet.

She trailed up the hall, exclaiming, grunting and wheezing. One of her legs was bandaged. The noises, he noticed, were not unlike those he himself made getting into bed.

In the living room the television was on, as it would be all the time. She would watch one soap opera while videoing others, catching up with them late at night or early in the morning.

It gave him pleasure to turn the television off.

The small house seemed tidy but he remembered Mother as a dirty woman. The cupboards, cups and cutlery were smeared and encrusted with old food.

Mother hadn't bathed them often. He had changed his underwear and other clothes only once a week. He thought it normal to feel soiled. He wondered if this was why other children had disliked and bullied him.

Mother had always watched television from the late afternoon until she went to bed. She hadn't wanted Harry or his brother or father to speak. If they opened their mouths, she told them to shut up. She didn't want them in the room. She preferred the faces on television to the faces of her family.

She was an addict.

Alexandra had recently started—among what he considered other eccentricities—'a life journal'.

When Harry left for work, she sat in the kitchen overlooking the fields, blinking rapidly.

She would write furiously across the page in a crooked slope, picking out different coloured children's markers from a plastic wallet and throwing other markers down, flinging them right on to the floor where they could easily upend him.

'Why are you doing this writing?'

He walked around the table, kicking the lethal markers away. It was like saying, why don't you do something more useful?

'I've decided I want to speak,' she said. 'To tell my story—'

'What story?'

'The story of my life—for what it is worth, if only to myself.'

'Can I read it?'

'I don't think so.' A pause. 'No.'

He said, 'What do you mean, people want to speak?'

'They want to say what happiness is for them. And the other thing. They want to be known to themselves and to others.'

'Yes, yes… I see.'

'Harry, you would understand that,' she said. 'As a journalist.'

'We keep to the facts,' he said, heading for the door.

'Is that right?' she said. 'The facts of life and death?'

'Yes.'

Perhaps Mother was ready to speak. That may have been why she had invited him on this journey.

If she'd let little in or out for most of her life, what she had to say might be powerful.

He was afraid.

This was the worst day he'd had for a long time.

He didn't go upstairs to the two small bedrooms, but waited for her at the door.

He knew every inch of the house, but he'd forgotten it existed as a real place rather than as a sunken ship in the depths of his memory.

It was the only house in the street which hadn't been knocked through or extended. Mother hadn't wanted noise or 'bother'. There was still an air-raid shelter at the end of the garden, which had been his 'camp' as a child. There was a disused outside toilet which hadn't been knocked down. The kitchen was tiny. He wondered how they'd all fitted in. They'd been too close to one another. Perhaps that was why he'd insisted that he and Alexandra buy a large house in the country, even though it was quite far from London.

He would, he supposed, inherit his mother's house, sharing it with his brother. They would have to clear it out, selling certain things and burning others, before disposing of the property. They would have to touch their parents' possessions and their own memories again, for the last time.

Somewhere in a cupboard were photographs of him as a boy wearing short trousers and wellington boots, his face contorted with anguish and fear.

Harry was glad to be going to Father's grave. He saw it as reparation for the 'stupid' remark he'd made not long before Father died, a remark he still thought about.

He led Mother up the path to the car.

'Hasn't it been cold?' she said. 'And raining non-stop. Luckily it cleared up for us. I looked out of the window this morning and thought God is giving us a good day out. It's been raining solid here— haven't you noticed? Good for the garden! Doesn't make us grow any taller! We're the same size! Pity!'

'That's right.'

'Hasn't it been raining out where you are?' She pointed at the ragged front lawn. 'My garden needs doing. Can't get anyone to do it. The old lady up the road had her money stolen. Boys came to the door, saying they were collecting for the blind. You don't have to worry about these things—'

Harry said, 'I worry about other things.'

'There's always something. It never ends! Except where we're going!'

He helped Mother into the car and leaned over her to fasten the seat belt.

'I feel all trapped in, dear,' she said, 'with this rope round me.'

'You have to wear it.'

He opened the window.

'Ooo…I'll get a draught,' she said. 'It'll cut me in two.'

'It'll go right through you?'

'Right through me, yes, like a knife.'

He closed the window and touched the dashboard.

'What's that wind?' she said.

'The heater.'

'It's like a hairdryer blowing all over me.'

'I'll turn it off but you might get cold.'

'I'm always cold. My old bones are froze. Don't get old!'

He started the engine.

With a startlingly quick motion, she threw her head back and braced herself. Her fingers dug into the sides of the seat. Her short legs and swollen feet were rigid.

When he was young, there were only certain times of the day when she would leave the house in a car, for fear they would be killed by drunken lunatics. He remembered the family sitting in their coats in the front room, looking between the clock and Mother, waiting for the moment when she would say it was all right for them to set off, the moment when they were least likely to be punished for wanting to go out.

To him now, the engine sounded monstrous. He had begun to catch her fears.

'Don't go too fast,' she said.

'The legal speed,' he said.

'Oh, oh, oh,' she moaned as the car moved away.

Awake for most of the previous night, Harry had thought that she was, really, mad, or disturbed. This realization brought him relief.

'She's off her head,' he repeated to himself, walking about the house.

He fell on his knees, put his hands together and uttered the thought aloud to all gods and humans interested and uninterested.

If she was 'ill' it wasn't his fault.

He didn't have to fit around her, or try to make sense of what she did.

If he only saw this now, it was because people were like photographs which took years to develop.

Harry's smart, grand friend Gerald had recently become Sir Gerald. Fifteen years ago they briefly worked together. For a long time they played cricket at the weekends.

Gerald had become a distinguished man, a television executive who sat on boards and made himself essential around town. He liked power and politics. You could say he traded in secrets, receiving them, hoarding them and passing them on like gold coins.

Harry considered himself too unimportant for Gerald, but Gerald had always rung every six months, saying it was time they met. Gerald took him to his regular place where there were others like him. He was always seated in a booth in the corner where they could be seen but not overheard.

Gerald liked to say whatever was on his mind, however disconnected. Harry didn't imagine that Gerald would do this with anyone else.

Last time Gerald said: 'Harry, I'm older than you and I've been alive for sixty years. If you requested any wisdom I'd have fuck all to pass on, except to say: you can't blame other people for your misfortunes. More champagne? Now, old chap, what's on your mind?'

Harry told Gerald that Alexandra had taken up with a female hypnotist; a hypnotherapist.

'She's done what?' said Gerald.

'It's true.'

Gerald was chuckling.

Harry noticed that Mother was trembling.

On the way to see her, Harry had worried about her liking the new Mercedes, which he called 'God's chariot'.

The car and what it meant had no interest for her. Her eyes were closed.

He was trying to control himself.

A year ago a friend had given him and Alexandra tickets for a 'hypnotic' show in the West End.

They had gone along sceptically. She preferred serious drama and he none at all. He couldn't count the Ibsens he had slept through. However he did often recall one Ibsen which had kept his attention; the one in which a character tells the truth to those closest to him, and destroys their lives.

The hypnotist was young, his patter amusing, reassuring and confident. Members of the audience rushed to the stage to have his hands on them. Under the compère's spell they danced like Elvis, using broom handles as microphone stands. Others put on big ridiculous glasses through which they 'saw' people naked.

After, he and Alexandra went to an Italian restaurant in Covent Garden for supper. She liked being taken out.

'What did you think of the show?' she asked.

'It was more entertaining than a play. Luckily, I wasn't taken in.'

'Taken in? You thought it was fake? Everyone was paid to pretend?'

'Of course.'

'Oh I didn't think that at all.'

She couldn't stop talking about it, about the 'depths' of the mind, about what was 'underneath' and could be 'unleashed'.

The next day she went into town and bought several books on hypnotism.

She hypnotized him to sleep in the evenings. It wasn't difficult. He liked her voice.

Harry was thirteen when Father crashed the car. They were going to the seaside to stay in a caravan. All summer he had been looking forward to the holiday. But not only had Mother been screeching from the moment the car left their house, but—a non-driver herself—she had clutched at Father's arm continually, and even dragged at the steering wheel itself.

She was successful at last.

They ran into the front of an oncoming van, spent two nights in hospital and had to go home without seeing the sea. Harry's face looked as though it had been dug up with a trowel.

He looked across at Mother's formidable bosom, covered by a white polo-neck sweater. Down it, between her breasts, dangled a jewel-covered object, like half a salt pot.

At last she opened her eyes and loudly began to read out the words on advertising hoardings; she read the traffic signs and the instructions written on the road; she read the names on shops.

She was also making terrible noises from inside her body, groaning, he thought, like Glenn Gould playing Bach.

Visiting Father's grave had been her idea. 'It's time we went back again,' she had said. 'So he knows he hasn't been forgotten. He'll hear his name being called.'

But it was as if she were being dragged to her death.

If he said nothing she might calm down. The child he once was would be alarmed by her terrors, but why shouldn't she make her noises? Except that her babbling drove out everything else. She ensured there was no room in the car for any other words.

He realized what was happening. If she couldn't actually take the television with her in the car, she would become the television herself.

Alexandra was interested in the history of food, the garden, the children, novels. She sang in the local choir. Recently she had started to take photographs and learn the cello.

She was a governor of the local school and helped the children with their reading and writing. She talked of how, inexplicably, they suffered from low self-esteem. It was partly caused by 'class' but she suspected there were other, 'inner' reasons.

Her curiosity about hypnotism didn't diminish.

A friend introduced Alexandra to a local woman, a hypnotherapist. 'Amazing Olga', Harry called her.

'What does she do?' he asked, imagining Alexandra walking about with her eyes closed, her arms extended in front of her.

'She hypnotizes me. Suddenly I'm five years old and my father is holding me. Harry, we talk of the strangest things. She listens to my dreams.'

'What is this for?'

For Harry, telling someone your dreams was like going to bed with them.

'To know myself,' she said.

'Amazing Olga' must have told Alexandra that Harry would believe they were conspiring against him.

She touched his arm and said, 'Your worst thoughts and criticisms about yourself—that's what you think we're saying about you in that room.'

'Something like that,' he said.

'It's not true,' she said.

'Thank you. You don't talk about me at all?'

'I didn't say that.'

'Nobody likes to be talked about,' he said.

'As if it weren't inevitable.'

In the train to work, and in the evenings when he fed the animals, he thought about this. He would discuss it with Gerald next time.

Faith healers, astrologers, tea-leaf examiners, palm readers, aura photographers: there were all manner of weirdo eccentrics with their hands in the pockets of weak people who wanted to know what was going on, who wanted certainty. Uncertainty was the one thing you couldn't sell as a creed and it was, probably, the only worthwhile thing.

What would he say about this?

He did believe there was such a thing as a rational world view. It was based on logic and science. These days 'enlightenment values' were much discredited. It didn't follow they were worthless. It was all they had.

'If you or one of the children fell sick, Alexandra—' he put to her one night.

It was dark but he had switched the garden lights on. They were sitting out, eating their favourite ice cream and drinking champagne. His trees shaded the house; the two young Labradors, one black, one white, sat at their feet. He could see his wood in the distance, carpeted with bluebells in the spring, and the tree house he would restore for his grandchildren. The pond, stifled by duckweed, had to be cleaned. He was saving up for a tennis court.

This was what he had lived for and made with his labour. He wasn't old and he wasn't young, but at the age when he was curious about, and could see, the shape of his whole life, his beginning and his end.

'You'd go to a doctor, wouldn't you? Not to a faith healer.'

'That's right,' she said. 'First to a doctor.'

'Then?'

'And then, perhaps to a therapist.'

'A therapist? For what?'

'To grasp the logic—'

'What logic?'

'The inner logic...of the illness.'

'Why?'

'Because I am one person,' she said. 'A whole.'

'And you are in control?'

'Something in me is making my life—my relationships I mean—the way they are, yes.'

Something in him opposed this but he didn't know what to say.

She went on, 'There are archaic unknown sources which I want to locate.'

She quoted her therapist, knowing that at university Harry had studied the history of ideas, 'If Whitehead said that all philosophy is footnotes to Plato, Freud taught us that maturity is merely a footnote to childhood.'

He said, 'If it's all been decided years ago, if there's no free will but only the determinism of childhood, then it's pointless to think we can make any difference.'

'Freedom is possible.'

'How?'

'The freedom that comes from understanding.'

He was thinking about this.

His car had left the narrow suburban streets for bigger roads. Suddenly he was in a maze of new one-way systems bounded by glittering office blocks. He drove through the same deep highway several times, with the same accompaniments from Mother.

Setting off from home that morning, he had been convinced that he knew how to get to the cemetery, but now, although he recognized some things, it was only a glancing, bewildered familiarity. He hadn't driven around this area for more than twenty-five years.

Mother seemed to take it for granted that he knew where he was. This might have been the only confidence she had in him. She loved 'safe' drivers. She liked coaches; for some reason, coach drivers, like some doctors, were trustworthy. Being safe mattered more than anything else because, in an inhospitable world, they were always in danger.

He didn't want to stop to ask the way, and he couldn't ask Mother for fear his uncertainty would turn her more feverish. Cars driven by tattooed south London semi-criminals with shaven heads seemed to be pursuing them; vans flew at them from unexpected angles. His feet were cold but his hands were sweating.

If he didn't keep himself together, he would turn into her.

He hadn't spoken to Mother for almost three months. He had had an argument with his brother—there had almost been a fist fight in the little house—and Mother, instead of making the authoritative intervention he wished for, had collapsed weeping.

'I want to die,' she wailed. 'I'm ready!'

The forced pain she gave off had made him throw up in the gutter outside the house.

He had looked up from his sick to see the faces of the neighbours at their windows—the same neighbours, now thirty years older, he'd known as a child.

They would have heard from Mother that he was well paid.

Sometimes he was proud of his success. He had earned the things that other people wanted.

He worked in television news. He helped decide what the News was. Millions watched it. Many people believed that the News was the most important thing that had happened in the world that day. To be connected, they needed the News in the way they needed bread and water.

He remembered how smug he had been, self-righteous even, as a young man at university. Some went to radical politics or Mexico; others sought a creative life. The women became intense, quirkily intelligent and self-obsessed. Being lower middle-class, he worked hard, preparing his way. The alternative, for him, he knew, was relative poverty and boredom. He had learned how to do his job well; for years he had earned a good salary.

He had shut his mouth and pleased the bosses. He had become a boss himself; people were afraid of him and tried to guess what he was thinking.

He worried there was nothing to him, that under his thinning hair he was a 'hollow man', a phrase from the poetry he'd studied at school. Being 'found out' Gerald called it, laughing, like someone who had perpetrated a con.

Harry's daughter Heather talked of wanting confidence. He understood that. But where could confidence originate, except from a parent who believed in you?

There she was next to him, vertiginous, drivelling, and scratching in fear at the seat she sat on, waving, in her other hand, the disconnected seat-belt buckle.

It wasn't long before Alexandra started to call it 'work'.

The 'work' she was doing on herself.

The 'work' with the different coloured pens.

The 'work' of throwing them on the floor, of being the sort of person who threw things about if she felt like it.

'Work,' he said, with a slight sneer. 'The "work" of imagining an apple and talking to it.'

'The most important work I've done.'

'It won't pay for the barn to be cleared and rebuilt.'

'Why does that bother you so much?'

Money was a way of measuring good things. The worth of a man had to be related to what he was able to earn. She would never be convinced by this.

Her 'work' was equivalent to his work. No; it was more important. She had started to say his work was out of date, like prisons, schools, banks and politics.

She said, 'The cost and waste of transporting thousands of people from one part of the country to another for a few hours. These things continue because they have always happened, like bad habits. These are nineteenth-century institutions and we are a few months from the end of the twentieth century. People haven't yet found more creative ways of doing things.'

He thought of the trains on the bridges over the Thames, transporting trainloads of slaves to futility.

In the suburbs where Mother still lived, the idea was to think of nothing; to puzzle over your own experience was to unsettle yourself gratuitously. How you felt wasn't important, only what you did, and what others saw.

Yet he knew that if he wasn't looking at himself directly, he was looking at himself in the world. The world had his face in it! If you weren't present to yourself, you'd find yourself elsewhere!

Almost all the men in the street where he had lived had lighted sheds at the end of the garden—or on their allotments—to which they retreated in the evenings. These men were too careful for the pub.

The sheds were where the men went to get away from the women; the women who weren't employed and had the time, therefore, to be disturbed. It was a division of labour: they carried the madness for the men.

'All right Mother?' he said at last. 'We aren't doing so badly now.'

They had escaped the highway and regained the narrow, clogged suburban roads.

'Not too bad, dear,' she sighed, passing the back of her hand across her forehead. 'Oh watch out! Can't you look where you're going! There's traffic everywhere!'

'That means we go slower.'

'They're so near!'

'Mother, everyone has an interest in not getting killed.'

'That's what you think!'

If Mother had kept on repeating the same thing and squealing at high volume, he would have lost his temper; he would have turned the car round, taken her home and dumped her. That would have suited him. Alexandra was coming back tomorrow; he had plenty to do.

But after a few minutes Mother calmed down and even gave him directions.

They were on their way to the cemetery.

It was easy to be snobbish and uncharitable about the suburbs, but what he saw around him was ugly, dull and depressing. He had, at least, got away.

But like Mother continuing to live here when there was no reason for it, he had put up with things unnecessarily. He had never rebelled, least of all against himself.

He had striven—up to a point—before the universe, like his mother, had shut like a door in his face.

He had been afraid Alexandra would fall in love with Thailand, or some exotic idea, and never want to return. Mother's irritability and indifference had taught him that women wanted to escape. If they couldn't get away, they hated you for making them stay.

There was a couple he and Alexandra had known for a long time. The woman had laboured for years to make their house perfect. One afternoon, as he often did, Harry drove over for tea in their garden. The woman cultivated wild flowers; there was a summer house.

Harry sighed and said to the man, 'You have everything you could want here. If I were you, I'd never go out.'

'I don't,' the man replied. He added casually, 'If I had my way, of course, we wouldn't live here but in France. They have a much higher standard of living.'

The man did not notice but at this the woman crumpled, as if she'd been shot. She went inside, shut the windows and became ill.

She could not satisfy her husband, couldn't quell his yearnings. It was impossible, and, without him asking her to do it, she had worn herself out trying.

If Alexandra was seeking cures, it was because she didn't have everything and he had failed her.

Yet their conflicts, of which there were at least one a week—some continued for days—weren't entirely terrible. Their disagreements uncovered misunderstandings. Sometimes they wanted different things but only in the context of one another. She was close to his wishes, to the inner stream of him. They always returned to one another. There was never a permanent withdrawal, as there had been with Mother.

There were times when it was a little paradise.

In the newspapers he learned of actors and sportsmen having affairs. Women wanted these people. It seemed easy.

There were attractive women in the office but they were claimed immediately. They weren't attracted to him. It wasn't only that he looked older than his years, as his wife had informed him. He looked unhealthy.

Plastic, anonymous, idealized sex was everywhere; the participants were only young and beautiful, as if desire was the exclusive domain of the thin.

He didn't think it was sex he wanted. He liked to believe he could get by without excessive pleasure, just as he could get by without drugs. He kept thinking that the uses of sex in the modern world were a distraction. It didn't seem to be the important thing.

What was important? He knew what it was—impermanence, decay, death and the way it informed the present—but couldn't bring himself to look straight at it.

'Where is Alexandra today?' Mother asked. 'I thought she might come with us. She never wants to see me.'

Mother's 'madness' had no magnetism for Alexandra; her complaints bored her; Alexandra had never needed her.

He said, 'She's gone to Thailand. But she sends beautiful letters to me—by fax—every day.'

He explained that Alexandra had gone to a centre in Thailand for a fortnight to take various courses. There were dream, healing, and 'imaging' workshops.

Mother said, 'What is she doing there?'

'She said on the phone that she is with other middle-aged women in sandals and bright dresses with a penchant for Joni Mitchell. The last I heard she was hugging these women and taking part in rituals on the beach.'

'Rituals?'

He had said to Alexandra when she rang, 'But you can't dance, Alexandra. You hate it.'

'I can dance badly,' she replied. 'And that's what I do, night after night.'

Dancing badly.

Harry said to Mother, 'She told me she looked up and the moon was smiling.'

'At her in particular?' said Mother.
'She didn't itemize,' said Harry.
'This is at your expense?'

Alexandra, somewhat patronizingly, had felt she had to explain it wasn't an infidelity.

'There's no other man involved,' she said before she left, packing a few things into their son's rucksack. 'I hope there's not even any men there.'

He looked at her clothes.

'Is that all you're taking?'

'I will rely on the kindness of strangers,' she replied.

'You'll be wearing their clothes?'

'I don't see why not.'

It was an infidelity if she was 'coming alive', as she put it. What could be a more disturbing betrayal than 'more life' even as he felt himself to be fading!

He was a conventional man, and he lived a conventional life so that she, and the children presumably, one day, could live unconventional ones.

Was he, to her, a deadweight? He feared losing sight of her, as she accelerated, dancing, into the distance.

'Anyway,' Mother said, 'thank you, Harry dear—'

'For what?'

'For taking me to Dad's—Dad's—'

He knew she couldn't say grave.

'That's OK.'

'The other sons are good to their mothers.'

'Better than me?'

'Some of them visit their mums every week. They sit with them for hours, playing board games. One boy sent his mother on a cruise.'

'On the Titanic?'

'Little beast you are! Still, without you I'd have to take three buses to see Dad.'

'Shame you didn't learn to drive.'

'I wish I had.'

He was surprised. 'Do you really?'

'Then I would have got around.'

'Why didn't you?'

'Oh I don't know now. Too much to do, with the washing and the cleaning.'

He asked, 'Is there anything else that you would like me to do for you?'

'Thank you for asking,' she said. 'Yes.'

'What is it?'

'Harry, I want to go on a Journey.'

One morning when Alexandra was scribbling he said, 'I'll say goodbye.'

She came to the door to wave, as she always did if she wasn't driving him to the station.

She said she was sorry he had to go into the office—'such a place'—every day.

'What the hell is wrong with it?' he asked.

The building was a scribble of pipes and wires, inhabited by dark suits with human beings inside. The harsh glow of the computer and TV screens reflected nothing back—nothing reflected into eternity.

Something changed after she said this.

He travelled on the train with the other commuters. The idea they shared was a reasonable though stifling one: to live without—or to banish—inner and outer disorder.

He was attempting to read a book about Harold Wilson, prime minister when Harry was young. There was a lot about the 'balance of payments'. Harry kept wondering what he had been wearing on his way to school the day that Wilson made a particular speech. He wished he had his school exercise books, and the novels he had read then. This was a very particular way of doing history.

He had to put his face by the train window but tried not to breathe out for fear his soul would fly from his body and he would lose everything that had meaning for him.

At work he would feel better.

He believed in work. It was important to sustain ceaseless effort.

Making; building—this integrated the world. It was called civilization. Otherwise the mind, like an errant child, ran away. It wanted only pleasure and nothing would get done.

The 'News' was essential information.

Without it you were uninformed, uneducated even. You couldn't see the way the world was moving. The News reminded you of other people's lives, of human possibility and destructiveness. It was part of his work to glance at the French, German, American and Italian papers every day.

However, an image haunted him. He was taking his university finals and a kid in his class—a hippy or punk, a strange straggly peacock—turned over the exam paper, glanced at the question and said, 'Oh I don't think there's anything here for me today,' and left the room, singing 'School's Out'.

Beautiful defiance.

Couldn't Harry walk into the office and say, 'There's nothing here for me today!' Or, 'Nothing of interest has happened in the world today!'

He remembered his last years at school, and then at university. The other mothers helped their student kids into their new rooms, unpacking their bags and making the beds. Mother had disappeared into herself, neither speaking nor asking questions. As the size of her body increased, her self shrank, the one defending the other. He doubted she even knew what courses he was taking, whether he had graduated or not or even what 'graduation' was.

She didn't speak, she didn't write to him, she hardly phoned. She was staring into the bright light, minute after minute, hour after hour, day after day, week after week, year after year. Television was her drug and anaesthetic, her sex her conversation her friends her family her heaven her...

Television did her dreaming for her.

It couldn't hear her.

After the television had 'closed down', and Father was listening to music in bed, she walked about the house in her dressing gown and slippers. He had no idea what she could be thinking, unless it was the same thing repeatedly.

It was difficult to be attached to someone who could only be attached to something else. A sleeping princess who wouldn't wake up.

He wondered if he'd gone into television so that he would be in front of her face, at least some of the time.

At this, he laughed.

'Don't shake like that,' she said. 'Look where you're going.'

'What journey?' he said.

'Oh yes,' she said. 'I haven't told you.'

On the way to work he had started to feel that if he talked with anyone they would get inside him; parts of the conversation would haunt him; words, thoughts, bits of their clothing would return like undigested food and he would be inhabited by worms, gnats, mosquitoes.

Going to a meeting or to lunch, if human beings approached, his skin prickled and itched.

If he thought, Well, it's only a minor irritation, his mind became unendurable, as if a landscape of little flames had been ignited not only on the surface of his skin, but within his head.

The smell, the internal workings of every human being, the shit, blood, mucus swilling in a bag of flesh, made him mad. He felt he was wearing the glasses the stage hypnotist had given people, but instead of seeing them naked, he saw their inner physiology, their turbulence, their death.

At meetings he would walk up and down, constantly going out of the room and then out of the building, to breathe. From behind pillars in the foyer, strangers started to whisper the 'stupid' remark at him, the one he had made to Father.

His boss said, 'Harry you're coming apart. Go and see the doctor.'

The doctor informed him there were drugs to remove this kind of radical human pain in no time.

Harry showed the prescription to Alexandra. She was against the drugs. She wouldn't even drink milk because of the 'chemicals' in it.

He told her, 'I'm in pain.'

She replied, 'That pain...it's your pain. It's you—your unfolding life.'

They went to a garden party. The blessed hypnotherapist would be there. It would be like meeting someone's best friend for the first time. He would see who Alexandra wanted to be, who she thought she was like.

He spotted 'Amazing Olga' on the lawn. She wore glasses. If she had a slightly hippy aspect it was because her hair hung down her back like a girl's, and was streaked with grey.

Alexandra had copied this, he realized. Her hair was long now, making her look slightly wild; different, certainly, to the well-kempt wives of Harry's colleagues.

The hypnotherapist looked formidable and self-possessed. Harry wanted to confront her, to ask where she was leading his wife, but he feared she would either say something humiliating or look into his eyes and see what he was like. It would be like being regarded by a policeman. All one's crimes of shame and desire would be known.

He didn't like Alexandra going away because he knew he didn't exist in the mind of a woman as a permanent object. The moment he left the room they forgot him. They would think of other things, and of other men, better at everything than he.

He was rendered a blank. This wasn't what the women's magazines—which his daughter Heather read—called low self-esteem. It was being rubbed out, annihilated, turned into nothing by a woman he was too much for.

Sometimes he and Alexandra had to attend dull dinners with work colleagues.

'I always have to sit next to the wives,' he complained, resting on the bed to put his heavy black shoes on. 'They never say anything I haven't heard before.'

Alexandra said, 'If you bother to talk and listen, it's the wives who are interesting. There's always more to them than there is to the husbands.'

He said, 'That attitude makes me angry. It sounds smart but it's prejudice.'

'There's more to the women's lives.'

'More what?'

'More emotion, variety, feeling. They're closer to the heart of things—to children, to themselves, to their husbands and to the way the world really works.'

'Money and politics are the engine.'

'They're a cover story,' she said. 'It's on top, surface.'

He was boring. He bored himself.

She was making him think of why she would want to be with him; of what he had to offer.

When he came home from school with news spilling from him, Mother never wanted to know. 'Quiet, quiet,' she said. 'I'm watching something.'

Gerald had said, 'Even when we're fifty we expect our mummy and daddy to be perfect but they are only ever going to be just what they are.'

It would be childish to blame Mother for what he was now. But if he didn't understand what had happened, he wouldn't be free of his resentment and couldn't move on.

Understand it! He couldn't even see it! He lived within it, but like primitive man almost entirely ignorant of his environment—and trying to influence it by magic—in the darkness he couldn't make anything out!

Gerald had said, 'Children expect too much!'

Too much! Affection, attention, love—to be liked! How could it be too much?

On their wedding day he had not anticipated that his marriage to Alexandra would become more complicated and interesting as time passed. It hadn't become tedious or exhausted; it hadn't even settled into a routine. He lived a life his university friends would have despised for its unadventurousness. Yet, every day it was strange, unusual, terrifying.

He had wanted a woman to be devoted to him, and when, for years, she had been, he had refused to notice.

Now she wasn't; things had got more lively, or 'kicked up', as his son liked to say.

Alexandra blazed in his face, day after day.

Mother, though, hadn't changed. She was too preoccupied to be imaginative. He wasn't, therefore, used to alteration in a woman.

Last night—

He had found himself searching through Alexandra's clothes, letters, books, make-up. He didn't read anything, and barely touched her belongings.

He had read in a newspaper about a public figure who had travelled on trains with a camera concealed in the bottom of his suitcase in order to look up women's skirts, at their legs and underwear. The man said, 'I wanted to feel close to the women.'

When it comes to love, we are all stalkers.

Last night Harry checked the house, the garden and the land. He fed the dogs, Heather's horse, the pig and the chickens.

Alexandra kept a tape deck in one of the collapsing barns. He had seen her, dancing on her toes, her skirt flying, singing to herself. He'd recalled a line from a song, 'I saw you dancing in the gym, you both kicked off your shoes...'

On an old table she kept pages of writing; spread out beside them were photographs she had been taking to illustrate the stories.

She said, 'If there's a telephone in the story, I'll take a picture of a phone and place it next to the paragraph!'

In the collapsing barn he put on a tape and danced, if dancing was the word for his odd arthritic jig, in his pyjamas and wellington boots.

That was why he felt stiff this morning.

'There is a real world,' Richard Dawkins the scientist had said.

Harry had repeated this to himself and then passed it on to Alexandra as an antidote to her vaporous dreaming.

She had laughed and said, 'Maybe there is a real world. But there is no one living in it.'

It was inevitable: they were nearing the churchyard and a feeling of dread came over him.

Mother turned to him, 'I've never seen you so agitated.'

'Me? I'm agitated?'

'Yes. You're twitching like a St Vitus dance person. Who d'you think I'm talking about?'

Harry said, 'No, no—I've got a lot to think about.'

'Is something bothering you?'

Alexandra had begged him not to take medication. She promised to support him. She'd gone away. The 'strange' had never come this close to him before.

But it was too late for confidences with Mother.

He had made up his mind about her years ago.

Mother hated cooking, housework and gardening. She hated having children. They asked too much of her. She didn't realize how little children required.

He thought of her shopping on Saturday, dragging the heavy shopping home, and cooking the roast on Sunday. The awfulness of the food didn't bother him; the joylessness which accompanied the futile ritual did. It wasn't a lunch that started out hopefully, but one which failed from the start. The pity she made him feel for her was, at that age, too much for him.

She couldn't let herself enjoy anything and she couldn't flee.

If he had made a decent family himself it was because Alexandra had always believed in it: any happiness he experienced was with her and the children. She had run their lives, the house and the garden, with forethought, energy and precision. Life and meaning had been created because she had never doubted the value of what they were doing. It was love.

If there was anguish about 'the family' it was because people knew it was where the good things were. He understood that happiness didn't happen by itself; making a family work was as hard as running a successful business, or being an artist.

To him it was doubly worthwhile because he had had to discover this for himself. Sensibly—somehow—he had wanted what Alexandra wanted.

She had kept them together and pushed them forward.

He loved her for it.

Now it wasn't enough for her.

He said, 'Would it be a good idea to get some flowers?'

'Lovely,' said Mother. 'Let's do that.'

They stopped at a garage and chose some.

'He would have loved these colours,' she said.

'He was a good man,' murmured Harry.

'Oh yes, yes! D'you miss him?'

'I wish I could talk to him.'

She said, 'I talk to him all the time.'

The cemetery was busy, a thoroughfare, more of a park than a burial ground. Women pushed prams, school kids smoked on benches, dogs peed on gravestones.

Father had a prime spot to rot in, at the back, by the fence.

Mother put her flowers down.

Harry said, 'Would you like to get down, Mother? You can use my jacket.'

'Thank you dear, but I'd never get up again.'

She bent her head and prayed and wept, her tears falling on the grave.

Harry walked about, weeping and muttering his own prayer, 'At least let me be alive when I die!'

Father would have been pleased by their attendance.

He thought: dying isn't something you can leave to the last moment.

He was like the old man, too. He had to remember that. Being pulled in two directions had saved him.

He walked away from Mother and had a cigarette. His boss had told him unequivocally to 'rest'. He said, 'To be frank, you're creating a bad atmosphere in the office.'

Harry's fourteen-year-old daughter Heather had run away from boarding school. Returning from the shops two days after Alexandra had left for Thailand, he found her sitting in the kitchen.

'Hello there, Dad,' she said.

'Heather. This is a surprise.'

'Is it OK?'

She looked apprehensive.

He said, 'It's fine.'

They spent the day together. He didn't ask why she was there.

He got on well with the boy who seemed, at the moment, to worship him. He would, Gerald said, understand him for another couple of years, when the boy was fourteen, and then never again.

Over Heather he felt sorry and guilty about a lot of things. If he thought about it, he could see that her sulks, fears and unhappinesses—called adolescence—were an extended mourning for a lost childhood.

After lunch, when she continued to sit there, looking at him, he did say, 'Is there anything you want to ask me?'

'Yes,' she said. 'What is a man?'

'Sorry?'

'What is a man?'

'Is that it?'

She nodded.

What is a man?

She hadn't said, 'What is sex?' Not, 'Who am I?' Not even, 'What am I doing here in this kitchen and on earth?' But, 'What is a man?'

She cooked for him. They sat down together in the living room and listened to a symphony. He put her in her own bed; he read to her from *Alice in Wonderland*.

He wanted to know her.

It had taken him a while to see—the screechings of the feminists had made him resistant—that the fathers had been separated from their children by work, though provided with the consolations of power. The women, too, had been separated from important things. It was a division he had had in the back of his mind—had taken for granted—most of his life.

They were lower middle-class; his father had had a furniture shop. He had worked all day his entire life and had done well. By the end he had two furniture shops; they did carpeting, too.

Harry and his brother had helped in the shops.

It was the university holidays when Harry accompanied his father

125

on the train to Harley Street. Father had retired. He was seeking help for depression.

'I'm feeling too down all the time,' he said. 'I'm not right.'

As they sat in the waiting room, Father said of the doctor, 'He's the top man.'

'How d'you know?'

'There's his certificate. I can't make out the curly writing from here, but I hope it's signed.'

'It is signed.'

'You've got good eyes then.' Father said, 'This guy will turn me into Fred Astaire.'

Father was smiling, full of hope for the first time in weeks.

'How can I help?' said the doctor, a man qualified to make others better.

The doctor listened to Father's terse, urgent account of inner darkness and spiritual collapse before murmuring, 'Life has no meaning, eh?'

'The wrong meaning,' said Father, carefully.

'The wrong meaning,' repeated the doctor.

'You've got it,' said Father.

The doctor scribbled a prescription for tranquillizers. They'd hardly been in there for half an hour.

As they went away, Harry didn't want to point out that the last thing tranquillizers did was make you happy.

Harry was puzzled and amused by Father striking out for happiness. It seemed a little late. What did he expect? Why couldn't he sink into benign, accepting old age? Isn't that what he, Harry, would have done?

He was taking Mother's side. This was the deep, wise view. Happiness was impossible, undesirable even, an unnecessary distraction from the hard, long, serious business of unhappiness. Mother would not be separated from the sorrow which covered her like a shroud.

In life Harry chose the dullest things—deliberately at first, as if wanting to see what it felt like to be Mother. Then it became a habit. Why did he choose this way rather than his father's?

His daughter Heather had always been fussy about her food.

By the time she was thirteen at every meal she sat at the table with her head bent, her fork held limply between her fingers, watched by her mother, brother and father. Could she eat or not?

Harry was unable to bear her 'domination of the table' as she picked at her food, shoved it around the plate and made ugly faces before announcing that she couldn't eat today. It disgusted him. If he pressurized her to eat, Heather would weep.

He saw that it isn't the most terrible people that we hate, but those who confuse us the most. His power was gone; his compassion broke down. He mocked and humiliated her. He could have murdered this little girl who would not put bread in her mouth.

He had, to his shame, refused to let Heather eat with them. He ordered her to eat earlier than the family, or later, but not with him, her mother or brother.

Alexandra had said that if Heather wasn't allowed to eat with them, she wouldn't sit at the table either.

Harry started taking his meals alone in another room, with a newspaper in front of him.

Alexandra had been indefatigable with Heather, cooking innumerable dishes until Heather swallowed something. This made him jealous. His mother had never been patient with him. He wanted Alexandra to tell him whether he was warm enough, what time he should go to bed, what he should read in the train.

Perhaps this was why Heather had wanted to go to boarding school.

His resentment of her had gone deep. He had come to consider her warily. It was easier to keep away from someone; easier not to tangle with them. If she needed him, she could come to him.

A distance had been established. He understood that a life could pass like this.

Father, always an active, practical man, had taken the tranquillizers for a few days, sitting on the sofa near Mother, waiting to feel better, looking as though he'd been hit on the head with a mallet. At last he threw the pills away, saying, 'It's going to take more than a couple of pills to make me smile!'

Father resumed his pilgrimage around Harley Street. If you were sick, you went to a doctor. Where else could you go, in a secular age, to find liberating knowledge?

It was then that Harry made the stupid remark.

They were leaving another solemn surgery, morbid with dark wood, creaky leather and gothic certificates. After many tellings, Father had made a nice story of his despair and wrong meanings. Harry turned to the doctor and said, 'There's no cure for living!'

'That's about right,' replied the doctor, shaking his pen.

Then, with Father looking, the doctor winked.

No cure for living!

As Father wrote the cheque, Harry could see he was electric with fury.

'Shut your big mouth in future!' he said, in the street. 'Who's asking for your stupid opinion! There's no cure! You're saying I'm incurable?'

'No, no—'

'What do you know! You don't know anything!'

'I'm only saying—'

Father was holding him by the lapels. 'Why did we stay in that small house?'

'Why did you? What are you talking about?'

'The money went on sending you to a good school! I wanted you to be educated but you've turned into a sarcastic, smart-arsed idiot!'

The next time Father visited the doctor, Harry's brother was deputed to accompany him.

Harry had a colleague who spent every lunch time in the pub, with whom Harry would discuss the 'problem' of how to get along with women. One day this man announced he had discovered the 'solution'.

Submission was the answer. What you had to do was go along with what the woman wanted. How, then, could there be conflict?

To Harry this sounded like a recipe for fury and murder but he didn't dismiss it.

Hadn't he, in a sense—not unlike all children—submitted to his Mother's view of things? And hadn't this half killed his spirit and left him frustrated? He wasn't acting from his own spirit, but like a slave, and his inner spirit, alive still, hated it.

Order form

Subscribe and save:

○ I'd like to subscribe and save:

   ○ 38% with a 3-year subscription (12 issues) for £67.00

   ○ 35% with a 2-year subscription (8 issues) for £46.50

   ○ 30% with a 1-year subscription (4 issues) for £24.95

   Please start the subscription with issue no:_____

My name: _____

Address: _____

Country/postcode: _____

Share and save:

○ I'd like to give a gift subscription, for:

   ○ 3 years (£67) ○ 2 years (£46.50) ○ 1 year (£24.50)

   Please start the subscription with issue no:_____

Recipient's name: _____

Address: _____

Country/postcode: _____

Gift message (optional): _____

Postage The prices above include postage in the UK. For the rest of Europe, please add £8 per year. For the rest of the world, please add £15 per year. (Airspeeded delivery).

Payment Total amount: £_____ by: ○ Cheque (to 'Granta') ○ Visa, Mastercard, AmEx:

Card no / __ / __ / __ / __ / __ / __ / __ / __ / __ / __ / __ / __ / __ / __ / __ / __ /

Expires / __ / __ / __ / Signature _____

Return You can either post ('Freepost' if you live in the UK), using the address label below. Or e-mail, fax or phone your details, if paying by credit card.

In the UK: **FreeCall 0500 004 033** (phone & fax).

Elsewhere: tel: 44 171 704 0470, fax 44 171 704 0470. E-mail: subs@grantamag.co.uk

00CBG690

○ Please tick if you'd prefer not to receive information from compatible organizations.

Granta Magazine

FREEPOST
2/3 Hanover Yard
Noel Road
London
N1 8BR

GRANTA

'Harry, Harry!' Mother called. 'I'm ready to go now.'

He walked across the grass to her. She put her handkerchief in her bag.

'All right, Mother!' He added, 'Hardly worth going home now.'

'Yes, dear. It is a lovely place. Perhaps you'd be good enough to put me here. Not that I'll care.'

'Right,' he said.

Father, the day he went to see the doctor, remembered how he had once loved. He wanted that loving back. Without it, living was a cold banishment.

Mother couldn't let herself remember what she loved. It was not only the unpleasant things that Mother wanted to forget, but anything that might remind her she was alive. One good thing might be linked to others. There might be a flood of disturbing happiness.

Before Father refused to have Harry accompany him on his doctor visits, Harry became aware, for the first time, that Father thought for himself. He thought about men and women, about politics and the transport system in London, about horse racing and cricket, and about how someone should live.

Yet his father never read anything but newspapers. Harry recalled the ignorant, despised father in *Sons and Lovers*.

Harry had believed too much in people who were better educated. He had thought that the truth was in certain books, or in the thinkers who were current. It had never occurred to Harry that one could—should—work these things out for oneself. Who was he to do this?

Father had paid for his education yet it gave Harry no sustenance; there was nothing there he could use now, to help him grasp what was going on.

He was a journalist—he followed others, critically of course. But he served them; he put them first.

Television and newspapers bored Alexandra. 'Noise' she called it. She had said: You'd rather read a newspaper than think your own thoughts.

He and Mother made their way back to the car.

She had never touched, held or bent down to kiss him; her body was as inaccessible to him as it probably was to her. He had never slept in her bed. Now she took his arm. He thought she wanted him to support her, but she was steady. Affection, it might have been.

One afternoon, when Alexandra had returned from the hypnotherapist and was unpacking the shopping on the kitchen table, Harry asked her, 'What did Amazing Olga say today?'

Alexandra said, 'She told me something about what makes us do things, about what motivates us.'

'What did Mrs Amazing say? Self-interest?'

'Falling in love with things,' she said. 'What impels us to act is love.'

'Shit,' said Harry.

The day she ran away from school, after the two of them had eaten and listened to music, Heather wanted to watch a film that someone at school had lent her. She sat on the floor in her pyjamas, sucking her thumb, wearing her Bugs Bunny slippers.

She wanted her father to sit with her, as she had as a kid, when she would grasp his chin, turning it in the direction she required. The film was *The Piano*, which, it seemed to him, grew no clearer as it progressed. When they paused the film to fetch drinks and food, she said that understanding it didn't matter, adding, 'Particularly if you haven't been feeling well lately.'

'Who's not feeling well?' he said. 'Me, you mean?'

'Maybe,' she said. 'Anyone. But perhaps you.'

She was worried about him; she had come to watch over him.

He knew she had got up later to watch the film another couple of times. He wondered whether she had stayed up all night.

In the morning, when he saw how nervous she looked, he said, 'I don't mind if you don't want to go back to school.'

'But you've always emphasized the "importance of education".'

Here she imitated him, quite well. They did it, the three of them, showing him how foolish he was.

He went on, feebly he thought, but on, nevertheless: 'There's so much miseducation.'

'What?' She seemed shocked.

'Not the information, which is mostly harmless,' he said. 'But the ideas behind it, which come with so much force—the force that is called "common sense".'

She was listening and she never listened.

She could make of it what she wanted. His uncertainty was important. Why pretend he had considered, final views on these matters? He knew politicians: what couldn't be revealed by them was ignorance, puzzlement, the process of intellectual vacillation. His doubt was a kind of gift, then.

He said, 'About culture, about marriage, about education, death... You receive all sorts of assumptions that it takes years to correct. The fewer the better, I say. It's taken me years to correct some of the things I was made to believe early on.'

He was impressed by how impressed she had been.

'I will go back to school,' she said. 'I think I should, for Mum.'

Before he took her to the station, she sat where her mother sat, at the table, writing in a notebook.

He had to admit that lately he had become frustrated and aggressive with Alexandra, angry that he couldn't control or understand her. By changing, she was letting him down; she was leaving him.

Alexandra rarely mentioned his mother and he never talked seriously about her for fear, perhaps, of his rage, or the memory of rage, it would evoke. But after a row over 'Olga' Alexandra said, 'Remember this. Other people aren't your mother. You don't have to yell at them to ensure they're paying attention. They're not half dead and they're not deaf. You're wearing yourself out, Harry, trying to get us to do things we're doing already.'

Alexandra had the attributes that Mother never had. He hadn't, at least, made the mistake of choosing someone like his mother, of living with the same person forever without even knowing it.

Oddly, it was the ways in which she wasn't like Mother that disturbed him the most.

He thought: a man was someone who should know, who was supposed to know. Someone who knew what was going on, who had a vision of where they were all heading, separately and as a family. He couldn't fall, fail or see the surface of his brain as a lunar surface illuminated by random flares. Sanity was a great responsibility.

'Why did you run away from school?' he asked Heather at last.

Placing her hands over her ears, she said there were certain songs she couldn't get out of her head. Words and tunes circulated on an endless loop. This had driven her home to Father.

He said, 'Are the noises less painful here?'

'Yes.'

He would have dismissed it as a minor madness, if he hadn't, only that afternoon—

He had been instructed to rest, and rest he would, after years of work. He had gone into the garden to lie on the grass beneath the trees.

There, at the end of the cool orchard, with a glass of wine beside him, his mind became possessed by brutal images of violent crime, of people fighting and devouring one another's bodies, of destruction and the police; of impaling, burning, cutting.

Childhood had sometimes been like this: hatred and the desire to bite, kill, kick.

He had been able to lie there for only twenty minutes. He walked, then, thrashing his head as if to drive the insanity away.

A better way of presenting the News might be this: a screaming woman dripping blood and guts, holding the corpse of a flayed animal. A ripped child; armfuls of eviscerated infants; pieces of chewed body.

This would be an image—if they kept it on screen for an hour or so—that would not only shock but compel consideration as to the nature of humankind.

He had run inside and turned the television on.

If he seemed to know as much about his own mind as he did about the governance of Zambia, how could his daughter's mind not be strange to her?

There was no day of judgement, when a person's life would be evaluated, the good and the bad, in separate piles. No day but every day.

Alexandra was educating him: a pedagogy of adjustment and strength. These were the challenges of a man's life. It was pulling him all over the place. The alternative wasn't just to die feebly, but to self-destruct in fury because the questions being asked were too difficult.

If he and Alexandra stayed together, he would have to change. If he couldn't follow her, he would have to change more.

A better life was only possible if he forsook familiar experiences for seduction by the unfamiliar. Certainty would be a catastrophe.

The previous evening Alexandra had rung from her mobile phone. He thought the background noise was the phone's crackle, but it was the sea. She had left the taverna and was walking along the beach behind a group of other women.

'I've decided,' she said straight away, sounding ecstatic.

'What is it, Alexandra?'

'It has become clear to me, Harry! My reason...let's say. I will work with the unconscious.'

'In Thailand?'

'In Kent. At home.'

'I guess you can find the unconscious everywhere.'

'How we know others. What sense we can make of their minds. That is what interests me. When I'm fully trained, people will come—'

'Where? Where?' He couldn't hear her.

'To the house. We will need a room built, I think. Will that be all right?'

'Whatever you want.'

'I will earn it back.'

He asked, 'What will the work involve?'

'Working with people, individually and in groups—in the afternoons and evenings—helping them understand their imaginations. It'll be a training in possibility.'

'Excellent.'

'Do you mean that? I know this work is alien to you. Today, today—a bunch of grown-ups—we were talking to imaginary apples!'

'Somehow it wouldn't be the same,' he said, 'with bananas! But I am with you—at your side, always...wherever you are!'

He had had intimations of this. There had been an argument.

He had asked her, 'Why do you want to help other people?'

'I can't think of anything else as interesting.'

'Day after day you will listen to people droning on?'

'After a bit, the self-knowledge will make them change.'

'I've never seen such a change in anyone.'

'Haven't you?'

'I don't believe I have,' he said.

'Haven't you?'

He said agitatedly, 'Why d'you keep repeating that like a parrot?' She was looked at him levelly. He went on, 'Tell me when and where you've seen this!'

'You're very interested.'

'It would be remarkable,' he said. 'That's why I'm interested.'

'People are remarkable,' she said. 'They find all sorts of resources within themselves that were unused, that might be wasted.'

'Is it from that "Amazing" woman that you get such ideas?'

'She and I talk, of course. Are you saying I don't have a mind of my own?'

He said, 'Are you talking about a dramatic change?'

'Yes.'

'Well,' he said. 'I don't know. But I'm not ruling it out.'

'That's something,' she smiled. 'It's a lot.'

He had wanted to tell Heather that clarity was not illuminating; it kept the world away. A person needed confusion and muddle—good difficult knots and useful frustrations. Someone could roll up their sleeves and work, then.

He got Mother into the car and started it.

She said, 'Usually I lie down and shut the tops of me eyes at this time. You're not going to keep me up are you?'

'Only if you want to eat. D'you want to do that?'

'That's an idea. I'm starving. Tummy's rumbling. Rumblin'!'

'Come on.'

In the car he murmured, 'You were rotten to me.'

'Oh was I so terrible?' she cried. 'I only gave you life and fed and clothed you and brought you up all right, didn't I? You were never late for school!'

'Sorry? You couldn't wait for us to get out of the house!'

'Haven't you done better than the other boys? They're plumbers! People would give their legs to have your life!'

'It wasn't enough.'

'It's never enough is it! It never was! It never is!'

He went on, 'If I were you, looking back on your life now, I'd be ashamed.'

'Oh would you,' she said. 'You've been so marvellous have you, you miserable little git!'

'Fuck you,' he told his mother. 'Fuck off.'

'You're terrible,' she said. 'Picking an old woman to pieces the day she visits her husband's grave. I've always loved you,' she said.

'It was no use to me. You never listened and you never talked to me.'

'No, no,' she said. 'I spoke to you but I couldn't say it. I cared but I couldn't show it. I've forgotten why. Can't you forget all that?'

'No. It won't leave me alone.'

'Just forget it,' she said, her face creasing in anguish. 'Forget everything!'

'Oh Mother, nothing is forgotten, even you know that.'

'Father took me to Venice and now I want to go again. Before they have to carry me wheelchair over the Wotsit of Cries.'

'You'll go alone?'

'You won't take me—'

'I wouldn't walk across the road with you,' he said, 'if I could help it. I can't stand the sight of you.'

She closed her eyes. 'No, well... I'll go with the other old girls.'

He said, 'You want me to pay for you?'

'I thought you wouldn't mind.' She said, 'I might meet a nice chap! A young man! I could get off! I'm a game old bird in me old age!'

She started to cackle.

'Like what?' Heather asked. 'What educational ideas are no good?'

'I think I have believed that if I waited, if I sat quietly at the table, without making a noise or movement—being good—the dish of life would be presented to me.'

He should have added, People want to believe in unconditional love, that once someone has fallen in love with you, their devotion will continue, whether you spend the rest of your life lying on the sofa drinking beer or not. But why should they? If love was not something that could be contrived, it still had to be kept alive.

Mother said, 'Children are selfish creatures. Only interested in themselves. You get sick of them,' she said. 'You bloody hate them, screaming, whining, no gratitude. And that's about it!'

'I know,' he said. 'That's true. But it's not the whole story!'

The restaurant was almost empty, with a wide window overlooking the street.

Mother drank wine and ate spare ribs with her fingers. The wine reddened her face; her lips, chin and hands became greasy.

'It's so lovely, the two of us,' she said. 'You were such an affectionate little boy, following me around everywhere. Then you got quite rough, playing football in the garden and smashing the plants and bushes.'

'All children are affectionate.' He said, 'I'm fed up with it, Mother.'

'What are you fed up with now?' she said, as if his complaints would never cease.

'My job. I feel I'm in a cult, there.'

'A cult? What are you talking about?'

'The bosses have made themselves into little gods. I am a little god, to some people. Can you believe it? I walk in—people tremble. I could ruin their lives in a moment—'

'A cult?' she said, wiping her mouth and dipping her fingers in a bowl of water. 'Those things they have in America?'

'It's like that but not exactly that. It's a cheerleader culture. There are cynics about, but they are all alcoholics. What the bosses want is to win awards and display ridiculous little statuettes on their shelves. They want to be written about by other journalists—the little praise of nobodies. Mother, I'm telling you, it's a slave ideology.'

He had become overenthusiastic.

He said more mildly, 'Still, it's the same for everyone. Even the Prime Minister must sometimes think, first thing in the morning—'

'Oh don't do it,' she said. 'Just don't.'

'I knew you wouldn't understand.'

'Don't I?' she said. 'You never give me a chance to understand things.'

'Alexandra and the kids wouldn't like it if I suddenly decided to leave for Thailand. I have four people to support.'

'You don't support me,' she said.

'Certainly not.'

'That's your revenge is it?'

'Yes.'

'Excuse me for saying so, dear, we're both getting on now. You could drop dead any minute. You've been sweating all day. Your face is damp. Is your heart all right?'

She touched his forehead with her napkin.

'My friend Gerald had a heart attack last month,' he said. 'He's not the only one.'

'No. Your dad, bless him, retired and then he was gone. What would your wife and the kids do then?'

'Thank you, Mother. What I'm afraid of, is that I will just walk out of my job or insult someone or go crazy like those gunmen who blaze away at strangers.'

'You'd be on the news instead of behind it.' She was enjoying herself. 'You'd be better off on your own—like me. I've got no one bothering me. Peace! I can do what I want.'

'I want to be bothered by others. It's called living.' He went on, 'Maybe I feel like this because I've been away for a week. I'll go in on Monday and find I don't have these worries.'

'You will,' she said. 'Once a worry starts—'

'You'd know about that. But what can I do?'

'Talk to Alexandra about it. If she's getting all free and confident about herself, why can't you?'

'Yes, perhaps she can support me now.'

They were about to order pudding when a motorcyclist buzzed down the street in front of them, turned left into a side street, hit a car, and flew into the air.

The waiters ran to the window. A crowd gathered; a doctor forced his way through. An ambulance arrived. The motorcyclist lay on the ground a long time. At last he was strapped on to a stretcher and carried to the ambulance which travelled only a few yards before turning off its blue light and klaxon.

'That's his life done,' said Mother. 'Cheerio.' The ruined motorcycle was pushed on to the pavement. The debris was swept up. The traffic resumed. Harry and Mother put their knives and forks down.

'Even I can't eat any more,' she said.

'Nor me.'

He asked for the bill.

He parked outside the house and walked her to the door.

She made her milky tea. With a plate of chocolate biscuits beside her, she took her seat in front of the television.

The television was talking at her; he could feel she didn't want him there. She would sit there until bedtime.

He kissed her.

'Goodbye, dear.' She dipped her biscuit in her tea. 'Thank you for a lovely day.'

'What are you going to do now? Nothing?'

'Have a little rest. It's not much of a life is it?'

'No.'

He noticed a travel agent's brochure on the table.

He said, 'I'll send you a cheque shall I, for the Venice trip.'

'That would be lovely.'

'When will you be going?'

'As soon as possible. There's nothing to keep me here.'

'No.'

While Heather was at home, Alexandra rang but Harry didn't say she was there. It was part of what a man sometimes did, he thought, to be a buffer between the children and their mother.

In the morning, before she left, Heather said she wanted to read him a poem she had written.

He listened, trying not to weep. He could hear the love in it.

Heather had come to cheer him up, to make him feel that his love worked, that it could make her feel better.

After Alexandra had rung from the beach, Harry rang Gerald and told him about the 'imaging', the 'visualization', the 'healing', the whole thing. Gerald, convalescing, took his call.

'I used to know a psychoanalyst,' he said cheerfully. 'I've always fancied talking about myself for a long time to someone. But it's not what the chaps do. It's good business, though, people buying into their own pasts—if Alexandra can think like that. Before, women wanted to be nurses. Now they want to be therapists.'

'It's harmless, you're saying.'

Gerald said, 'And sometimes useful.' He laughed, 'Turning dreams into money for all of you, almost literally.'

Gerald imagined it was almost the only way that Harry could grasp what Alexandra was doing.

But it wasn't true.

Harry drove around the old places after leaving Mother. He wanted to buy a notebook and return to write down the thoughts his memories inspired. Maybe he would do it tonight, his last evening alone, using different coloured markers.

It started to rain. He thought of himself on the street in the rain as a teenager, hanging around outside chip shops and pubs—not bored, that would underestimate what he felt—but unable to spit out or swallow the amount of experience coming at him.

It had been a good day.

Walking along a row of shops he remembered from forty years ago, he recalled a remark of some philosopher that he had never let go. The gist of it was: happiness is wanting one thing. The thing was love, if that was not too pallid a word. Passion, or wanting someone, might be better. In the end, all that would remain of one's years would be the quality of one's link with others, of how far one had gone with them.

Harry turned the car and headed away from his childhood.

He had to go to the supermarket. He would buy flowers, cakes, champagne and whatever attracted his attention. He would attempt to tidy the house; he would work in the garden, clearing the leaves.

The next morning he would pick Alexandra up from the airport and if the weather was good they would eat and talk in the garden. She would be healthy, tanned and full of ideas.

He had to phone Heather to check whether she was all right. It occurred to him to write to her. If he knew little of her day-to-day life, she knew practically nothing of him, his past and what he did most of the time. Parents wanted to know everything of their children, but withheld themselves.

He thought of Father under the earth and of Mother watching television; he thought of Alexandra and his children. He was happy.

□

GRANTA

BORN IN ROMANIA

PHOTOGRAPHS AND TEXT
BY KENT KLICH

In 1989, the first television pictures from Romania's children's homes shocked the world. More than 100,000 undernourished children were kept in institutions reminiscent of Nazi concentration camps: left lying in their own faeces, bound hand and foot, maltreated by their 'guards'. No one touched them gently.

Soon it was found that thousands of the children had been infected with HIV, either through transfusions of infected blood or by syringes that had been reused without being sterilized. The fact that low-birthweight children in Romania would be given micro-transfusions of blood to help their chance of survival only increased the risk of transmitting HIV.

According to President Ceausescu, HIV and Aids did not exist in Romania—which is why, for a decade before his downfall in 1990, the virus was able to spread so quickly. Under his regime, families were required to have as many children as possible—the norm was five children to each woman—which put an impossible burden on the poor. Contraceptives were forbidden, abortion was illegal. The result was thousands of primitive abortions and tens of thousands of children abandoned to state institutions.

Children make up ninety per cent of the Aids figures in Romania. The latest estimate of 6,000 Romanian children with HIV/Aids constitutes sixty per cent of the total paediatric HIV cases in Europe. Seventy-five per cent of the Romanian cases are children born between 1988 and 1990 (babies born before 1988 would not have been identified as having Aids; after 1991, better medical practice reduced the numbers). An average of 400 new cases from this 1988–90 period are still discovered every year.

When I first went to Romania in 1994, HIV-positive children, whose life expectancy was assumed to be no more than two or three years, were at the bottom of the heap when it came to care. Many of the children I photographed were not orphans but had parents who could not look after them at home (a child found to be HIV-positive would not be allowed in school), or wanted their condition kept secret.

The state orphanage in Cernavoda sits in the hills overlooking the entrance to the Danube-Black Sea Canal. Of the 200 children living there in 1994, around thirty, in ward eighteen, were HIV-positive. Their rooms were bare, the metal beds stood in rows, there was no sign of toys or pictures. Although the children were allowed to play outside, I often found them sitting quietly in their dormitories, doing nothing. None of them had clothes of their own—every garment was marked with a number eighteen. Their meals of soup, porridge and bread were served at tremendous speed and eaten in the same way. Children who ate slowly were made to hurry up. The local staff were supplemented by volunteers from Nightingales, a British charity which began working in Cernavoda in 1993. There were no medicines, no gloves, no disposable syringes.

At the Colentina Hospital in Bucharest at least there were playrooms and staff to play with the children. Health Aid, a British organization which has worked with HIV-positive children in Romania since 1990, had brought in medical supplies and were helping to train Romanian carers to work in the three small homes they had established for HIV-positive children. In one of them, in Snagoff, a village near Bucharest, eight children live as a family with people who love them, and they receive lessons from a tutor paid for by the state.

In Snagoff the children have a history. Each child has his or her own photo album in which they make a record of the events in their lives. When one of the children dies—as, inevitably, some do—their memory is kept alive by photographs. While I was there I noticed a picture of a boy who had died a couple of months earlier hanging on the living-room wall. His memory lived on within the family.

There are now seven Aids centres in Romania: in Bucharest, Constanta, Brasov, Cluj, Iasi, Timisoara and Craiova. The government has agreed to pay for HIV medication, and gives allowances for HIV-positive children living at home. But lack of money, trained staff and adequate supplies of medicine are still problems. It can cost £5,000 a year to care for one patient—and this in one of the poorest countries in Europe. As in other European countries, Romania now has a growing number of infected babies born to HIV-positive mothers.

In 1998, twenty children from the orphanage in Cernavoda moved into a new building run by Nightingales, where they live and go to school. Health Aid now has six homes instead of three. Sadly, some of the children I photographed have already died. For the survivors, the next step is to prepare them for a life outside. □

These photographs were taken between 1994 and 1999.

These sandals belong to Iliaz Ali, born 1 January 1989, in the hospital in Constanta. He first tested HIV-positive a year later, though he was clear at birth. In September 1998 he moved from the Cernavoda orphanage into the Nightingales home, the Casa Fericirii, the 'House of Happiness', where he attends school.

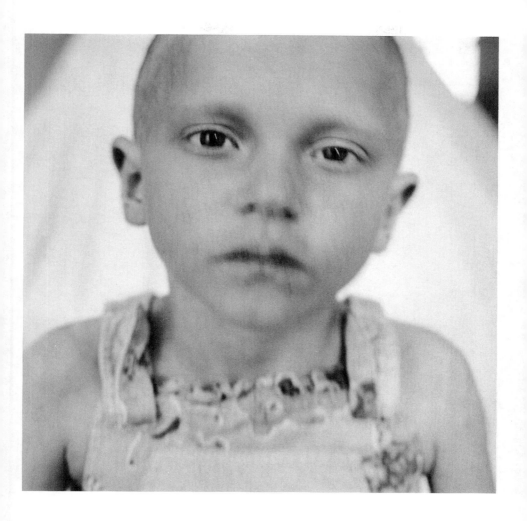

Ionica Visan was born 30 February 1990. She spent three years in the orphanage at Pucioasa, a small town in the mountains north-west of Bucharest. In January 1994 she was admitted to St Laurence's Children's Hospice in Cernavoda, run by Children in Distress, a British charity working in Romania.

Niculeta, at the municipal hospital in Constanta, the Black Sea port which has a quarter of all HIV/Aids cases in Romania.

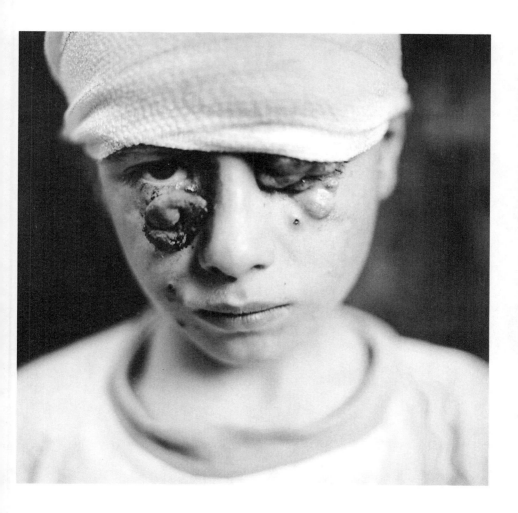

Mehai, at the municipal hospital, Constanta. He is suffering from a chronic viral skin disorder which can be successfully treated in its early stages. It can develop in institutions where children have close contact with each other, and in the case of these children, when their immune system is depleted.

Stefan, Hospital Number 3, Galati.

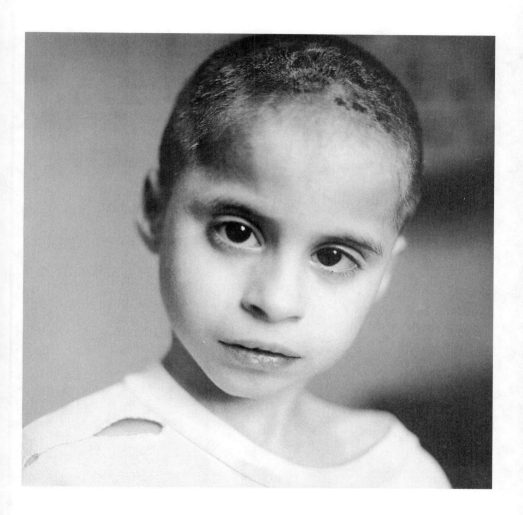

Giurgiu Elena Tita, known as 'Tita', was born 28 September 1987. In February 1990 she tested HIV-positive. In 1998 she was moved to the Casa Fericirii, the 'House of Happiness', in Cernavoda, which is specifically for children with HIV. *Also overleaf.*

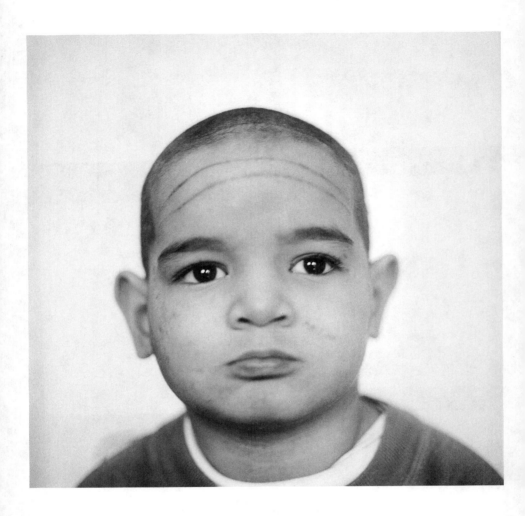

Simona, at the Victor Babes Hospital in Bucharest. Many HIV-positive children still live on hospital wards, even when they present no symptoms of illness. It is the aim of Health Aid and other charities working with HIV children to move them out of hospitals and into smaller family units where they can be given schooling.

Valerica Hira was born 5 February 1987 in the hospital in Constanta. Her mother and father were getting divorced when she was born and her mother gave her up at birth. She tested HIV-positive in January 1990 and in 1991 moved to the orphanage at Cernavoda. In 1998 she moved into the Casa Fericirii.

Ionica Visan (also page 145) was thought to have been abandoned on a rubbish dump when she was about one year old. It was then that rats chewed away some of her toes and fingers. After being moved from the orphanage at Pucioasa in 1994, she died in the hospice at Cernavoda 13 October 1998.

Daniel Enache was born 4 February 1989. He lived at home until 1993, when he was admitted to hospital, and then to the Cernavoda hospice. His sister also had Aids. His father visited him regularly, sometimes with his mother. He died 26 May 1997. *Overleaf:* The Vidra hospital for HIV-positive children in eastern Romania.

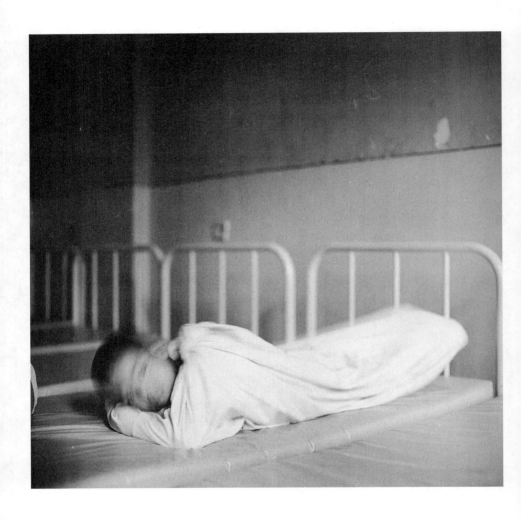

Vervel, at the Victor Babes Hospital, Bucharest.

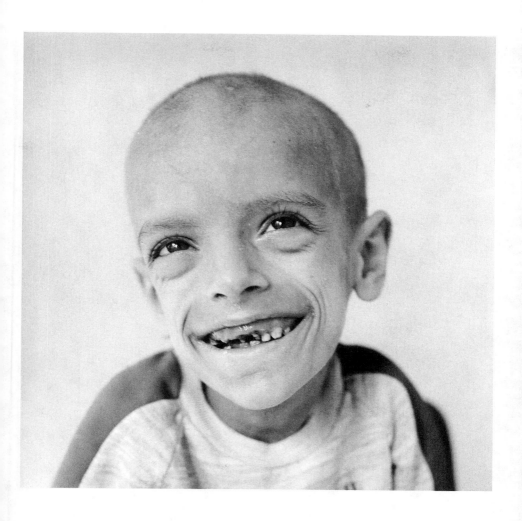

A child at the hospital in Bacau, eastern Romania. *Overleaf:* Children playing in a summer rainstorm on the roof of the hospice at Cernavoda. The boy in the foreground is Sebastian Jacob, born 2 September 1987. He was abandoned at birth and admitted to the hospice in 1992.

Cornelia Ciobanu was born 27 December 1988. She stayed at home with her family for the first few years of her life, until her mother could not care for her any longer. She was admitted to the Cernavoda hospice in October 1994 where her mother visits her several times a year.

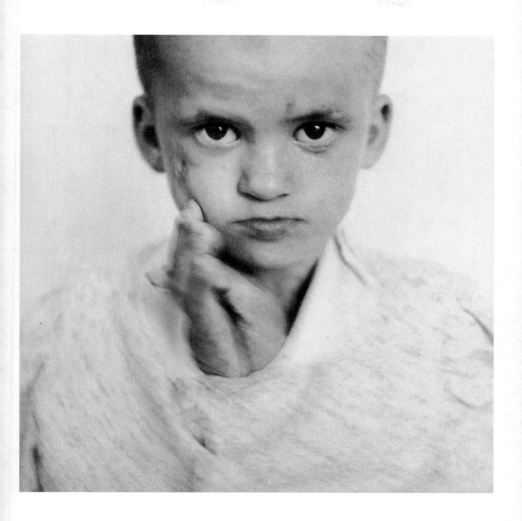

Carmen, at the hospice in Cernavoda.

A child at the hospital in Vidra, which cares for HIV-positive children.

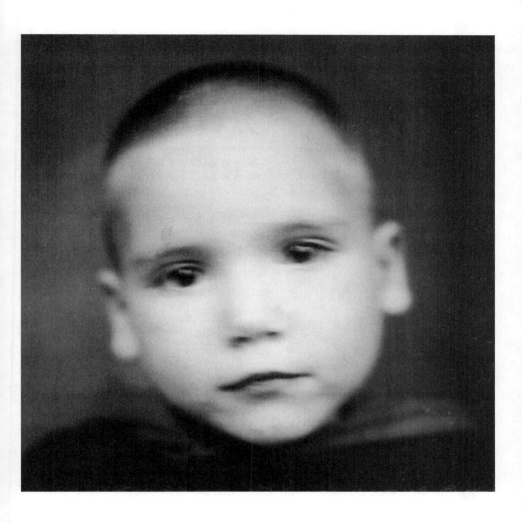

Georgiana, at the Victor Babes Hospital in Bucharest.

THE DRAMA OF EVERYDAY LIFE

KARL E. SCHEIBE

Drama, Scheibe reminds us, is no more confined to the theater than religion is to the church or education to the schoolroom. Accordingly, he brings to his reflection on psychology the drama of literature, poetry, philosophy, history, music, and theater. The essence of drama is transformation: the transformation of the quotidian world into something that commands interest and stimulates conversation. It is this dramatic transformation that Scheibe seeks in psychology as he pursues a series of suggestive questions, such as: Why is boredom the central motivational issue of our time? Why are eating and sex the biological foundations of all human dramas? Why is indifference a natural condition, caring a dramatic achievement? Why is schizophrenia disappearing? Why does gambling have cosmic significance?

Writing with elegance and passion, Scheibe asks us to take note of the self-representation, performance, and scripts of the drama that is our everyday life. In doing so, he challenges our dispirited senses and awakens psychology to a new realm of dramatic possibility.

$24.95 / £15.50 cloth

HARVARD UNIVERSITY PRESS

US: 800 448 2242 • UK: 0171 306 0603 • www.hup.harvard.edu

GRANTA

OUR NICKY'S HEART
Graham Swift

Frank Randall had three sons: Michael, Eddy and Mark. That was fine by him. A farmer whose business is rearing livestock knows that the sums extend to his own offspring. Sons are a good investment. His wife couldn't argue. She'd married a farmer with her eyes open and knew the score. Three sons in nine years at almost exact three-year intervals, and that was that. But she could have done with a daughter to leaven the male dough. So when she became pregnant a fourth time, and a little unexpectedly, she set her hopes high. She even named her Sally secretly to herself. I know because she told me, years later.

When Sally turned out to be Nick she put a good face on her disappointment and never made a grudge of it. All the same, I think Nicky must have known he was meant to have been a girl because when he grew up all his emphasis was in the other direction. More than any of his brothers, he was the cocky, reckless young stud and, being such, was indulged like none of his brothers had been—his mother's favourite despite, or because of, not being a girl. She doted on him, I think, more than if he *had* been a girl, while to the males of the family he was always the baby and something of an amusement. Michael, nearly twelve when Nick was born, could almost have felt he could be Nick's father, though in practice the image hardly worked, since Michael seemed not to get around to women till he was past twenty, and then in no great rush.

By contrast, I can remember catching Nicky once in front of the bathroom mirror when he hadn't seen me, running a comb again and again through his hair and giving himself a steady slow burn of a stare. He was only sixteen but he had the looks and the way about him, and he knew it. He wasn't a girl but he got them. As many at least as there were to be had in our corner of the county.

He never saw me looking at him—too busy with himself. That comb was like a knife with which he was sculpting the last touches to his head, but he put it aside anyway to run a claw of a hand through the results.

When men, or boys, look at themselves like this in a mirror, which way round does it work? Do they see the girl in their own face in the glass, or is the girl inside them, getting the stare and going weak-kneed?

Sometimes it wasn't Nicky who ran that final rough hand through his hair. It was Mum. She'd see him all slicked and preened and she'd go and muss it up for him, just a bit. He got the habit from her.

I was the odd one out in my own way: Mark, the 'clever one', the renegade—or the one with ambition and sense. Michael and Eddy stuck to Dad and the farm, I went to veterinary college. As it turned out, I never became a farmer's vet. I live in Exeter now and my practice is mostly domestic pets. All this might have just earned me the family's scorn—cats and dogs! Guinea pigs for God's sake! But, as things have gone, they're in no position to mock.

At one time I might even have opted for general medicine. Vets will always seem like thwarted doctors. It's not true of course, and anyway it's different when animals were what you grew up with. I like my practice, my cats and dogs. I like the attachment, the care, their owners have for them. It rests on simple affection, not on a way of life.

Besides, I have a link with human medicine. My wife is a theatre sister at the Devon and Exeter.

All this—I mean remembering Nicky combing his hair in front of the mirror—seems far off now, across a divide. If you'd said to my father even then—it's only sixteen years ago—that one day meat and stock prices would plunge, that one day there'd be talk of 'mad cows', one day he'd only be punishing himself, bringing bull calves into the world just to send them to slaughter, he'd have laughed in your face, looked round at the yard and called you an idiot.

If you'd said to him that one day, soon, what had always been a given, the way a farmer works not just for himself but for what he hands on, wouldn't seem like a given at all but like something teetering on its edge, he'd have called you more than a fool. And if you'd said it wouldn't be so rare for a farmer at the end of the twentieth century to go into his barn with a shotgun and never walk out... Well, you wouldn't have said that, even if you'd known.

I didn't know. I couldn't read the future. I just went my own way. What happened to Nicky clinched it. Now it seems, of course, except to my mother, that I was the traitor, the deserter, making my escape safe, leaving a sinking ship.

Nicky was no girl. When he was seventeen he somehow scraped together the cash to buy a six-year-old Yamaha on which he careered round the lanes and burned up and down the main roads, discovering, I think, that for all its throb and roar—what could you expect with the money he'd paid?—the thing was pretty short on power. Michael and Eddy would never have been allowed to do this, nor would I, if I'd wanted, but with Nicky it was somehow all right. Somehow it went with Nicky. Mum would have hated stopping him having his own way—he could twist her round his finger. All the same, I could see her dreading the worst, and it happened.

As far as we know, he tried to overtake a lorry and cut in before the bend, but he didn't judge the speed, or didn't have it, and the wet road was against him. After the accident it was a matter of less than two days before he was dead, but those days were like months, they were like a shift into a different time, a different world, one in which the farm and all that sure sense it could give you of how things lived and died, safe in the bosom of the land, didn't count for a thing. Nicky was in his own little lost bubble of a world, held there by tubes and drips and wires, and the man who was in charge of Nicky and was seeing us now was carefully trying to explain that, because of the brain injury, Nicky would never regain consciousness again.

There was only one decision to be made.

They found us somewhere to sit, to think it through. It was three o'clock in the morning. As if we could think. There are times when a family has to cling together but those same times can make a family seem like a pretty clumsy piece of apparatus. The tubes going into Nicky seemed more efficient. Dad looked at me as if maybe I should pronounce—as if being in my final year at vet college gave me an authority in situations like this. Anyhow, hadn't I always been so keen to show it? That I was the one with the brains in the family? He started to shake his head slowly and mechanically from side to side.

Then Mum, who was drawing every breath like some long, deep adventure, took Dad's hand, squeezed it and they got up. They asked me to go with them—as if I should be some kind of interpreter— and I saw Michael and Eddy shoot me looks I'd never seen them shoot me before but that I realized they must have been giving me all my life behind my back. I'll never know what they said to each other, left by themselves.

Back with the doctor, Dad looked at Mum first, then he cleared his throat and said that we understood. I never heard him say anything further from the truth.

And that should have been the end of it. But the doctor said there was another doctor who wanted to speak to us, he was on his way. He glanced at his watch.

At that moment, I remember, a sudden light came into my mother's face and I realized later that she must have thought for a few wild seconds that this other doctor was some super-special specialist who had overruled the first doctor and was coming to tell us that, after all, Nicky could be saved. But the second doctor said that he understood what we must be going through but in these situations more than one decision had to be made. He had his own careful way of saying what he said next—it must have come from training and practice—but the gist was that Nicky was (he didn't say 'had been') a very healthy young man and we should consider whether his organs should be made available to others.

In particular, the heart.

In my memory of that night I try to keep to the essentials, to remove the daze of sheer shock and amazement in which everything occurred, the dither of secondary complications, like those looks from Michael and Eddy.

In such a situation—to speak like an outsider—there are two opposing arguments. First, that only the victim has authority over his own body and since the victim is beyond all power of intelligence, how do we know that he would have been willing? (I'm sure it never entered Nicky's mind.) On the other hand, how do we know, if we suppose the victim were able to judge his own situation, that he would *not* be willing?

Time, of course, was of the essence.

I remember looking at my parents and thinking there simply was no readiness for this. The one decision, or inevitable acceptance, was enough—too much. Now this. I remember too how they began to look suddenly like guilty, disobedient parties, placed more and more, as each moment passed by, in a position of blameworthy obstinacy, backsliders who wouldn't come round. They looked like they were under arrest.

And as more time passed, it changed into something worse. I could see the picture seeping into at least my mother's head (the second doctor hadn't painted it for her but perhaps it was part of his training to let it take shape) of some person, perhaps not very far away, perhaps just down a corridor in this very hospital, some person in a situation, in its way, not unlike Nicky's, some person, in fact, not unlike *Nicky*, a kind of second Nicky, and she was—we were—denying him life.

We ought to have discussed it with Michael and Eddy. Not sharing it with them might be a bad move, it might only store up permanent trouble. (It did.) But I said nothing and I could see that democratic debate was far from my mother's thoughts. If word had to be given and given quickly, it could only be given under the pressure of whatever imaginings were right then rushing through her head. *Her* head—since I could see that my father was simply going to defer to her. Twenty-five years of being in charge of 400 acres and all that lived on it, generations of Randalls ruling the roost, of which he was the latest heir, hadn't made him capable at that moment of being the one to step forward and speak.

My mother nodded. She said, 'Yes. OK.' The second doctor left a just measurable pause (that, also, might have been in the training), then nodded too, gave a squeeze to his mouth. There were forms that had to be signed.

First and foremost, they needed the heart.

My father walked out of that room a second-in-command, but he had the task, he knew it, of telling Michael and Eddy what had been decided upon without their knowing.

If you'd said to him, years back, that one day they'd be able to take out someone's heart and put it in someone else, he'd have thought you were crazy too.

In the subsequent days and weeks my mother's grief went through terrible lurches and swings. She was torn, I know, between the thought that she'd signed away the last living part of her son—what mother could do that?—and the knowledge that part of her son lived on, giving life to another. Wasn't that some small answer to grief? But then, if part of her son lived on in another, wasn't it just a new kind of agony not to know who or where? Wasn't it worse? She had only denied her grief its completion. It was like knowing someone was missing but never knowing, finally, that they were dead. Or knowing they were dead and never knowing the whereabouts of the remains.

As for my own grief, I kept it suppressed, even vaguely concealed, like something that had an edge of shame. My mother had taken on for herself a pitch of anguish that none of the men in her family could match.

The heart, what is it? It's a piece of muscle, a pump.

In more recent years, I've come to see my practice, my cats and dogs, as my principal cushion—a solace, a kind of immunization even—against the worst things life can bring. It sounds like mere softness, an evasion, I know. But I think we demean what they give us, the animals we choose to keep by our side, by calling them 'pets'. In those weeks after Nicky's death it wasn't the cows in the shed, with their own lot of doom, that either comforted or troubled me. It was our border collie, Ned, who knew there was a gap, an unclosable space. We all rubbed against each other strangely harshly and cruelly, but we were all of us more tender than we'd ever been with Ned.

It's a regular part of my job to put down animals, to 'send them to sleep'. I never take it lightly. I know that the brave or matter-of-fact face their owners put on things—their 'let's not be silly, it's only a dog'—isn't the whole story at all. Usually, the animal comes to me. Sometimes, because of the circumstances, I have to go to the house. I always take a heavy-duty black plastic sack. After the procedure is over I might be seen off with the same householderly mannerliness with which the man who's fixed the washing machine is shown on his way. But more than once, barely a pace or two down the front path, I've been stopped like a thief in my tracks by the sudden sob, wail even, of genuine grief coming from behind the closed door.

I think it was in those weeks after Nicky's death that I decided that when I became a vet, it wouldn't be of the kind that visits farms.

Nicky, after all—it's not to make light or soft, either—had been a kind of pet.

As for that space that my mother could never close, her not knowing where Nicky's heart had *gone*, it seemed to become more of an issue for her, not less, not a secondary thing but somehow the nub—I can't say the other word—of the matter.

She understood, of course, that there were strict rules about preserving the anonymity of the recipient—understood, but didn't understand, though I tried to explain some of the reasons. She wanted to know, at least—didn't she have the right?—what had happened to Nicky's heart during that first astonishing stage of disconnection, when it had been removed from Nicky and before it was lodged with its new owner.

I said that first (as if I really knew) you had to think of it from the other end. Someone—they might have been close or hundreds of miles away—would have received a phone call, been woken from sleep, perhaps in those same early hours in which we sat, sleepless and disbelieving, in the hospital. A phone call they had been given to understand could come at any time—soon or maybe years ahead (if they were still there to receive it), maybe never—a phone call they knew would allow them only seconds to agree and prepare.

They would have gone through an instant, perhaps, of wishing that this wished-for call *hadn't* come, that life as they'd known it, with all its risk and distress, might simply go on as it had and not be subject to this imminent, immense change. Then they would have swallowed that thought with the thought that this moment, this chance, might never come again.

They would have been told what to do, to pack the things needed for a stay in hospital, where and to whom to present themselves.

Amid everything else, they would know there was only one way, a necessary prior event, in which this could be happening.

Meanwhile, I said—as I went on it seemed more and more like some impossible fairy-tale, like something I must be making up—Nicky's heart would have been placed in a container, a container perhaps a bit like a picnic cool-box, and then it would have been transported by special priority service, by a network of links that exists for such things. Who knows—it might even have been put on a plane? But almost certainly at some stage in the journey it would have been carried in the special pannier of a motorcycle—the quickest way through traffic. There were motorcyclists who volunteered for such tasks. And almost certainly (but I didn't offer this thought to my mother) it would occur to such motorcyclists that motorcyclists themselves formed a significant portion of the stock of organ donors. They tended to be young and fit. They had fatal accidents.

But it seemed my mother, even after months, would not give up her yearning. Surely, she had the right? To think that someone, somewhere, was walking around. A whole new person, with a whole new life. A lease of life. A deliverance.

In the end I did something irresponsible, foolish perhaps. By this time I knew Pauline, my future wife. She was only a junior nurse in those days, she didn't even work at the hospital where Nicky had died. She knew no more than I did, and if she was about to make clandestine enquiries it could be at the risk of her job. All she suggested—I could have come up with this myself—was that I phone up the office of Reynolds (that was the second doctor), hassle the secretary, play the distraught relative (but I was a distraught relative), see what might not, in a moment's exasperation, be let slip over the phone.

She said, 'But are you sure about this? It could all backfire.'

I made the call. I pleaded. The secretary insisted: she simply didn't have access, even if she could release it, to this information. In the end she went away, for some while, came back. 'All I can tell you,' she said, 'is that the recipient was female and forty-six.' She didn't say it as if she were whispering a secret that could get her dismissed. She said it as if it was meaningless knowledge: it hardly narrowed things down.

A female. I hadn't really thought it or imagined it, though of course it was always possible. Nicky's seventeen-year-old heart had ended up in the body of a forty-six-year-old woman. And of course that was a possibility too—the difference in age. That the organs of the young might be received by those older. Not the very old but, still, in this case, someone a lot older than Nicky.

But I didn't say this to my mother. This has been my one big lie, the biggest lie of my life. I said I'd found out something. I'd been 'ferreting around'. Contacts, I said, through vet college (as if there should have been any). I said there was absolutely nothing more to be found out, but I'd learned something: Nicky's heart had gone to a girl. 'A girl,' I said, 'a young woman. That's all I know.'

I said, 'Keep this between you and me.'

The biggest lie of my life. But it gave my mother something with which to close, almost completely, that gap. Something to content her with never knowing more. It was only a half lie too, of sorts, false only by a span of years. If I'd told my mother that Nicky's heart was inside the body of an older woman, a woman, in fact, not so far from my mother's age, I know what my mother would have thought from that moment on. I know what I'd spared her from.

If only, she would have thought, it had not been that other woman's fate to have the dicky ticker, if only it could have been herself. If only she had not been a strong, robust woman, a mother of four, doomed to carry on being strong and robust while a farm and all that it stood for seemed to crumble away around her, and the men on it, a husband and two sons, seemed to crumble too, so it seemed it was left to her to put things right, to change things back. As if she could do that, as if she could wave a wand.

If only she hadn't been that robust woman but a woman, in her middle years, with an incurable complaint of the heart. Then of course it wouldn't have been terrible or even difficult to have made that decision that night, it wouldn't have been the source for ever afterwards of confusion, mystery and remorse. They wouldn't even have needed motorcyclists. She would have said, yes, let them take out Nicky's heart and meanwhile cut her open and take out her iffy one, and then tuck Nicky's up safely inside her. Then everything would have been all right. □

GRANTA

EDITING VIDIA
Diana Athill

Good publishers are supposed to 'discover' writers, and perhaps they do. To me, however, they just happened to come. In 1956, four years after the launch of André Deutsch Limited, of which I was a director, Mordecai Richler (whose first novel we had just published) introduced me to Andrew Salkey. Andrew was a writer from Jamaica who was then keeping a roof over his head by working for the BBC's Caribbean Service and who was always generous towards other writers. When he heard that I was Mordecai's editor he immediately asked if he could send me a young friend of his who regularly freelanced for the same service and had just written something very good. A few days later V. S. Naipaul came to a coffee bar near our office and handed over *Miguel Street*.

He was in his very early twenties and looked even younger, but his manner was grave—even severe—and unsmiling. This I attributed to nervousness—but I felt that it was the nervousness of someone essentially serious and composed, and that it would be impertinent to think in terms of 'putting him at his ease'. It was a surprise to discover that *Miguel Street* was funny: delicately funny, with nothing overdone. It was a portrait of a street in Trinidad's Port of Spain, in the form of stories which each centred on a street character; its language that of the street, and its balance between amusement and sympathy perfectly judged. I was delighted by it, but worried: it was a publishing dogma to which André Deutsch strongly adhered that stories didn't sell unless they were by Names. So before talking to him about it I gave it to Francis Wyndham who was with us as part-time 'Literary Adviser', and Francis loved it at once and warmly. This probably tipped the balance with André, whose instinct was to distrust as 'do-gooding' my enthusiasm for a little book by a West Indian about a place which interested no one and where the people spoke an unfamiliar dialect. I think he welcomed its being stories because it gave him a reason for saying 'no': but Francis's opinion joined to mine made him bid me find out if the author had a novel on the stocks and tell him that if he had, then that should come first and the stories could follow all in good time. Luckily Vidia was in the process of writing *The Mystic Masseur*.

In fact we could well have launched him with *Miguel Street*, which has outlasted his first two novels in critical esteem, because in the Fifties it was easier to get reviews for a writer seen by the British as black than it was for a young English writer, and reviews influenced readers a good deal more then than they do now. Publishers and reviewers were aware that new voices were speaking up in the newly independent colonies, and partly out of genuine interest, partly out of an optimistic if ill-advised sense that a vast market for books lay out there, ripe for development, they felt it to be the thing to encourage those voices. This trend did not last long, but it served to establish a number of good writers.

Vidia did not yet have the confidence to walk away from our shilly-shallying, and fortunately it did him no real harm. Neither he nor we made any money to speak of from his first three books, *The Mystic Masseur*, *The Suffrage of Elvira* and *Miguel Street*, but there was never any doubt about the making of his name, which began at once with the reviews and was given substance by his own work as a reviewer, of which he got plenty as soon as he became known as a novelist. He was a very good reviewer, clearly as widely read as any literary critic of the day, and it was this rather than his first books which revealed that here was a writer who was going to reject the adjective 'regional', and with good reason.

We began to meet fairly often, and I enjoyed his company because he talked well about writing and people, and was often funny. At quite an early meeting he said gravely that when he was up at Oxford—which he had not liked—he once did a thing so terrible that he would never be able to tell anyone what it was. I said it was unforgivable to reveal that much without revealing more, especially to someone like me who didn't consider even murder literally unspeakable, but I couldn't shift him and never learned what the horror was—though someone told me later that when he was at Oxford Vidia did have some kind of nervous breakdown. It distressed me that he had been unhappy at a place which I loved. Having such a feeling for scholarship, high standards and tradition he ought to have liked it…but no, he would not budge. Never for a minute did it occur to me that he might have felt at a loss when he got to Oxford because of how different it was from his background, still less because of any form of racial insult: he appeared to me far too impressive a person to be subject to such discomforts.

The image Vidia was projecting at that time, in his need to protect his pride, was so convincing that even when I read *A House for Mr Biswas* four years later, and was struck by the authority of his account of Mr Biswas's nervous collapse, I failed to connect its painful vividness with his own reported 'nervous breakdown'. Between me and the truth of his Oxford experience stood the man he wanted people to see.

At that stage I did not know how or why he had rejected Trinidad, and if I had known it, still wouldn't have understood what it is like to be unable to accept the country in which you were born. Vidia's books (not least *A Way in the World*, not written until thirty-seven years later) were to do much to educate me; but then I had no conception of how someone who feels he doesn't belong to his 'home' and cannot belong anywhere else is forced to exist only in himself; nor of how exhausting and precarious such a condition (blithely seen by the young and ignorant as desirable) can be. Vidia's self—his very being—was his writing: a great gift, but all he had. He was to report that ten years later in his career, when he had earned what seemed to others an obvious security, he was still tormented by anxiety about finding the matter for his next book, and for the one after that...an anxiety not merely about earning his living, but about existing as the person he wanted to be. No wonder that while he was still finding his way into his writing he was in danger; and how extraordinary that he could nevertheless strike an outsider as a solidly impressive man.*

This does not mean that I failed to see the obvious delicacy of his nervous system. Because of it I was often worried by his lack of money, and was appalled on his behalf when I once saw him risk losing a commission by defying *The Times Literary Supplement*. They had offered their usual fee of twenty-five pounds (or was it guineas?) for a review, and he had replied haughtily that he wrote nothing for less than fifty. 'Oh silly Vidia,' I thought. 'Now they'll never offer him anything again.' But lo! they paid him his fifty and I was filled with admiration. Of course he was right: authors ought to know their own value and refuse the insult of derisory fees.

I was right to admire that self-respect, at that time, but it was going to develop into a quality difficult to like. In all moral qualities the line between the desirable and the deplorable is imprecise—

---

*Since writing this I have read the letters which Vidia and his father exchanged while Vidia was at Oxford. Letters Between a Father and Son fully reveals the son's loneliness and misery, and makes the self he was able to present to the world even more extraordinary.

between tolerance and lack of discrimination, prudence and cowardice, generosity and extravagance—so it is not easy to see where a man's proper sense of his own worth turns into a more or less pompous self-importance. In retrospect it seems to me that it took eight or nine years for this process to begin to show itself in Vidia, and I think it possible that his audience was at least partly to blame for it.

For example, after a year or so of meetings in the pubs or restaurants where I usually lunched, I began to notice that Vidia was sometimes miffed at being taken to a cheap restaurant or being offered a cheap bottle of wine—and the only consequence of my seeing this (apart from my secretly finding it funny) was that I became careful to let him choose both restaurant and wine. And this carefulness not to offend him, which was, I think, shared by all, or almost all, his English friends, came from an assumption that the reason why he was so anxious to command respect was fear that it was, or might be, denied him because of his race; which led to a squeamish dismay in oneself at the idea of being seen as racist. The shape of an attitude which someone detests in themselves, and has worked at extirpating, can often be discerned from its absence, and during the first years of Vidia's career in England he was often coddled for precisely the reason the coddler was determined to disregard.

Later, of course, the situation changed. His friends became too used to him to see him as anything but himself, and those who didn't know him saw him simply as a famous writer—on top of which he could frighten people. Then it was the weight and edge of his personality which made people defer to him, rather than consideration for his sensitivity, and it was easy to underestimate the pain and strain endured by that sensitivity when he had first pulled himself up out of the thin, sour soil in which he was reared and was striving to find a purchase in England where, however warmly he was welcomed, he could never feel that he wholly belonged.

During the Sixties I visited the newly independent islands of Trinidad and Tobago twice, with intense pleasure: the loveliness of tropical forests and seas, the jolt of excitement which comes from *difference*, the kindness of people, the amazing beauty of Carnival (unlike Vidia, I like steel bands; oh, the sound of them coming in from the fringes of Port of Spain through the four-in-the-morning darkness of the opening day!). On my last morning in Port of Spain I felt a sharp pang as I listened to the keskidee (a bird which really does say '*Qu'est ce qu'il dit?*') and knew how unlikely it was that I should ever hear it again. But at no time was it difficult to remember that mine was a visitor's Trinidad and Tobago; so three other memories, one from high on the country's social scale, the others from lower although by no means from the bottom, are just as clear as the ones I love.

One. Vidia's history of the country, *The Loss of El Dorado*, which is rarely mentioned nowadays but which I think is the best of his non-fiction books, had just come out. Everyone I had met, including the Prime Minister of Trinidad and Tobago, Eric Williams, and the poet Derek Walcott, had talked about it in a disparaging way and had betrayed as they did so that they had not read it. At last, at a party given by the leader of the opposition, I met someone who had: an elderly Englishman just retiring from running the coastguard. We were both delighted to be able to share our pleasure in Vidia's book and had a long talk about it. As we parted I asked him: 'Can you really be the only person in this country who has read it?' and he answered sadly: 'Oh, easily.'

Two. In Tobago I stayed in a delightful little hotel, where on most evenings the village elders dropped in for a drink. One such evening a younger man—a customs officer in his mid-thirties seconded to Tobago's chief town, Scarborough, from Port of Spain— invited me to go out on the town with him. We were joined by another customs officer and a nurse from the hospital. First we went up to Scarborough's fort—its Historic Sight—to look at the view. Then, when conversation fizzled out, it was suggested that we should have a drink at the Arts Centre. It looked in the darkness little more than a shed, and it was shut, but a man was hunted up who produced the key, some Coca-Cola and half a bottle of rum...and there we stood, under a forty-watt lamp in a room of utter dinginess which contained nothing at all but a dusty ping-pong table with a very old copy of the *Reader's Digest* lying in the middle of it. We sipped our drinks in an atmosphere of embarrassment—almost shame—so heavy that it silenced us. After a few minutes we gave up and went to my host's barely furnished but tidy little flat—I remember it as cold, which it can't have been—where we listened to a record of 'Yellow Bird' and drank another rum. Then I was driven back to the hotel.

The evening's emptiness—the really frightening feeling of nothing to do, nothing to say—had made me feel quite ill. I knew too little about the people I had been with to guess what they were like when at ease: all I could discern was that my host was bored to distraction at having to work in the sticks; that he had been driven by his boredom to make his sociable gesture and had then become nervous to the extent of summoning friends to his aid; and that all three had quickly seen that the whole thing was a mistake and had been overtaken by embarrassed gloom. And no wonder. When I remember the Arts Centre I see why, when Vidia first revisited the West Indies, what he felt was fear.

Three. And it is not only people like Vidia, feverish with repressed talent, who yearn to escape. One day I was trying on a swimsuit in a store in Port of Spain when I overheard a conversation in the changing-cubicle next to mine. An American woman, accompanied by her husband, was also buying something, and they were obviously quite taken by the pretty young woman who was serving them. They were asking her questions about her family, and the heightened warmth of their manner made me suspect that they found it almost exciting to be kind to a black person. When the customer had made her choice and her husband was writing a cheque, the saleswoman's voice suddenly changed from chirpiness to breathlessness and she said, 'May I ask you something?' The wife said, 'Yes, of course,' and the poor young woman plunged into desperate pleading: please, please would they help her, would they give her a letter inviting her to their home which she could show to the people who issued visas, she wouldn't be any trouble, and if they would do this for her... On and on she went, the husband trying to interrupt her in an acutely embarrassed voice, still wanting to sound kind but only too obviously appalled at what his entirely superficial amiability had unleashed. Soon the girl was in tears and the couple were sounding frantic with remorse and anxiety to escape—and I was so horrified at being the invisible and unwilling witness of this desperate young woman's humiliation that I abandoned my swimsuit, scrambled into my dress and fled, so I do not know how it ended.

Vidia had felt fear and dislike of Trinidad ever since he could remember. As a schoolboy he had written a vow on an endpaper of his Latin primer to be gone within five years (it took him six). He remembered this in *The Middle Passage*, his first non-fiction book, published in 1962, in which he described his first revisiting of the West Indies and did something he had never done before: examined the reasons why he feared and hated the place where he was born.

It was a desperately negative view of the place, disregarding a good half of the picture; and it came out with the fluency and force of something long matured less in the mind than in the depths of the nervous system. Trinidad, he said, was and knew itself to be a mere dot on the map. It had no importance and no existence as a nation, being only somewhere out of which first Spain, then France, then Britain could make money: grossly easy money because of using slaves to do the work, and after slaves indentured labour which was almost as cheap. A slave-based society has no need to be efficient, so no tradition of efficiency exists. Slave-masters don't need to be intelligent, so 'in Trinidad education was not one of the things money could buy; it was something money freed you from. Education was strictly for the poor. The white boy left school "counting on his fingers" as the Trinidadian likes to say, but this was a measure of his privilege... The white community was never an upper class in the sense that it possessed a superior speech or taste or attainments; it was envied only for its money and its access to pleasure.'

When this crude colonial society was opened up because the islands were no longer profitable and the British pulled out, what Vidia saw gushing in to fill the vacuum was the flashiest and most materialistic kind of American influence in the form of commercial radio (television had yet to come) and films—films at their most violent and unreal. ('British films,' he wrote, 'played to empty houses. It was my French master who urged me to go to see *Brief Encounter*; and there were two of us in the cinema, he in the balcony, I in the pit.') Trinidad and Tobago was united only in its hunger for 'American modernity', and under that sleazy veneer it was split.

It was split between the descendants of slaves, the African Trinidadians, and the descendants of indentured labourers, the Indians, both groups there by an accident of history, neither with any roots to speak of. In *The Middle Passage* Vidia called the Africans 'Negroes', which today sounds shocking. Reading the book one has to keep reminding oneself that the concept of Black Power had yet to be formulated. Black people had not yet rejected the word 'Negro': it was still being widely used and 'black' was considered insulting. And in this book his main criticism of Trinidadians of African descent is that they had been brainwashed by the experience of slavery into 'thinking white'—into being ashamed of their own colour and physical features. What he deplored—as many observers of West Indian societies had done—was precisely the attitudes which people of African descent were themselves beginning to deplore, and would soon be forcing themselves to overcome.

The Indians he saw as less unsure of themselves because of the pride they took in the idea of India; but he also saw that idea as being almost meaningless—they had no notion of what the subcontinent was really like. It was also dangerous in that it militated against attempts to bridge the rift. Theirs was 'a peasant-minded, money-minded community, spiritually static, its religion reduced to rites without philosophy, set in a materialist, colonialist society'. The Trinidadian Indian was a 'complete colonial, even more philistine than the white'.

He sums up his account of racial friction thus: 'Like monkeys pleading for evolution, each claiming to be whiter than the other, Indians and Negroes appeal to the unacknowledged white audience to see how much they despise one another. They despise one another by reference to the whites; and the irony is that their antagonism should have reached its peak today, when white prejudices have ceased to matter.'

This was a fair assessment: everyone, apart from Tourist Board propagandists, to whom I talked about politics deplored this racial tension, and most of them either said outright, or implied, that blame lay with the group to which they did not belong. No one remarked on the common sense which enabled people to rub along in spite of it (as they still do), any more than Vidia did. The rift, which certainly was absurd and regrettable, became more dramatic if seen as dangerous, and therefore reflected a more lurid light on whoever was being presented as its instigator. People did make a bid for the outsider's respect—did 'appeal to the unacknowledged white audience'. But to what audience was Vidia himself appealing? It was *The Middle Passage* which first made black West Indians call him 'racist'.

The book was admired in England and disliked in Trinidad, but it was not addressed to the white audience in order to please it. Its whole point was to show that Caribbean societies are a mess because they were callously created by white men for the white men's own ends, only to be callously administered and finally callously abandoned. Vidia was trying to write from a point of view above that of white or brown or black; he was trying to look at the people now inhabiting the West Indies with a clear-sighted and impartial intelligence, and to describe what he saw honestly, even if honesty seemed brutal. This he felt, and said, had to be done because a damaged society shuffling along with the help of fantasies and excuses can only become more sick: what it has to do is learn to know itself, and only its writers can teach it that. Caribbean writers had so far, he claimed, failed to do more than plead their own causes. If he expected Trinidadians to welcome this high-minded message he was naive—but I don't suppose he did. He was pursuing his own understanding of the place, and offering it, because that is what a serious writer can't help doing. If anyone resented it, too, bad.

Of course they did resent it—who doesn't resent hearing disagreeable truths told in a manner verging on the arrogant? But I think the label 'racist' which they stuck on him was, so to speak, only a local one. I saw him as a man raised in, and frightened by, a somewhat disorderly, inefficient and self-deceiving society, who therefore longed for order, clarity and competence. Having concluded that the lack of these qualities in the place where he was born came from the people's lack of roots, he overvalued a sense of history and respect for tradition, choosing to romanticize their results rather than to see the complex and far from admirable scenes with which they often coexist. (His first visit to India, described in *An Area of Darkness*, left him in a state of distress because it showed him that an ancient civilization in which he had dared to hope that he would find the belonging he hungered for, could be just as disorderly and inefficient as the place where he was born.) Although both England and the United States were each in its own way going to fall short of his ideal society, Europe as a whole came more close, more often, to offering a life in which he could feel comfortable. I remember driving, years ago, through a vine-growing region of France and coming on a delightful example of an ancient expertise taking pleasure in itself: a particularly well-cultivated vineyard which had a pillar rose—a deep pink pillar rose—planted as an exquisite punctuation at the end of every row. Instantly—although it was weeks since I had seen or thought of him—he popped into my head: 'How Vidia would like that!'

But although I cannot see Vidia as racist in the sense of wanting to be white or to propitiate whites, I do think it is impossible to spend the first eighteen years of your life in a given set of circumstances without being shaped by them: and Vidia spent the first eighteen years of his life as a Trinidadian Indian. Passionate though his determination to escape the limitations imposed by this fate was, and near though it came to achieving the impossible, it could not wholly free him from his conditioning.

In Chapter One of *The Middle Passage*, when he has only just boarded the boat train which will take him to Southampton, there begins the following description. Into the corridor, out of the compartment next to Vidia's, had stepped 'a very tall and ill-made Negro... He went to the window, opened the ventilation gap, pushed his face through, turned slightly to his left, and spat. His face was grotesque. It seemed to have been smashed in from one cheek. One eye had narrowed; the thick lips had bunched into a circular swollen protuberance; the enormous nose was twisted. When, slowly, he opened his mouth to spit, his face became even more distorted. He spat in slow, intermittent dribbles; and when he worked his face back in, his eyes caught mine.'

Vidia makes a slight attempt to give this man a role in the story of his journey by saying that he began to imagine that the poor creature was aware of him in a malign way, that after that one glance, in the buffet car there he was again...but in fact once he has been described the man has no part to play, he is done with; in spite of which Vidia could not resist placing him right at the start of the book and *describing him in greater physical detail than anyone else in all its 232 pages.* I am not saying that this man was invented or that he may have been less dreadfully unattractive than we are told he was; but by choosing to pick him out and to *fix* on him, Vidia has given an indelible impression less of the man than of his own reaction: the dismayed recoil of a fastidious Trinidad Indian from what he sees as an inferior kind of person. And I believe that if I were black I should from time to time, throughout his work, pick up other traces of this flinching presence hidden in the shadow behind one of the best English-language novelists we have. And even as part of the white audience I cannot help noticing the occasional touch of self-importance (increasing with the years) which I suspect to have its roots far back in the Trinidad Indian's nervous defiance of disrespect.

Vidia's mother, handsome and benignly matronly, welcomed his publishers very kindly when they visited Trinidad, and gave the impression of being the beloved linchpin of her family. When I first met them, long before they had been stricken by the close-together deaths of one of the daughters and of Shiva, Vidia's younger and only brother, they impressed me as a flourishing lot: good-looking, intelligent, charming, successful. A married daughter told me that Mrs Naipaul 'divides her time between the temple and the quarry'— the latter being a business belonging to her side of the family, in which she was a partner. That she was not simply a comfortable mother-figure became apparent when she told me that she had just got home from attending a seminar on welding and was very glad that she hadn't missed it because she had learned enough at it to be able to cut the number of welders they employed at the quarry by half. Soon afterwards she threw more light on her own character by making a little speech to me, after noticing my surprise when she had appeared to be indifferent to some news about Vidia. She had been, she said, a well-brought-up Hindu girl of her generation, so she had been given no education and was expected to obey her parents in everything, and that was what she did. Then she was married ('And there was no nonsense about falling in love in those days'), whereupon it was her husband she had to obey in everything, and that was what she did. Then she had her children, so of course it was her job to devote herself entirely to them and bring them up as well as possible, and that was what she did ('and I think I can say I made a good job of it'). 'But then I said to myself, when I am fifty—FINISH. I will begin to live for myself. And that is what I am doing now and they must get on with their own lives.'

It was an impressive little thumbnail autobiography, but it left questions in my mind. I had, after all, read *A House for Mr Biswas*, the novel Vidia had based on his father's life, and had gained a vivid picture of how humiliated Mr Biswas had been after his marriage into the much richer and more influential Tulsi family—although I don't think I knew at that stage that Seepersad Naipaul, Vidia's father, had once had a mental breakdown and had vanished from his home for months. Clearly this attractive and—I was now beginning to think—slightly formidable woman was greatly oversimplifying her story, but I liked her; as I told Vidia when, soon after this, he asked me if I did. 'Yes, very much,' I said; to which he replied: 'Everyone seems to. I hate her.'

I wish I had asked him what he meant by that. It was not the first time that I heard him, in a fit of irritation, strike out at someone with a fierce word, so I didn't think it was necessarily true (and anyway, dislike of a mother usually indicates damaged love). But uncertain though I remained about his feelings towards his mother, I knew that he loved his father, who had died soon after Vidia left Trinidad to come to Oxford. He wrote a moving introduction to the little volume of his father's stories which he gave us to publish in 1976, and he spoke about the way his father had introduced him to books. Seepersad Naipaul had possessed a remarkably strong and true instinct for writing which had overcome his circumstances to the point of giving him a passion for such English classics as had come his way, and steering him into a writing job on the local newspaper. He had passed his passion on by reading aloud to Vidia and Kamla, the sister nearest to him, making the children stand up as he read to keep them from falling asleep—which seems to have impressed the importance of the ritual on them rather than to have put them off. Seepersad's own few stories were about Trinidadian village life, and the most important lesson he gave his son was 'Write about what you know', thus curing him of the young colonial's feeling that 'literature' had to be exotic—something belonging to the faraway world out of which came the books he found in the library. And I know of another piece of advice Seepersad gave his son which speaks for the truth of his instinct. Vidia had shown him a piece of would-be comic writing, and he told him not to strive for comedy but to let it arise naturally out of the story. It is sad to think of this man hobbled by the circumstances of his life (see *A House for Mr Biswas*) and dying before he could see his son break free. The mother was part of the 'circumstances' and the child sided with his father against her, of that I feel sure.

I cannot remember how long it was—certainly several months, perhaps even a year—before I learned that Vidia was married. 'I have found a new flat', he would say; 'I saw such-and-such a film last week'; 'My landlady says': not once had he used the words 'we' or 'our'. I had taken it for granted that he lived in industrious loneliness, which had seemed sad. So when at a party I glimpsed him at the far end of a room with a young woman—an inconspicuously, even mousily pretty young woman—and soon afterwards saw him leaving with her, I was pleased that he had found a girlfriend. The next time he came to the office I asked who she was—and was astounded when he answered, in a rather cross voice, 'My wife, of course.'

After that Pat was allowed to creep out of the shadows, but only a little: and one day she said something that shocked me so much that I know for certain that I am remembering it word for word. I must have remarked on our not meeting earlier, and she replied: 'Vidia doesn't like me to come to parties because I'm such a bore.'

From that moment on, whenever I needed to cheer myself up by counting my blessings, I used to tell myself: 'At least I'm not married to Vidia.'

It did not exactly turn me against him, I suppose because from the beginning I had thought of him as an interesting person to watch rather than as a friend. The flow of interest between us had always been one-way—I can't remember ever telling him anything about my own affairs, or wanting to—so this odd business of his marriage was something extra to watch rather than something repellent. Had he ever loved her—or did he still love her in some twisted way? They had married while he was at Oxford: had he done it out of loneliness, to enlarge the minuscule territory he could call his own now that he was out in the world? Or was it because she could keep him? She was working as a teacher and continued to do so well into their marriage. Or was it to shelter him from other women? He had once asked a man of my acquaintance: 'Do you know any *fast* women?' which my friend found funny (particularly as he was gay) but which seemed touching to me. As did Vidia's only attempt to make a pass at me. Pat was away and I had asked him to supper. Without warning he got to his feet, came across the room and tried to kiss me as I was coming through the door carrying a tray loaded with glasses. It hardly seemed necessary to put into words the rebuff which most of him was clearly anxious for, but to be on the safe side I did. Our friendship, I said gently, was too valuable to complicate in any way—and his face brightened with relief. That someone so lacking in sexual experience and so puritanical should have to resort to prostitutes (as he told *The New Yorker* in 1994, and as a passage in *The Mimic Men* suggests) is natural; though I guess he did so infrequently, and with distaste.

The little I saw of Vidia and Pat together was depressing: there was no sign of their enjoying each other, and the one whole weekend I spent with them they bickered ceaselessly, Pat's tetchiness as sharp as his (developed as a defence, I thought). When he was abroad she was scrupulously careful of his interests; she did research for him; sometimes he referred to showing her work in progress: he trusted her completely, and with reason, because he was evidently her raison d'être. And she made it unthinkable to speak critically of him in her presence. But always her talk was full of how tiresome it was for him that she was sick in aeroplanes, or fainted in crowds, or couldn't eat curries…and when I tried to introduce a subject other than him that would interest us both, such as West Indian politics or her work as a teacher, she never failed to run us aground yet again on some reference to her own inadequacy. At first I took it for granted that he had shattered her self-confidence, and I am still sure he did it no good. But later I suspected that she had always been negative and depressing, someone who enjoyed being squashed.

In *A Way in the World*, writing (as usual) as though he were a single man, Vidia described himself as 'incomplete' in 'physical attractiveness, love, sexual fulfilment'. How terrible for a wife to be publicly wiped out in this way! Everyone who knew the Naipauls said how sorry they were for Pat, and I was sorry for her, too. But whatever Vidia's reason for marrying, he cannot have foreseen the nature of this sexless, loveless (on his part) union with such a discouraging little person. He, too, probably deserved commiseration.

When his Argentinian friend Margaret first came to London he brought her to lunch with me. She was a lively, elegant woman who, though English by descent, was 'feminine' in the Latin-American style, sexy and teasing, with the appearance of having got him just where she wanted him. And he glowed with pride and pleasure. Afterwards he said he was thinking of leaving Pat, and when I was dismayed (could she exist without him?), said that the thought of giving up 'carnal pleasure' just when he'd discovered it was too painful to bear. Why not stay married and have an affair, I asked; which he appeared to think an unseemly suggestion, although it was what he then did for many years. What happened later I don't know, but in the early years of their relationship there was no sign of his squashing Margaret. He did, however, make one disconcerting remark. Did I not find it interesting, he asked, that there was so much cruelty in sex.

What began to wear me down in my dealings with Vidia (it was a long time before I allowed myself to acknowledge it) was his depression.

With every one of his books—and we published eighteen of them—there was a three-part pattern. First came a long period of peace while he was writing, during which we saw little of him and I would often have liked to see more, because I would be full of curiosity about the new book. Then, when it was delivered, there would be a short burst of euphoria during which we would have enjoyable meetings and my role would be to appreciate the work, to write the blurb, to hit on a jacket that pleased both him and us, and to see that the script was free of typist's errors (he was such a perfectionist that no editing, properly speaking, was necessary). Then came part three: post-publication gloom, during which his voice on the telephone would make my heart sink—just a little during the first few years, deeper and deeper with the passing of time. His voice became charged with tragedy, his face became haggard, his theme became the atrocious exhaustion and damage (the word damage always occurred) this book had inflicted on him, and all to what end? Reviewers were ignorant monkeys, publishers (this would be implied in a sinister fashion rather than said) were lazy and useless: what was the point of it all? Why did he go on?

It is natural that a writer who knows himself to be good and who is regularly confirmed in that opinion by critical comment should expect to become a best-seller, but every publisher knows that you don't necessarily become a best-seller by writing well. Of course you don't necessarily have to write badly to do it: it is true that some best-selling books are written astonishingly badly, and equally true that some are written very well. The quality of the writing—even the quality of the thinking—is irrelevant. It is a matter of whether or not a nerve is hit in the wider reading public as opposed to the serious one which is composed of people who are interested in writing as an art. Vidia has sold well in the latter, and has pushed a good way beyond its fringes by becoming famous—at a certain point many people in the wider reading public start to feel that they *ought* to read a writer—but it was always obvious that he was not going to make *big* money. An old friend of mine who reads a great deal once said to me apologetically, 'I'm sure he's very good, but I don't feel he's for me'—and she spoke for a large number of reading people.

Partly this is because of his subject matter, which is broadly speaking the consequences of imperialism: people whose countries once ruled empires relish that subject only if it is flavoured, however subtly, with nostalgia. Partly it is because he is not interested in writing about women, and when he does so usually does it with dislike: more women than men read novels. And partly it is because of his temperament. Once, when he was particularly low, we talked about surviving the horribleness of life and I said that I did it by relying on simple pleasures such as the taste of fruit, the delicious sensations of a hot bath or clean sheets, the way flowers tremble very slightly with life, the lilt of a bird's flight: if I were stripped of those pleasures...better not to imagine it! He asked if I could really depend on them and I said yes. I have a clear memory of the sad, puzzled voice in which he replied: 'You're very lucky, I can't.' And his books, especially his novels (after the humour which filled the first three drained away) are coloured—or perhaps I should say 'discoloured'—

by this lack of what used to be called animal spirits. They impress, but they do not charm.

He was, therefore, displeased with the results of publication, which filled him always with despair, sometimes with anger as well. Once he descended on me like a thunderbolt to announce that he had just been into Foyle's of Charing Cross Road and they didn't have a single copy of his latest book, published only two weeks earlier, in stock: not one! Reason told me this was impossible, but I have a lurking tendency to accept guilt if faced with accusation, and this tendency went into spasm: suppose the sales department really had made some unthinkable blunder? Well, if they had I was not going to face the ensuing mayhem single-handed, so I said: 'We must go and tell André at once.' Which we did; and André Deutsch said calmly: 'What nonsense, Vidia—come on, we'll go to Foyle's straight away and I'll show you.' So all three of us stumped down the street to Foyle's, only two minutes away, Vidia still thunderous, I twittering with nerves, André serene. Once we were in the shop he cornered the manager and explained: 'Mr Naipaul couldn't find his book: will you please show him where it is displayed.'—'Certainly Mr Deutsch' and there it was, two piles of six copies each, on the table for 'Recent Publications'. André said afterwards that Vidia looked even more thunderous at being done out of his grievance, but if he did I was too dizzy with relief to notice.

Vidia's anxiety and despair were real: you need only compare a photograph of his face in his twenties with one taken in his forties to see how it has been shaped by pain. It was my job to listen to his unhappiness and do what I could to ease it—which would not have been too bad if there had been anything I *could* do. But there was not: and exposure to someone else's depression is draining, even if only for an hour or so at a time and not very often. I felt genuinely sorry for him, but the routine was repeated so often… The truth is that as the years went by, during these post-publication glooms I had increasingly to force myself into feeling genuinely sorry for him, in order to endure him.

Self-brainwashing sometimes has to be a part of an editor's job. You are no use to the writers on your list if you cannot bring imaginative sympathy to working with them, and if you cease to be of use to them you cease to be of use to your firm. Imaginative sympathy cannot issue from a cold heart so you have to like your writers. Usually this is easy; but occasionally it happens that in spite of admiring someone's work you are—or gradually become—unable to like the person.

I thought so highly of Vidia's writing and felt his presence on our list to be so important that I simply could not allow myself not to like him. I was helped by a foundation of affection laid down during the early days of knowing him, and I was able to believe that his depressions hurt him far more than they hurt me—that he could not prevent them—that I ought to be better at bearing them than I was. And as I became more aware of other things that grated—his attitude to Pat and to his brother Shiva (whom he bullied like an enraged mother hen in charge of a particularly feckless chick)—I called upon a tactic often employed in families: Aunt Emily may have infuriating mannerisms or disconcerting habits, but they are forgiven, even enjoyed, because they are *so typically her*. The offending person is put into the position of a fictional, almost a cartoon, character, whose quirks can be laughed or marvelled at as though they existed only on a page. For quite a long time seeing him as a perpetrator of 'Vidia-isms' worked rather well.

In 1975 we received the thirteenth of his books—his eighth work of fiction—*Guerrillas*. For the first time I was slightly apprehensive because he had spoken to me about the experience of writing it in an unprecedented way: usually he kept the process private, but this time he said that it was extraordinary, something that had never happened before: it was as though the book had been given to him. Such a feeling about writing does not necessarily bode well. And as it turned out, I could not like the book.

It was about a Trinidad-like island sliding into a state of decadence, and there was a tinge of hysteria in the picture's dreadfulness, powerfully imagined though it was. A central part of the story came from something that had recently happened in Trinidad: the murder of an Englishwoman called Gail Benson who had changed her name to Halé Kimga, by a Trinidadian who called himself Michael X and who had set up a so-called 'commune'. Gail had been brought to Trinidad by her lover, a black American known as Hakim Jamal (she had changed her name at his bidding). Both of the men hovered between being mad and being con-men, and their linking-up had been Gail's undoing. I knew all three, Gail and Hakim well, Michael very slightly: indeed, I had written a book about them (which I had put away—it would be published sixteen years later) called *Make Believe*. This disturbed my focus on large parts of *Guerrillas*. The people in the book were not meant to be portraits of those I had known (Vidia had met none of them). They were characters created by Vidia to express his view of post-colonial history in places like Trinidad. But the situation in the novel was so close to the situation in life that I often found it hard to repress the reaction: 'But that's not true!' This did not apply to the novel's Michael X character who was called Jimmy Ahmed: Jimmy, and the half-squalid half-pathetic ruins of his 'commune', is a brilliant and wholly convincing creation. Nor did it apply to Roche, Vidia's substitute for Hakim Jamal. Roche is a liberal white South African refugee working for a big commercial firm, whose job has involved giving cynical support to Jimmy. Roche was so evidently not Hakim that the question did not arise. But it certainly did apply to Jane, who stood in for Gail in being the murdered woman.

The novel's Jane, who comes to the island as Roche's mistress, is supposed to be an idle, arid creature who tries to find the vitality she lacks by having affairs with men. Obtuse in her innate sense of her superiority as a white woman, she drifts into such an attempt with Jimmy: an irresponsible fool playing a dangerous game for kicks with a ruined black man. Earlier, Vidia had written an account for a newspaper of Gail's murder which made it clear that he saw Gail as that kind of woman.

She was not. She was idle and empty, but she had no sense of her own superiority as a white woman or as anything else. Far from playing dangerous games for kicks, she was clinging on to illusions for dear life. The people she had most in common with were not the kind of secure Englishwomen who had it off with black men to demonstrate their own liberal attitudes, but those poor wretches who followed the American 'guru' Jones to Guyana in 1977, and ended by committing mass suicide at his bidding. She was so lacking in a sense of her own worth that it bordered on insanity.

It was therefore about Jane that I kept saying to myself, 'But that's not true!' Then I pulled myself together and saw that there was no reason why Jane should be like Gail: an Englishwoman going into such an affair for kicks was far from impossible and would be a perfectly fair example of fraudulence of motive in white liberals, which was what Vidia was bent on showing.

So I read the book again—and this time Jane simply fell to pieces. Roche came out of it badly, too: a dim character, hard to envisage, in spite of revealing wide-apart molars with black roots whenever he smiled (a touch of 'clever characterization' which should have been beneath Vidia). But although he doesn't quite convince, he almost does; you keep expecting him to emerge from the mist, while Jane becomes more and more like a series of bits and pieces that don't add up, so that finally her murder is without significance. I came to the conclusion that the trouble must lie with Vidia's having cut his cloth to fit a pattern he had laid down in advance: these characters existed in order to exemplify his argument, he had not been *discovering* them. So they did not live; and the woman lived less than the man because that is true of all Vidia's women.

From the professional point of view there was no question as to what I ought to do: this was one of our most valuable authors; even if his book had been really bad rather than just flawed we would certainly have published it in the expectation that he would soon be back on form; so what I must say was 'wonderful' and damn well sound as though I meant it.

Instead I sat there muttering 'Oh my god, what am I going to say to him?' I had never lied to him—I kept reminding myself of that, disregarding the fact that I had never before needed to lie. 'If I lie now, how will he be able to trust me in the future when I praise something?' The obvious answer to that was that if I lied convincingly he would never know that I had done it, but this did not occur to me. After what seemed to me like hours of sincere angst I ended by persuading myself that I 'owed it to our friendship' to tell him what I truly thought.

Nothing practical would be gained. A beginner writer sometimes makes mistakes which he can remedy if they are pointed out, but a novelist of Vidia's quality and experience who produces an unconvincing character has suffered a lapse of imagination about which nothing can be done. It happened to Dickens whenever he attempted a good woman; it happened to George Eliot with Daniel Deronda. And as for my own attitude—I had often seen through other people who insisted on telling the truth about a friend's shortcomings: I knew that *their* motives were usually suspect. But my own were as invisible to me as a cuttlefish becomes when it saturates the surrounding water with ink.

So I told him. I began by saying how much I admired the many things in the book which I did admire, and then I said that I had to tell him (*had* to tell him!) that two of his three central characters had failed to convince me. It was like saying to Conrad, '*Lord Jim* is a very fine novel except that Jim doesn't quite come off.'

Vidia looked disconcerted, then stood up and said quietly that he was sorry they didn't work for me, because he had done the best he could with them, there was nothing more he could do, so there was no point in discussing it. As he left the room I think I muttered something about its being a splendid book all the same, after which I felt a mixture of relief at his appearing to be sorry rather than angry, and a slight (only slight!) sense of let-down and silliness. And I supposed that was that.

The next day Vidia's agent called André to say that he had been instructed to retrieve *Guerrillas* because we had lost confidence in Vidia's writing and therefore he was leaving us.

André must have fought back because there was nothing he hated more than losing an author, but the battle didn't last long. Although I believe I was named, André was kind enough not to blame me. Nor did I blame myself. I went into a rage. I fulminated to myself, my colleagues, my friends: 'All those years of friendship, and a mere dozen words of criticism—*a mere dozen words!*—send him flouncing out in a tantrum like some hysterical prima donna!' I had long and scathing conversations with him in my head; but more satisfying was a daydream of being at a huge and important party, seeing him enter the room, turning on my heel and walking out.

For at least two weeks I seethed…and then, in the third week, it suddenly occurred to me that never again would I have to listen to Vidia telling me how damaged he was, and it was as though the sun came out. *I didn't have to like Vidia any more!* I could still like his work, I could still be sorry for his pain; but I no longer faced the task of fashioning affection out of these elements in order to deal as a good editor should with the exhausting, and finally tedious, task of listening to his woe. 'Do you know what,' I said to André, 'I've begun to see that it's a release.' (Rather to my surprise, he laughed.) I still, however, failed to see that my editorial 'mistake' had been an act of aggression. In fact I went on failing to see that for years.

Guerrillas was sold to Secker and Warburg the day after it left us.

A month or so after this I went into André's office to discuss something and his phone rang before I had opened my mouth. This always happened. Usually I threw myself back in my chair with a groan, then reached for something to read, but this time I jumped up and grabbed the extension. 'Why—Vidia!' he had said. 'What can I do for you?'

Vidia was speaking from Trinidad, his voice tense: André must call his agent *at once* and tell him to recover the manuscript of *Guerrillas* from Secker and Warburg and deliver it to us.

André, who was uncommonly good at rising to unexpected occasions, became instantly fatherly. Naturally, he said, he would be delighted to get the book back, but Vidia must not act too impetuously: whatever had gone wrong might well turn out to be less serious than he now felt. This was Thursday. What Vidia must do was think it over very carefully without taking action until Monday. Then, if he still wanted to come back to us, he must call his agent, not André, listen to his advice, and if that failed to change his mind, instruct him to act. André would be waiting for the agent's call on Monday afternoon or Tuesday morning, hoping—of course— that it would be good news for us.

Which—of course—it was. My private sun did go back behind a film of cloud, but in spite of that there was satisfaction in knowing that he thought himself better off with us than with them, and I had no doubt of the value of whatever books were still to come.

Vidia never said why he bolted from Seckers, but his agent told André that it was because when they announced *Guerrillas* in their catalogue they described him as 'the West Indian novelist'.

The books still to come were, indeed, worth having (though the last of them was his least important): *India: a Wounded Civilization, The Return of Eva Perón, Among the Believers, A Bend in the River* and *Finding the Centre*. I had decided that the only thing to do was to behave exactly as I had always done in our pre-*Guerrillas* working relationship, while quietly cutting down our extra-curricular friendship, and he apparently felt the same. The result was a smooth passage, less involving but less testing than it used to be. Nobody else knew—and I myself was unaware of it until I came to look back—that having resolved never again to utter a word of criticism to Vidia, I was guilty of an absurd pettiness. In *Among the Believers*, a book which I admired very much, there were two minor points to which in the past I would have drawn his attention, and I refrained from doing so: thus betraying, though luckily only to my retrospecting self, that I was still hanging on to my self-righteous interpretation of the *Guerrillas* incident. Vidia would certainly not have 'flounced out like some hysterical prima donna' over matters so trivial. One was a place where he seemed to draw too sweeping a conclusion from too slight an event and could probably have avoided giving that impression by some quite small adjustment; and the other was that when an Iranian speaking English said 'Sheep' Vidia, misled by his accent, thought he said 'ship', which made some dialogue as he reported it sound puzzling. To keep mum about that! There is nothing like self-deception for making one ridiculous.

When Vidia really did leave us in 1984 I could see why—and even why he did so in a way which seemed unkind, without a word of warning or explanation. He had come to the conclusion that André Deutsch Limited was going downhill. It was true. The recession, combined with a gradual but relentless shrinkage in the readership of books such as those we published, was well on the way to making firms of our size and kind unviable; and André had lost his vigour and flair. His decision to sell the firm, which more or less coincided with Vidia's departure, was made (so he felt and told me) because publishing was 'no fun any more', but it was equally a matter of his own slowly failing health. The firm continued for ten years or so under Tom Rosenthal, chuntering not-so-slowly downwards all the time (Tom had been running Seckers when they called Vidia a West Indian, so his appearance on the scene did nothing to change Vidia's mind).

A writer of reputation can always win an even bigger advance than he is worth by allowing himself to be tempted away from publisher A by publisher B, and publisher B will then have to try extra hard on his behalf to justify the advance: it makes sense to move on if you time it right. And if you perceive that there is something going seriously wrong with publisher A you would be foolish not to do so. And having decided to go, how could you look in the eye someone you have known for over twenty years, of whom you have been really quite fond, and tell him, 'I'm leaving because you are getting past it'? Of course you could not. Vidia's agent managed to conceal from André what Vidia felt, but André suspected something: he told me that he thought it was something to do with himself and that he couldn't get it out of the agent, but perhaps I might have better luck. I called the agent and asked him if there was any point in my getting in touch with Vidia, and he—in considerable embarrassment—told me the truth; whereupon I could only silently agree with Vidia's silence, and tell poor André that I'd been so convincingly assured of the uselessness of any further attempt to change Vidia's mind, that we had better give up.

So this leaving did not make me angry, or surprised, or even sad, except for André's sake. Vidia was doing what he had to do, and it seemed reasonable to suppose that we had enjoyed the best of him, anyway. Many years later Mordecai Richler, in at the story's end, oddly enough, as well as its beginning, told me that he had recently seen Vidia with his new and much younger wife, Nadira (they met in Pakistan in 1995 and married the next year, soon after Pat's death). He was, said Mordecai, 'amazingly jolly'; and I was pleased to find that this news made me very glad indeed. □

GRANTA

NEVER LOVE
A GAMBLER
Keith Ridgway

There was the roar of a bus, a shuddering agitation in the warm air, and then a rotten smell that came wafting in the open door from the street, and then a second later a dog, an awful nightmare of a dog, a cur, who strolled by with something dead in the clamp of his jaw.

'Ah Jaysus,' moaned Dodo, hiding her eyes. 'What's he got? What's he got?'

The dog went on, dripping, and there was a trail led after him, of something dark and thick that was not blood.

'A rat I think,' said Jimmy, squinting.

'Or a cat. A little kitten.'

Another bus roared away from the lights and Dodo picked up her half of stout and put it down again. Jaysus. The smell lingered. It hung and she could see it, a red-black colour like a winter nose bleed. In her leg the pain began. She glanced at her son and burst into tears.

'Ah Mam, don't cry for Christ's sake. What's wrong with you?'

She put down the glass and pulled a sky-blue handkerchief from her pocket and blew her nose and dabbed at her eyes and picked up the glass again and drank. A skinny drunk woman looked down at her sideways from the counter of the bar.

'Nothing,' she said.

'Is it Da?'

His father his father. Her son and his father and the pain in her leg.

'No.'

'What then?'

'My leg hurts.'

'Is that it?'

'Feels like there's something living in me knee. It's killin me Jimmy. Turns and twists and turns like it can't get asleep.'

'We'll go to the doctor tomorrow.'

'What do you want to go for?'

'You go on your own so.'

'He's useless.'

'He's alright.'

'He looks down at me, turns up his nose.'

She drank, and watched him out of the corner of her eye as he stuck a finger in his whiskey and sucked it. Her knee twisted itself again and she scrunched up her face and stuck out her tongue and let a moan out of her till it passed.

'Alright Dodo?' the barman called.

'Oh yes. It's me knee. Awful in the heat.'

'Awful in the cold. Awful in the in-between,' said Jimmy huffily, his eyes front ahead, his mess of hair in a greasy tumble over the bad skin of his forehead. Forehead from his father. Great domes, the two of them—made you think of clever, complicated men. They weren't that.

'I'd have thought it'd be better when it's dry,' said the barman. 'Dry and hot like it is. I thought the damp'd be worse.'

'No,' said Dodo, conscious of Jimmy smiling and shaking his head.

The barman lit a cigarette and flicked the flame from his match and tossed it smoking towards the door, but it fell short, landing on the colourless mat.

'Joints are awful things,' he said. 'Never trust them.'

Dodo nodded and stared into her stout. Jimmy watched the barman for a while and then lit a cigarette of his own, drawing in a big lungful of smoke and pausing for a long moment and hurling it out of him then in a great big rush towards the bright street.

'I wonder is it cigarettes?' said Dodo.

'You've been off them for years.'

'Not as long as I was on them. Rose Kelly's sister-in-law had a leg amputated and she was on forty a day and I was on forty a day too.'

Jimmy said nothing, only shook his head and drew again the soft grey smoke into himself and held it, as if it were necessary to test something, in his insides.

'There's that dog,' said Dodo, and Jimmy breathed out.

'He's eaten it.'

'Ah don't say that.'

'Swallowed it whole.'

'It's a fierce smell off him.'

The dog paused in the doorway and looked in, one eye gooey

and the other colourless and blind. His coat was dirty with dust and filth and he was of no particular breed. A scar ran down one side, and he dragged that hind leg, and he smelled hugely.

'Poor fella,' said Dodo. 'Bad leg too.'

'Forty a day man.'

Dodo smiled.

At the other end a door opened and in stepped Mossie Russell, and all the bar glanced up at him and away again, and there was a slight hush, all eyes. The skinny woman got up and left, going out the side door, stepping, almost falling, over the old dog who now lay panting on the pavement, staring at Dodo.

'Shite,' muttered Jimmy, cleared his throat, shifted in his seat.

Mossie Russell walked smiling across the room, for all the world like he had stepped out of a game show, as if there was applause going on, as if he was delighted, delighted, to be here, my word, with all these lovely lovely people. He nodded hugely at the barman and made a gun with his finger and fired it, clicking in his mouth, just a couple of times too often, so that it was funny, or past funny, a parody of that type of man, so that he showed he had the measure of himself, contained himself, stood beside himself, watched you watching, letting you know he was cleverer than he seemed, but keeping a secret still—just how much cleverer—as if the parody might itself be a joke, a double-cross, a parody of your smug amusement, a way of getting at you no matter who you were or what you thought. Here was Mossie Russell. And without once glancing at them as far as Dodo could see, he strode the length of the place in his swagger and came straight to her and Jimmy. He clapped his hands and rubbed them.

'Mrs Fitzgerald,' he said. 'Jimmy,' he said. He smiled at them and held his arms out wide and stood like that for a moment, a beaming cruciform shape, an exaggeration of himself, tempting comment. Jacket a kind of yellow. Go on. Say a word.

He sat at their table on a low stool with his back to the door and the dog. 'Mind if I join yous?' This after he was seated.

'We do yes,' said Jimmy.

'Ah shut up Jimmy,' said Mossie, delighted. 'What are yous havin?'

'I'm fine thanks,' said Dodo, chewing, which was what she did.

'Jimmy?'

'What?'

'What can I get you?'

'Large Black Bush.'

Mossie laughed and nodded at the barman. He reached into the pocket of his jacket then and pulled out a box of Extra Mild Silk Cut and a gold lighter and offered cigarettes to Dodo, who shook her head, and to Jimmy, even though he had one lit. Jimmy took one and dropped it into his shirt pocket. Mossie laughed again.

'You're great fuckin fun Jimmy, do you know that? What's that fuckin smell?'

'It's the dog,' said Dodo quickly, and nodded her head towards the open door. Mossie turned and looked and stood up then and went over to the dog and aimed a kick. But the dog had seen him coming and got out of the way with a speed that was shocking for a dog in his state. Gone he was.

Mossie came back to the table shrugging his jacket and nodding, as if acclaimed. Squinting eyes brought on by smiling. Smiling brought on by squinty eyes. The barman put down a pint and a large whiskey and went off again without asking for money.

'Grand,' said Mossie, sitting on the stool. 'Are you sure Mrs Fitzgerald that you won't have another?'

'No thanks Mossie. I'm fine now.'

'Right.'

He fell silent and stared at the table, and Dodo looked at the horseshoe of hair that sat on the top of his head, and at the taut honey-coloured scalp that he scratched now, as if her gaze was an irritation. He looked up at the ceiling and rubbed his chin and his throat, and Dodo looked at the two rings that he wore on his left hand and then glanced at his right hand that rested on the table top and saw the three rings there, and looked at his neck, expecting to see a chain, but seeing no such, just a tuft of dark hair poking out from under his black denim shirt. He wore a yellow, well, sandy, mustard, she wasn't sure, sandy sports jacket, and black jeans and a big buckled belt and soft brown shoes. There was a scent from him that was fresh and clean, and he held his cigarette between his pale fingers as if it was a permanent fixture, forgotten. But then, her irritant eyes again, he took a drag and blew the smoke upwards, away from her.

'Isn't this the weather?' he asked.

Dodo nodded. Jimmy scowled.

'It's global warming,' said Mossie. 'Global warming. The sun goes lethal and we get more of it. Get worse before it gets better. And of course some fools lap it up. Always have. Billy Lawlor from Phibsboro out on the grass in his knickers the first sign of it. That's some sight. Every time Mrs Sullivan looks out her window there he is spreadeagled like he's fallen off the roof, his shite brown legs and his scrawny body. She complains about it but you know I think it's the only reason she listens to the weather forecast. Makes sandwiches the night before if it's going to be hot. Sits there all day long drinking Diet Coke and munching her sambos, her eyes crawling all over Billy Lawlor's sorry corpse.'

He gave a great laugh, winked at Dodo, sipped his golden drink.

'Then Mrs Grealy calls by and wants to see the new wallpaper in the upstairs bedroom, new since 1979, and they sit there the two of them making Billy Lawlor wonder why he's so bleedin itchy. I'm a winter man. Warm coats and coal fires and hot drinks. But some people. Lie in the fuckin sun from dawn to dusk and not move a muscle. I never understood it. Jetting off to Spain and fuckin Florida. When I go away I go to cities. I go for the culture.'

He gave a wide smile and nodded. Roar of the fuckin crowd.

'Paris. Venice. Rome. Travelling to the sun is a fuckin joke. If you're looking for a holiday, Jimmy, take your mother to Paris. Take Mrs Fitzgerald to the Louvre.'

He took a drag of the cigarette and stared at Jimmy.

'It's an art museum. Mona Lisa.'

'I know.'

'Mona Lisa Mrs Fitz. About the size of a postcard. Big throng of nips around her yapping away. Mona Lisa and the way she might look at you. There's better pictures there. Better stuff than that.'

He sighed as if it was a great shame. He looked at his watch.

'Can't find Frank,' he said.

Dodo's knee twitched and she gasped and closed her eyes.

'What is it Mrs Fitz?' asked Mossie.

'My leg. My knee.'

'Hurts does it?'

She looked at him. His face that he lived in. His face that he pulled around and pushed at, him behind it somewhere, a skeleton with a smell, an earthy breath of bad thoughts. He could stay looking at you with the same expression for a long time, unflinching. While inside he ran around the angles. And even when he had not asked a question, he always looked as if he had.

'Yes,' she said.

He nodded.

'Where's your husband missus?'

Dodo sighed and sipped from her stout, the thin head gone warm in the heat.

'Why do you want to know?' asked Jimmy, making his voice hard and slow.

'I have business with him.'

'What kind of business?'

'He's in the flat,' said Dodo.

'What kind of business?'

'I was at the flat. There's no one there.'

Dodo shrugged.

'I asked you a question,' Jimmy said.

'I'm sorry Jimmy, I missed it. What did you say?'

'What kind of business do you have with my father?'

Mossie looked at the table top and ran his fingers along the edge of it, his cigarette burning low, his rings bright.

'None of your business business.' He laughed and looked up. 'You know the kind of thing.'

He stared at Jimmy, still smiling, and did not blink. Jimmy nodded and looked away. Mossie turned to Dodo.

'I was at the flat. There's no one there.'

'Maybe he has the telly on,' said Dodo. 'Can't hear you. Maybe he's fallen asleep.'

Mossie took a last sharp drag from his cigarette and stubbed it out in the ashtray, it hissing in the water and smoking and dying. Mossie drank and put his glass down and folded his arms.

'I thought that,' he said. 'I thought that might be it. But no.

There's no one in the flat at all, asleep or awake.'

His smile was gone and Dodo could not look at him.

'What do you mean?' asked Jimmy.

Mossie said nothing.

'Did you break into our fuckin flat?'

'Didn't know you still lived with your Mam Jimmy.'

Jimmy made a small hissing noise and Dodo glanced at the ashtray.

'Now Jimmy,' said Mossie. 'There's no call for that at all. Your Da invited me by not turning up. Me sittin like a fool on the steps outside the gallery, that's an invitation. Half-hour I was there. That's an invitation Jimmy. Given the circumstances.'

Jimmy did not say anything. He lifted his whiskey, the one he had bought for himself, and drank it all. The double Black Bush stayed where it was. Mossie watched him and turned again to Dodo.

'Lovely place you have missus. Nice view too, of the world. And you have all the gear. The telly and the video and all that. Deep fat fryer. Microwave.'

'We don't have a deep fat fryer,' said Dodo.

'Lovely view though. That height.'

'I don't know where he is,' said Dodo, and she sipped her stout.

Mossie nodded. He traced his fingers on the table top and cleared his throat.

'I've left a fella by the flat in case he comes home. You don't mind him. He's outside the door and he's a nice fella and you won't know he's there. In the meantime if you know where Frank might be, if it occurs to you suddenly like, then I'll be at my place and I'd love to hear from you. Right?'

Dodo nodded.

'Fuck off,' said Jimmy.

Mossie stood quickly and his stool fell over behind him and Dodo crouched back out of the way as he leaned across the table and grabbed Jimmy by the shoulder of his shirt and lifted him to his feet, the shirt ripping a little and a button popping out into the air, Dodo watching it, up and across and down like it was taking forever, through the air with her eyes on it all the way, and down then, plop, the sound maybe only in her head, who knows, into the Black Bush, like a body in the canal, in the sunset. Dodo was stuck on that for a moment. By the time she was back, brought round by a shaking in the whiskey's surface like a nice evening breeze, Mossie had pulled Jimmy towards him and the table was pinched by their thighs.

'Now Jimmy. Stop being a thick little shite and keep your fuckin mouth shut or we'll have to see how well you dangle. Do you hear me Jimmy?'

His face was so close to Jimmy's, and his voice so loud, as if Jimmy was in another room, that he spat on Jimmy with all the openings and closings of his mouth. Then he was still for a minute, glaring, with not a sound in the place, not even in the street or the whole of the city, so it seemed to Dodo, then he sniffed and let go, and Jimmy dropped to the seat wiping at his mouth.

'Fuck's sake,' he muttered.

'I'll be off,' said Mossie. He nodded at Dodo and his smile was back. He ran his hand over his head. 'I'll see you around Mrs Fitzgerald. See you soon.'

He nodded at the barman and walked back through the bar, stopping to talk to a couple at a table by the door, shaking hands with an old fella who stood up for it. He did not look back. Then he was gone, and the barman looked towards Dodo and Jimmy and shook his head slowly.

'Jesus Christ,' said Jimmy. 'He's a fucking bollox.'

'What does that mean?' Dodo asked.

'What?'

'We'll see how well you dangle. What does that mean?'

'They hung a fella off the top of the flats last week. Tied a rope around his ankle and the other end around a chimney stack or something and pushed him off. Fucking left him there. The fire brigade had to come. It's his new thing. Bungee jumping. The fella's leg was nearly ripped out of him.'

Dodo drank what was left of her stout. She reached for her stick.

'Come on,' she said.

'Where?'

'To find your father.'

Jimmy sighed and shook his head, but he did not argue. He fiddled with his shirt, looked for his button, felt the cheap material, patting himself, as if it might have slipped inside and be against his skin. Dodo watched him. As if something would be against his skin. She closed her eyes and told herself that that was a wrong thought. You love your son. Your children. Love.

She was about to tell him where it was, but that would give her away. Let him know that at his moment of danger, his pale body threatened, she, his very mother, had chosen to watch the gentle arc of a plastic button through slow motion air into whiskey. Which was, she thought, shocking. They moved away, her son helping her, a sash of his white stomach visible, the Black Bush staying where it was. She thought of some poor man coming across it and delighting in his good fortune and knocking it back and choking to death on the button of her son's shirt. The barman called 'Good luck,' and Dodo groaned with the pain in her leg and told her son that it would be fine after a minute. Once they got going, she said. Once they got going the pain would fall away.

Outside the evening was still as hot as the day had been and traffic waited at the lights and two children played on the steps of the wax museum. The dog was there, dozing by the wall in a shaft of sunlight. He looked up at them and got to his feet.

'Are you alright Mam?'

'I'm feckin crippled. I'm like that fella.'

She stopped and looked at the dog who took a step towards her and wagged its tail.

'We're for the vet's,' she said to him. 'You and me son. They'll be putting us to sleep soon, the two of us.'

The dog nodded and turned in a circle and wagged its tail and seemed happy at last. Happy at last. The end of the day and happy at last.

'Where'll we look?' asked Jimmy.

Dodo leaned on her stick and patted the handbag that was slung around her shoulders and pulled her handkerchief from the pocket of her cardigan and dabbed her mouth and her nose.

'I don't know love. We'll go around by the gallery I suppose. By the Garden. Maybe he's over in Barry's.'

She set off slowly, taking small steps. The dog watched her, Jimmy held her elbow. She remembered being other than this. Always that memory at the start. Fell away when she got going. Everything falls away when you get going.

After a few yards they moved a little faster. The pain in her leg made itself smaller. The dog followed. At the pedestrian crossing past The Granby, at the corner of the square, the lights were against them. If she stopped she'd have to start again. There was a bus approaching. Always a bus. She shook Jimmy loose and strode across the road against the red man.

'Jaysus Mam. Will ye fuckin wait.'

The bus blew a loud horn and Dodo hurried. The dog ran ahead of her, telescoping its arse up to its ears. Dodo tried something similar, regretted it, something in her hips clicking.

'If I stop it'll hurt,' she said.

'If you don't stop it'll fuckin kill you.'

The bus had slowed and moved around them. The driver leaned out of his window and shouted.

'Yeah yeah,' said Jimmy. 'Yeah yeah.'

They walked with the dog in tow and the leg pain diminishing, like a toddler rocked silent by travel, leaving off its scratching and its squeaking and fading into sleep. Dodo thought herself a ship with a child aboard, as she had in pregnancy, sailing through all those days of her life like a liner, and the thought made her thirsty again. They went on. Past the school and the parking meters and the cars parked head on, and into the clear space in front of the Hugh Lane Gallery of Modern Art. She squinted at the steps and slowed. Jimmy regarded her with suspicion as she tugged at him and dwindled and came to a stop. They looked at the closed doors.

'He's not here alright,' said Jimmy.

'Why meet here?'

She felt her son shrug and mutter something about Mossie and culture. She had met Mossie's mother once, a delicate woman, thin and smoky, a tireless talker, long hands that tapped ash and fear, fear and ash. Dodo stared upwards at the gallery, at first-floor windows and then at second-floor windows. A face looked down at her. A pale circle in the dusty air. Straight into her eyes. She gripped Jimmy's arm tightly and gasped, and he must have thought that it was her leg at her again because instead of looking up he looked down, at her knee, crouched and stared at it, as if he might catch a spasm, a ripple in the skin, a flutter of the kneecap. Dodo tugged at him, her eyes impatiently wandering for the slightest of seconds, but enough. Enough to lose it. Jimmy straightened and looked where she looked and saw nothing for there was nothing there.

'Oh,' said Dodo.

'What is it?'

'Nothing.' The dog wet a parking meter and nodded at her. It was his bad leg he lifted. 'Let's go on.'

They walked, the leg pain oddly quiet. Dodo could not glance back without stopping and they did not stop. The face had been a man's, and Dodo had been sure that he had looked directly at her, and that he was pale and saddened, and that he was dead and a ghost, or a spirit, or a memory in her own mind of a previous life, shone up on the glass of the window like a film or an old party trick from her days as a girl. Or perhaps God, or the devil, or a murdered soul, trapped, or an angel. One of those many things.

'What was that house?' she asked.

'What house?'

'The gallery. Who lived there before it was a gallery?'

'I don't know Mam. Some old English Lord or something. Maybe. I don't know.'

Dodo shuffled, her sore feet scuffing the ground.

'There'd be a lot of history there then.'

'Yes.'

'All old stories of murders and sad ladies and candles.'

Jimmy sighed. He was looking over towards the Garden of Remembrance.

'There'd be ghosts there too,' said Dodo. 'Or the hope of ghosts.'

She thought of the dead. They would be flighty. They would be cautious like children, like parents, conscious of the difference. They'd know the trouble of living and have soft sighing pity on her. On her and her husband and her sons and her daughters and their children who ran in small circles around her and dizzied her with giggling. They'd watch, the dead. She raised her eyes and sniffed the air. Over by the cross pool and the children of Lir. Ghosts. The uncertainty of them. Marks on the ground for them. Signs they might know. Calling out to them. Come here and hover. We shaped you a pool.

'Barry's, Ma?'

'We might as well have a look.'

They passed the tall mast of Findlater's church and waited at the lights this time, her leg very calm. Jimmy monitored her. The dog sat politely, its raggy coat splayed on the ground, some connection made in its simple brain between Dodo and the scent of its dreams. They crossed and she thought of sending Jimmy into the shop for a can of something, but said nothing and they went on into Gardiner Row and the high lights. It was gloomy now, the sun sickening behind them. They walked to the crack in the pavement that marked the end of Gardiner Row and the start of Great Denmark Street. She waited on the footpath with the dog, a hand on the black railings, while Jimmy ran into Barry's. She watched a grey-dressed school boy slowly idle by her, his big eyes on the ground. They were back from the holidays then. Poor things.

'Back already?' she said.

He heard her. She knew he'd heard her. It was in those big eyes, and in the tiny stiffness of his little head. But he didn't look up. He set his small mouth shut and went by, his hands in his pockets, his school bag shrugged up on his narrow back. He was a low thing, not up to her elbow. About eight maybe. New to the middle of the city. Don't talk to strangers.

Dodo let go of the railing and glanced at her palm. Flecked with black paint. She gripped things tightly now.

'Were you not collected?' she called to him.

He sort of paused, then continued, as if he'd stepped over a little bump in the ground.

'Belvo is it?'

He glanced back. Whatever she was to look at she was not a worry. She didn't look like a stranger. He stopped and nodded.

'Not collected? Did your Mam not come?'

'My father,' he said. He stayed where he was. He looked up the street and squinted. As if it was an inconvenience. Can't get good parents these days. But Dodo could see glinting trails on his baby cheeks.

'How late is he?'

'He was supposed to be here at five o'clock because I had to go to swimming at half-three. But he usually comes at half-three because that's the time that I usually finish so maybe he did and couldn't find me.'

He gave an awful moan out of him and a stuttering sob and his hands came out of his pockets and went to his eyes and he crouched over and before Dodo could think she was at his side with her arm around him telling him hush and not to worry and such things that she had not had to say in a long time and which filled her with memories of her own so that it was nearly the two of them in floods. And the dog dancing in a circle, wagging a terrible tail.

'Can you not ring him?'

His face jerked and his nose was a mess and Dodo gave him her handkerchief.

'I have no money.'

'Did the priests not help you?'

'It's too late. They're all locked up.'

She could give him the money. They'd take him to a phone box and he'd call home.

'What's your name?'

'Kilian.'

The poor child.

'Mine is Dodo.'

He looked at her.

'No it's not.'

'It is.'

'Dodo?'

'Yes. It's short for something.'

'What?'

She laughed and reddened and pretended that she was a little embarrassed and didn't want to say, which seemed to cheer him up a touch. But the truth was that she couldn't remember what it was short for. Something regal she thought. Something posh. But couldn't bring it to mind. Doreen. Dolores. Deirdre.

'Will we ring your parents?'

'I only have a father. I know the number though.'

'Will he not be worried?'

The child shrugged and hurt his shoulders with the weight of the bag. She helped him off with it and told him that they'd just wait for Jimmy and then go and find a phone box. He squinted up at her and wiped his face and offered up the sodden handkerchief. She took it.

'Jimmy is my son. Used to be your age, but is no longer. He's inside looking for my husband Frank who owes money. We're wandering around looking for him and finding ghosts and small boys instead.'

'Ghosts?'

She didn't answer. The dog sniffed the boy's shoes and fixed his rotting eyes on the school bag. It was a great mystery.

'What's your dog called?'

Dodo patted her cheek.

'Let's see now. Mossie. Little Mossie with the yellow tongue. We've been places, me and him. Her. Him.'

'It's a boy dog,' said the boy. 'He's very smelly.'

Jimmy bounded down the steps shaking his head, the gap in his shirt shifted now to reveal his dirty navel, a black eye in the dusk of a September evening. Dodo would have said something, but he saw the child.

'Billy's there hasn't seen him since Thursday who's this?'

'This is Killin.'

'Kilian.'

'His father was meant to collect him and didn't so we're going to help him phone. Isn't that right love?'

'Jaysus. Are you from the posh school?'

He nodded, ashamed.

'Jaysus. Do you not have a mobile or a car of your own or something? A credit card? Take a taxi for God's sake.'

Dodo sighed, ashamed. There was a pause and the sun was gone. They stood in a second of quiet, broken by the click of the bulb at the top of the curled silver wand that stood high beside them. The boy craned and saw it. Jimmy grinned. Dodo wondered whether Mr Kilian might not have had an accident. She wondered what had happened to the mother. Could she ask? Could she ask that question in the rattle of traffic and Jimmy's thin leer?

'You said ghosts.'

'I'll tell you later. Jimmy, where's there a phone?'

'Inside.'

'Oh. Right. Inside then.'

It was the steps. Only four of them but steep and tiled and the colour of sand. Mossie's jacket colour. Shifting in the dim light. The boy before she knew it was watching her approach, standing in the doorway of the hotel with his hands back in his pockets, sniffing. Jimmy held her. Helped her. She put her head down and stared at her awful feet. Then the boy before she knew it had moved again, this time to her side, his little hands on her swollen arm, his baby head whispering encouragement to her breast. The wholesomeness of it nearly sent her flying. And her knee. Waking up.

'Oh.'

'Alright Ma. Last one.'

The whispering boy. What was he saying? Was his mother dead in a car crash? Crushed? Had it happened again? Hmmm? Could that happen? Would they let her adopt at her age? Not at her age surely. With Frank dangling from the chimney and her unwashed son always smoking in the kitchen? Hmmm?

'Here we are. Top of the hill. Thank you boys. You're a good strong fella Killin.'

'Kilian.'

'Very strong love.'

He bent his body and picked up his bag and straightened again and was up the doorstep and down again, three steps ahead, turned, back again, a little jump, reaching his hands up on the wall to feel the wallpaper. Dodo was dizzy. Her knee was building up to a rage. A pure rage.

Behind her there was a little whimper, barely heard. She turned and waved.

'You stay there boy. We'll be back in a minute.' Mossie the dog nodded and flopped on the footpath, his chin at rest on two soft paws. Dodo envied that. Wished she could settle down for a snooze.

'There's the phone Ma.'

She stuck out her hand and Jimmy rummaged in his pocket and blew out a breath and Dodo didn't breathe in while it flowed by her.

The boy was looking happier now. He swayed on his little legs. A couple came by them, arm in arm, going in. A barman swung a bunch of keys and nodded at Jimmy and glanced at the boy and went through the glass doors whistling.

'What's the number love?'

He told her, one number at a time, as she pressed the buttons and heard the tones in her ear. It rang. And rang. No one exactly sitting by the phone. Then it opened on to air, a hiss, a space. A sleepy man's voice said:

'Hello there.' Her knee was on the verge of bursting.

'Hello. Mr...' She held her hand over the mouthpiece. 'What's your surname love?'

'Hickey.'

'Mr Hickey. My name is Dodo Fitzgerald...'

'Who?'

'Dodo Fitzgerald. I'm here with...'

'Dodo?'

'Yes. I'm here with your son. With Killin. Oh sweet Jesus Christ.'

It was her knee. It buckled and flexed like a fish. Something electric shot up her thigh and spewed a thick syrupy pain through her bowels and her pelvis and her shivering flesh. She vomited pain sounds.

'Hello?'

'Mam? Leg? Here.'

Jimmy took the phone while Dodo grabbed her knee and pressed, and backed her backside into the wall. She stood one foot on the other in an effort to confuse her senses. She thought she might faint. Through a dripping mist she saw the boy stare at her with an open mouth, fascinated. Wondering if she'd die maybe. Perhaps thinking of his mother. Dodo bit her cheek. Cried.

'We have your son Mr Hickey. What? No he's not, don't be stupid. You never collected him.'

It found a way across her hips, turning them to dust, and shot down the other leg. To the other knee. She was now dying in stereo. Being shot would not be as bad.

'Well whatever. We're at Barry's Hotel on Denmark Street and if you're not here in fifteen minutes we pull the trigger.'

And Jimmy hung up. The boy looked at him and Jimmy grinned.

'Alright Ma?'

'Don't mind him love, he was only joking with your father. Good lord.' It echoed through her like a bomb. Everything shook. Her body was a trembling bag of soft fraying strings and bubbles that burst.

'Are you alright?'

'I have a bad knee. It sometimes hurts very badly.'

She thought from his half-open mouth and his big eyes, blue as it happens, that he was about to say something, perhaps that his mother had had the same complaint and he hoped that Dodo would not die too, and she thought as well that maybe she had the same name as his mother, which was, which was...

'Is my father coming?'

'He is,' said Jimmy, looking out the door, lighting a cigarette. 'He's coming to get you. Be here soon. Thought someone else was doing it. Fuckin mortified.'

Jimmy showing off in front of a child, swaggering, acting like a film star with his cigarette, spitting towards the dog. Dodo leaned on the wallpaper, swung her leg from the knee, limped to the door and across to the steps, past Jimmy and his smells. The boy followed, scurried to the footpath like a dancer, offered her a white hand. Gentleman.

'Good fella. Thank you love. I need to pace. It calms the soreness.'

'Did you fall?'

The dog was on its feet, watching her carefully. Ready to catch her. It was easier going down. No sign of Jimmy. She put her weight on the little man. He took it.

'No. Thank you love. That's it. There we are. It grew on me. Crept up.'

'Like a ghost.'

'Exactly like that.'

'Where did you see a ghost?'

'I'm not sure love. In an old house maybe. It was probably just a cleaner. A man looking out the window. It was probably just that.'

He nodded. She thought that he would have pondered death.

That ghosts would have a hold on him in more than just the scary way. That he might have seen his mother in the dark of his bedroom just before the dawn.

'Have you ever seen a ghost?'

'No.'

He had forgotten crying. He lugged his bag and paced with her, turning at the end of the railings and coming back, turning again opposite Jimmy, the dog keeping up for a while then sitting at the kerb, puzzled at this nonsense.

They talked. He held back a bit when it came to his new school. He seemed undecided. He seemed to think it very old, odd, as if he had stepped into the past. 'The classes have funny names. Some of the teachers wear gowns.' She nodded, uncertain. Had no advice for that kind of thing. She told him about her children and their schools. Smoking rooms and clatter palaces. Stained, drizzling places to which she was occasionally summoned to be sneered at in words only understood later. 'Your daughter's behaviour is inappropriate Mrs Fitzgerald.' Much later. Told him Jimmy had cried his eyes out for days when he first went to school, which was not quite true, though nearly, there having been at that time in her family's life a general wailing, unconnected to circumstances, as far as she could remember, beyond the front door. The child chewed on the news, glanced back at Jimmy with a little admiration and a little understanding. He told her that he had two sisters and a brother who was nearly a doctor. That was nice. Told her that they lived in Clontarf, and he could see the sea from his room. She sighed at that, thought it lovely. Told her that he was a good swimmer, probably the best in all of Elements. And probably better than anyone in Rudiments as well. As good as that? Yes. Told her that his father was a businessman. And that he was left-handed (this information was half whispered), and that he took the boy and his two sisters to the cinema practically every week. Popcorn sickness was a family ailment. Told her that his friend in Clontarf, Paul, had fallen off a wall and broken a cheekbone. He had touched it and felt a soft, mushy give, and he shuddered slightly as he recalled it. Said Paul had screamed his head off.

About his mother, nothing.

'My mother,' said Dodo, trying to remember, 'was a singer.'

Silence. The dog was yawning.

'She sang old songs that you wouldn't know. Was an angel at a party or a wedding or a funeral or any class of gathering at all. She met my father in a chorus line. He was a chorus boy. She was a chorus girl. They fell in love and lived in Primrose Street. Music always. I had four brothers and two sisters. We were always fed and clothed and cared for. She lived to nearly ninety. She did. My mother.'

Nothing. Then he sighed. Rubbed at his nose.

'My mother left us.'

'She what?' It was a way of saying it surely?

'She left. She had this problem and she had to go away for it. Not to jail or anything, but she couldn't stay because it wasn't good for her to stay. Or for us. Or something.'

Well. She stood still for a moment, paused. Felt a tension start in her knee, a turning of a clammy screw. Looked at the light on the head of the boy. Moved off again.

'That's very sad.'

He gave his sigh.

'She writes.'

What did she write?

'Liked a drink did she?'

'No, not really.'

Well. Dodo frowned and tried to work it out. A lover. But her children? Was the woman maybe dead and the left-handed father and the doctor son telling lies and forging letters? Maybe she really was in jail. Though probably a lover. So easily found these days. So easily taken. A lover. A bright flame in a far town. Perhaps there was, oh, she knew, a breakdown. A mental collapse. An asylum.

'How long ago did she leave?'

'I don't know. A few years.'

Could a mad woman write letters?

They turned and came towards Jimmy again. Mulling things over. The boy seemed to whisper, or hum. Dodo tried to hear, but it was hard, above the traffic from the square, and the odd car that passed them, and the one or two people, and the planes in the sky. Jimmy cursed. Dodo looked at him frowning, fed up with his bare belly and his nicotine and his sharp skull. But he was staring off down the street nervously. Dodo looked. The night almost down. Figures in the gloom, moving into the light's glow, one of them briefly open-armed, as if advancing on an embrace. Not a specific embrace. A general embrace. The glad arms of many. Mossie Russell.

He sauntered. Up the street from Findlater's church as if the path disappeared behind him, a cigarette in his hand, a big thug at each shoulder, two thieves. Brutish shadows and Mossie bringing light. In the sky there was a red line like a cut on a black man. The evening smell. The chill air. Mossie dropped his arms and changed his tune. Slightly hunched now, not a television colour any longer but a late night black-and-white gangster, bright grey but for the red gash in the skin of the sky.

'You wait here love,' Dodo told the child, pressing him back a little so that he leaned against the railings. She moved away. Moved forward. Halted. Mossie in the open air at night-time was not a thing she'd choose. Jimmy was small in the door, not crouching, but small. Mossie Russell said something to his entourage. There was a nod.

'Mrs Fitz.' He stopped and beamed at her.

'No luck then?' Dodo asked in a steady voice.

'No.' He seemed delighted. 'Nor you?'

'No.'

'Isn't that an awful shame?' He was beside her, laid an arm across her shoulders, turned her gently to face the road, her back to her son. His party was lost to her, just shapes pushing gently at the air on her back.

'Not sight nor sign. Odd how a man like your Frank can be so, so, ubiquitous, that's the word, then gone. Gone! Like a ghost. Flitted away into the cracks in the ground. Like a ghost! Whoooosh! Poor Mrs Fitz.'

Behind them there was the sound of a scuffle, Jimmy cursing, protesting, flapping. Mossie's voice dropped into confidence. Between you and me.

'I'm just taking Jimmy off to the flat Mrs Fitz. You don't come home for a while now alright?'

She nodded, God forgive her. Nodded in the smoky light. From the corner of her eye she could see the boy, still as a pillar, small as a bead.

'We'll just see about settling Frank's account via a fair estimation of goods and suchlike. Nothing excessive I assure you. Sort out the whys and wherefores at a later date. No need to worry yourself. Suffices tonight to reach a round figure in terms of items in lieu. Need Jimmy for, eh, for guidance.'

Jimmy squealed like a pig in a dream and Dodo turned just enough to see his arm twisted up behind his back and his face in a scrunch. The gap in his shirt had grown bigger. It seemed to hold a patch of the ground. He was marched by one of the big men back down towards Parnell Square. His insect shadow attached to a tree.

'Don't do that thing with him,' said Dodo.

'What thing?'

'Dangling or whatever.'

Mossie looked at her. Looked into her eyes. Sucked his cigarette. 'OK.'

She nodded, but it was the way he held her gaze. It was too straight. Too solid. Honest and sincere and his word as a gentleman. Liar.

The dog brushed her leg. The second big man was out of sight. Somewhere back there, hands held loosely at his crotch, chewing probably, looking this way and that. Under control, Mr Russell. Again the brush of the dog and a waft of his decay. Mossie made a face. Looked down. Made a blubbery noise, shooed at the creature. The creature persisted.

Dodo glanced. And then, oh then, in the night that had finally fallen, with the cold air lapping her shoulders, Dodo heard, and it stopped all the clocks in her faltering world, the thin lovely voice of the boy.

'Mossie. Mossie. Come here.'

She opened her mouth to gasp or gape, or something. But her mouth caught the city and tasted the slowness of all things, the patience of time.

'Come here Mossie. Come here.'

Mossie the man let her go. Stood and peered into the gloom by the railings. Mossie the dog stayed where he was, looked up at Dodo. Dodo wondered at the sloth of sudden things. How they unravel.

Mossie the man stepped towards the boy, who cowered.

'What?' said Mossie. Astonishment really. The heavy squinting too. The boy shifted slightly. Straightened. Took stock of the state of things, his place in the world, decided now might be a good time to be more than he felt he was.

'I was not talking,' said the brave brave boy, 'to you. I was talking,' and here he flung out his small exasperated arm, 'to the dog.'

Dodo saw it all as if she was a ghost, hovering in living space, watching the play of small mistakes, the teasing out of moments.

'Fuckin cheek,' said Mossie and grabbed the little stick of flesh and pinned it to the black iron, and raised an arm of his own, and swept his hand down twice, the first time only brushing the boy's hair, the second time harder, the second time coinciding (and here is where Dodo came into her useless own, seeing all things from all angles without moving an inch), coinciding with the appalling arrival of sharp brakes, the Jimmy squeal of them, the opening of a car door, the flashing run of a strange man, eyes lit in fury, his raised left arm crashing past Dodo towards Mossie the man, just as a shout rings out—'BOSS!' or something, and Mossie turns and seems to arch in the air and come down somewhere else, his shoulder sinking into the man's ribs, the man faltering, the brute shadow arriving with a downward crash of doubled fists and a quick upwards kick to the man's lowered head, the man collapsing, Mossie cursing, Mossie kicking, the brutal shadow kicking, both of them kicking, the dog a mess of barking, the boy a huddle on the cold ground (Dodo watching, altered into infinity, as if the scene is a show in the heavens, the hells), the wretched flexing of the man on the hard ground, his head cracking, his back strangely shaped, Mossie kicking after his shadow has stopped, the shadow taking Mossie's arm, telling him to leave it, 'LEAVE IT!', Mossie patting down his hair, leaving it, cursing, kicking again one last time, the boy jerking, the father jerking, Mossie and his shadow leaving, leaving, walking off, Mossie spitting, tugging at his sleeves, a groaning from the body on the ground, the pool, the boy moving closer, his hands unnaturally stiff, pale, his white face holding nothing, and then from somewhere else, a gentle crash, seen without turning, a meshing of metal and a sprinkling of glass as the father's abandoned car rolls, with all the time in the world, as if everything, absolutely everything, is inevitable, written down and predetermined, into a parked white van with a side of gothic black lettering which reads CHARLEMONT CATERING. FINE FOOD FOR FORMAL AND INFORMAL FUNCTIONS. BUSINESS LUNCHES A SPECIALITY.

Mossie and his man were gone. The dog ceased barking and sniffed at the beaten man until Dodo chased it away. It. The boy sobbed and held his father's hand. There was a red mark on his shocked alabaster skin, where Mossie's hand had found him. He sat on the ground with his feet before him. A small crowd gathered. Someone called for an ambulance. By the time it had arrived Dodo was on the ground too, her knee a roaring furnace, her eyes scorched, her hand on the poor child's head, her voice ragged in the night, her mind a haul of wrong turns and missed chances and good ideas she had forgotten.

'Blast you Frank Fitzgerald,' she cried. 'I hope he finds you and I hope he hangs you and I hope it snaps, the rope, I hope it does, I pray to God the rope will snap.'

And in the gentle night, the swollen clouds roll across the city. And unlucky dogs bark at empty windows. All falls away when you get going. When you get going it all falls away. □

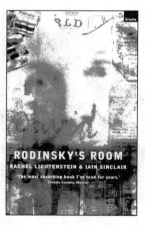  

GRANTA

GIFTED
Richard Williams

The interim report filed by the investigator from the coroner's bureau listed him as a black male, 5ft 7in tall, weighing 135lb. His birth date, 3 March 1929, made him sixty-four years old. He had died at 1.30 a.m. on 5 June 1993 at the Marina Convalescent Hospital, 3201 Fernside Boulevard, Alameda, California. The death certificate, filed at the county records office in Oakland, twenty-five miles away, specified cardiac arrest and a history of generalized arteriosclerosis and diabetes. He had a social security number: 448-18-5547. Place of birth: unknown. Father's and mother's names: unknown. Marital status: unknown. Education: unknown. Occupation: unknown. His only possession was a nineteen-inch colour television set. There was no mention of a trumpet.

The TV had gone with him to the hospital from the nursing home in which he had lived for the preceding six months. The owner of the home, when she was contacted by the coroner's bureau investigator, said that the dead man had left no cash, stocks, trusts or other material effects. The body had been taken to a mortuary for storage. There was no one to pay for a funeral, so on 1 July a cremation took place at the state's expense and the ashes were placed in a community crypt.

His full name was Dupree Ira Lewis Bolton, although his surname was misspelled 'Bolten' on all the official records relating to his death. He was also known, according to police records in two states, as Lewis Bolton, Lewis Dupree, Louis Dupree Balton, Walter Williams Jr, and Walter Jamil Glasby. He had a second social security number: 448-17-5542. There were scars on his back, his left arm, his abdomen and his left leg.

His sound was strong and brilliant, his attack swift and bright. The notes swarmed out of his horn, impatient to be heard, slanting back and forth across the chords and vaulting the bar lines. He tended to come out of the gate already moving through the music at full speed, as if he thought there was no time to waste, but he knew the value of a moment's unexpected silence, and he could stroke a ballad with an old-fashioned elegance while probing beneath its surface, deftly revealing unsuspected melodic planes and harmonic hinges. In none of his improvisations is there a sense of what musicians call 'running the changes', merely negotiating the harmonic obstacles. Like all great jazz soloists, from Louis Armstrong to Ornette Coleman, his playing somehow contained the past, the present and the future. Even under the fiercest pressure, weaving through complex chord sequences at the highest tempo, his phrases were unfolded with a confidence that seems strangely chilling now. He died with nothing, with no family or friends on hand to mourn him, without even an authentic identity. Yet to listen to his music today is to hear the sound of exhilaration, of transcendence, of beauty imagined into life.

Those who heard him in person during his best years still recall his special quality. The kind of jazz he played was called bebop, a music of blinding speed, jolting abruptness and oblique angles. The inventors of bebop—Charlie Parker, Dizzy Gillespie and Thelonious Monk—gloried in their rejection of the normal rules of entertainment. The complexity of the music was intended to be a trap for the unready. Dupree Bolton mastered its codes, but he brought to it an unusual directness and an emotional heat that you couldn't miss.

I was sixteen years old, and starting to learn about jazz, when I first heard of him. Listening to this sort of music wasn't a popular hobby for a schoolboy in England at the beginning of the Sixties. A dozen of us had formed a school jazz society, grudgingly permitted to convene at lunchtime once a week in a room in a Victorian house which served as an annex to the main school building. This seemed particularly appropriate. Jazz was not part of the curriculum of the life that had been planned for us. It wouldn't help us become lawyers or accountants or scientists. It was outcast music. And we liked to think of ourselves as outcasts, too, in a mild sort of way, bound together by our enthusiasm, forced to wear our school blazers and house ties but speaking to each other in our own codes.

We brought in our new records, and sometimes gave solemn little lectures. Using the school record-player, a primitive device encased in a big brown mahogany box to make it look like a piece of respectable furniture, we pieced together the mosaic that jazz, in its first half-century, had already become. This was where I first heard Charlie Parker and Miles Davis, and Muddy Waters at the Newport Jazz

Festival, and Johnny Hodges's pre-war small groups. We bought the *Melody Maker* and *Disc*, which carried news and record reviews each week, and eventually I found the only newsagent in my Midlands city that sold *Down Beat*, the fortnightly American magazine, which was almost like getting the news first-hand. At home I listened on the family's valve radio to Europe 1's *Aimez-vous le jazz?*, the nightly show presented by Frank Ténot and Daniel Filipacchi, and to the Voice of America's *Jazz Hour*, with Willis Conover, who announced the records slowly enough for his millions of listeners behind the Iron Curtain to understand. Ténot and Filipacchi introduced me to Miles Davis's *Kind of Blue*, a record which seemed (and still seems) to fulfil all the promises of beauty and intelligence that music had ever made, and the normally conservative Conover played John Coltrane's 'Olé' in between the bursts of static from the Soviet bloc's jamming stations.

So the music had a sense of discovery, of an introduction to emotional areas that were not a part of the English culture in which I grew up. We might have been members of the madrigal choir and the symphony orchestra and the cadet corps, but we were discovering that Duke Ellington's 'Rockin' in Rhythm', Thelonious Monk's 'Epistrophy' and *Jazz: Its Evolution and Essence* spoke more directly than 'Adieu Sweet Amaryllis' or 'Belshazzar's Feast' or *Scouting for Boys*. They meant more in terms of our own emotional lives, then taking shape, than all the prescribed texts of our formal education.

Of course, it would be foolish to deny that jazz also appealed because it was cool and different. Modern jazz certainly recreated for us the lure of the exotic and the forbidden that had attracted the first generation of European jazz fans to Louis Armstrong and Jelly Roll Morton. If you enjoyed this, you were already different. But with modern jazz, you really did have to enjoy it. Unlike traditional jazz, it was no good for dancing. You were there to listen, and to listen hard. People who were just pretending to like modern jazz soon gave up. It was too much trouble, too demanding, too astringent and awkward. That, I suppose, made the rest of us feel even better, in a perverse, outsiderish way.

I know when it was that I first read about Dupree Bolton because I still have the copy of *Down Beat*, dated 14 March 1963, containing the first published mention of his name. Bolton was singled out for special praise in a review of a group led by a saxophone player, Curtis Amy, which had appeared in Los Angeles at a place called the It Club. 'Thanks mainly to little-known trumpeter Bolton,' the piece began, 'Amy's current group is about the wildest thing in jazz on the West Coast today.' And the first hint of mystery appeared in the next sentence: 'Bolton, whose personal troubles kept him from the Los Angeles scene more than two years, returned home last fall. Since joining Amy, he's been turning heads around all over town. His sound is big and honest and sometimes so raw it all but rips a listener's head off.' The review was accompanied by a single-column photograph of Bolton, playing his trumpet. He was wearing a grey suit with a crisp white shirt and cufflinks, and he had a small moustache.

Half a dozen issues later, he was mentioned again in a feature about a group of musicians newly signed up by Pacific Jazz Records, a California label which had come to prominence ten years earlier with the hit recordings of Gerry Mulligan and Chet Baker. This time the writer, John Tynan, tried to discover something more about the trumpeter's background. But all Bolton would say was that he ran away from home when he was fourteen. His reluctance was ascribed to a biography that included 'jails and things'. Bolton, Tynan wrote, had needed to 'clean up' his personal affairs, but now he was ready 'to take care of his business, which is partly the business of becoming recognized as one of the most important trumpeters in jazz'.

That summer, I bought the only record released by the group in which Curtis Amy and Dupree Bolton shared the front line. It was called *Katanga!*, and when I took it home and played it I realized that Tynan hadn't exaggerated. Bolton had written the title track, which opened the album, and he took the first solo, leaping out of the tense, jabbing, up-tempo theme with enormous impact, building his short solo with firm declamatory flourishes and a perfect sense of dramatic contrast. In an era of verbosity, he seemed to have a gift for compression, and even at such speed he showed a sensitivity to the shading of the song's underlying harmonies. In only ninety-six bars of improvisation, occupying less than a minute and a quarter, he created a series of moods and pictures that changed shape and colour with the sort of divine blend of logic and unpredictability for which jazz musicians are always searching.

The very best thing about jazz, really, is the opportunity it gives a musician to be himself, to be an individual. Because improvisation is at its heart, the musician is handed a responsibility which can properly be discharged only by calling on his own resources, his own store of emotional experience. The relative narrowness of bebop's usual structures—the twelve-bar blues, the thirty-two-bar Broadway song, the 4/4 metre, the horns-and-rhythm format—tends to emphasize even the smallest variations of individual temperament. As a result, jazz contains a remarkable number of players who can genuinely claim originality, however limited it may be.

The briefest exposure to *Katanga!* was enough to establish that Dupree Bolton deserved a place among them. This was the sort of performance that defined the arrival of a new star, and the next steps in his career seemed obvious. He would appear with bigger names, he would form his own band, he would get a recording contract of his own. But John Tynan's words in *Down Beat* had given a warning that Bolton's career path might not be so straightforward. And for some jazz fans, including me, that only served to heighten his appeal.

This is a complicated matter that has something to do with the nature of jazz itself. A music based on improvising in public must necessarily have a constant and probably disturbing awareness of its own evanescence. How much great jazz, played in nightclubs, perhaps in front of unsympathetic audiences and without recording equipment, has simply escaped into the ether? That sense of impermanence seemed to influence the lives of its performers, and was exaggerated by the heroin epidemic. There wasn't much of a secret about it. When *Down Beat* attempted to camouflage the professional hiatus of a well-known musician by saying that he had been 'off the scene' due to 'personal problems', even the most naive fan knew what lay behind the euphemisms. In New York and Los Angeles, certainly, a majority of young jazz musicians were using heroin. Many of them were imitating their idols, some of whom, like Charlie Parker, tried to discourage such a destructive homage, although it was hard to persuade young men that Parker's genius had not been fuelled by the drug, or that shooting up was not integral to becoming a fully fledged bebopper. As a result, many of the most gifted musicians of Parker's generation conveyed the impression that, one way or another, they wouldn't necessarily have long in which to say their piece.

Dupree Bolton was definitely in that category, too, and it gave his work a special value, a kind of dark glamour which was only deepened when it became obvious that he would not be following the path to stardom. *Katanga!* turned out not to be the prologue to a glittering career. Not at all. And his failure to realize that extraordinary promise simply provoked an even greater interest in the few traces left by his passage through life.

What little I knew, from various jazz historians, books and magazines, was this. He had been born in Oklahoma City in 1929, and when he left home it was to join the band of the pianist Jay McShann, who had also provided Charlie Parker with an apprenticeship. McShann was based in Kansas City, which made it likely that Bolton had jumped on board when the band passed through his own home town. In 1944 he joined the big band of Buddy Johnson, a pianist and composer who specialized in genial blues-based dance tunes and mournful ballads. Their big hits were 'Since I Fell For You', a blues-ballad sung by the leader's sister, Ella Johnson, and 'Walk 'Em', a medium-tempo blues which Johnson wrote for the dancers at the Savoy Ballroom in Harlem, where the band had a residency. Bolton played in the four-man trumpet section on both hits. Towards the end of 'Walk 'Em' there is a twelve-bar trumpet solo, played with a bold tone and slightly unsteady attack, which is thought to be his first recorded improvisation.

At this stage he was just another Swing Era musician, technically proficient enough to take his place in the trumpet section of a leading band, and probably chafing at the restrictions. In his position, he would be lucky to be given one or two short solos a night in which to develop his self-expression. This was the frustration that gave birth to bebop, among men who could no longer put up with the disciplined regime of the big bands. The Benny Carter Orchestra was full of such musicians, and Bolton was in Carter's brass section for a couple of recording sessions in New York in October 1945 and

January 1946, playing on five tunes but taking no solos. When Carter's band recorded again, two days after the second of those sessions, he had gone. Dupree Bolton had fallen into the first of his long silences, and this one would last thirteen years.

In 1959 he had just finished a jail sentence—something to do with drugs, the records are lost—when he was heard in a Los Angeles club by Harold Land, a well-known saxophonist and bandleader. Land immediately enlisted him as part of a quintet which made an album titled *The Fox*. Recorded in a single night in a Hollywood studio, the music had an intellectual bite that raised it above all but a very small proportion of the jazz played anywhere in the world that year. At a time when California jazz was associated with young white men with blond crew-cuts and imported sports cars playing a pale-toned, slightly fey kind of music, the full-blooded sound of Land's quartet came as a surprise. In October 1959, months before the album was released, *Down Beat* published a page of pictures taken at the session. Musicians on the West Coast were reported to be 'flipping' over the playing of the unknown Bolton and the band's eighteen-year-old bassist, Herbie Lewis. The session was 'without doubt one of the best in spirit and quality ever to be recorded here'.

The critics liked *The Fox*, but by the time their reviews appeared Bolton was off the scene again. It would be three years and another spell in jail before he returned, newly signed to Pacific Jazz and given equal billing with Curtis Amy on *Katanga!* The title of his composition and the tribal mask on the cover were a reminder that this was the time of the civil-rights struggle at home and of liberation movements in Africa. He had named his piece after Moise Tshombe's breakaway republic, which seceded from the Belgian Congo in 1960 but was retaken by United Nations troops in 1963, only weeks before Bolton and Amy entered the recording studio. Again there were good reviews in the specialist magazines, and this time there was a piece of film.

Bolton is on view throughout the twenty-five-minute episode of a television series called *Frankly Jazz*, broadcast in the United States in 1962 and made commercially available in Europe much later on videotape. He plays with great confidence and invention, but what is immediately noticeable is his stance. The viewer never sees him

239

without the trumpet to his lips. His body is still. He barely opens his eyes. There are no gestures towards the audience. This is modern jazz as it existed between the Forties and the Sixties, a music in revolt against the last vestiges of its origins in minstrel shows, cotton fields, whorehouses and juke joints, determined to establish its seriousness of purpose as a token of its value.

His only words in the programme are spoken off-screen. 'Thank you,' he says, in response to praise from the show's host, a young Hollywood disc jockey named Frank Evans, for his recital of 'Laura', a standard ballad which Bolton plays with a brusque tenderness very characteristic of the way bebop musicians, proud of their resistance to sentimentality, handled romantic material.

'Yeah, Dupree,' Evans drawls as the tune ends, raising his cigarette an inch or two in a hipster's salute. 'That's awfully pretty. That's three-o'clock-in-the-morning type music. Charmingly played, too, by Dupree Bolton.'

And on that note, he faded once more. Over the next couple of years an occasional paragraph in *Down Beat*'s news columns suggested that he might be joining this or that band, or making a record under his own name, but nothing materialized. And before long even the rumours dried up.

The Fox and *Katanga!*, as it turned out, would be his only testaments. And perhaps that was why, as the years went by, his name slowly turned into a kind of password among a certain kind of jazz fan—one proud of his depth of knowledge, of his awareness of the often difficult and unrewarding conditions in which the musicians produced the art that gave him so much pleasure. Every now and then one of the jazz magazines would mention Dupree Bolton. Sometimes a reader would write in to request information on his whereabouts. And as he grew more remote, as the mystery intensified, so his stature increased. Other young trumpeters of his generation had been robbed by death of the chance to fulfil their potential— Fats Navarro by heroin and tuberculosis, Clifford Brown by a car crash, Booker Little by a kidney disorder. Bolton's story, on the other hand, had no resolution. No one knew for certain whether he had really stopped playing, or why.

From the mid-Sixties through the late Seventies there was

nothing but speculation. Around the turn of the Eighties, however, there were a couple of published sightings of a street musician in San Francisco answering to his name and description. Eventually he was said to have moved across the bay to Oakland, and to have given up music altogether, although not his other habit, for which he was receiving treatment on the methadone programme. One of these sightings resulted in the second and last encounter between Bolton and someone with a professional interest in hearing his story. Ted Gioia, the founder of the jazz studies programme at Stanford University, was researching a history of West Coast jazz when he was contacted by one of the people who had seen Dupree Bolton on the streets. The musicologist and the trumpeter met in a music shop and held a conversation, from which the author published only one detail. 'San Quentin,' Bolton had told him, 'was the worst.'

Over the years I wrote a great deal about music and met a lot of musicians, famous and obscure. But the story of Dupree Bolton, such as it was, stayed with me and developed a special resonance. The scholarship of jazz has many unanswered questions, and Dupree Bolton was mine. His life seemed to symbolize the relationship between a jazz musician and his listener. What did it mean to have listened to him, to have admired his playing and to have wondered, on and off for almost forty years, about his life? How could so little, in terms of measurable output and general effect, mean so much? And, if he was still alive, what did he think about it all?

Early in 1999 I spent a couple of nights in San Francisco, wandering the streets of North Beach and Fisherman's Wharf, peering somewhat foolishly at homeless people huddled in doorways and listening out for the sound of a trumpet. No success. One afternoon I took a cab to Oakland, and did the same thing. Again, no luck. Later in the evening I went to a jazz club. The music was terrific, but no one there could give me a lead to a trumpeter called Dupree Bolton. Afterwards I walked up the street and stood outside the office of the Alameda County social services department. And there, as I thought about going back to London empty-handed, I decided to try another route.

A few weeks later, with the help of a private investigator and the

Freedom of Information Act, the county records office was persuaded to release a handful of documents. The first of them provided the proof that I had been wasting my time searching the streets. Dupree Bolton was dead. He had died six years earlier, and had been buried in a pauper's grave. What became obvious was that no one who knew him in those last days had any idea of what he might once have done. And those who had known him in earlier times, or had known of what it was he did, the musicians and critics and historians, were ignorant of his fate. It was with them that I decided to make a start on the journey back into Dupree Bolton's life.

Growing up with jazz in the second half of the twentieth century was like wandering through a living museum. Most of the music's titans—Armstrong and Ellington, Monk and Mingus—were still around. Until comparatively recently it was possible to see and hear virtually all the phases of jazz's history, the generations existing alongside each other. That is no longer true. Very few of the great originators are still alive, which means that early forms of jazz exist only as recordings or in recreations by younger musicians. The stories of the historic figures, too, have been thoroughly researched. But there are still many unexplored corners. To try and shed some light on Dupree Bolton's early career, I talked to two of the great survivors, former bandleaders who are believed to have provided him with his first experience as a professional musician. But neither Jay McShann, born in 1915, nor Benny Carter, eight years older, was able to summon the recollection of a young trumpeter fitting his description.

This was not so surprising, since the big bands crossed the United States constantly during the Swing Era, dropping musicians and recruiting replacements as they travelled from coast to coast. The first memory of Dupree Bolton's professional existence came from the tail end of that time. Gerald Wilson, now eighty-two, who served his own apprenticeship with the bands of Duke Ellington and Jimmie Lunceford in the 1930s and 1940s, was still active as a bandleader and composer when I telephoned him in Los Angeles in the autumn of 1999. He hadn't known of Bolton's death and expressed regret at the manner of it. But he remembered their first encounter quite clearly. It was in 1945, when Bolton was playing with the Buddy Johnson band. Johnson was opening at a club called the Riviera, in St Louis, Missouri, where Wilson and his orchestra had just finished a run. 'We were leaving as they were coming in,' Wilson said. 'At that time he was a very nice trumpet player, playing real good, more or less in a swing style.'

Harold Land, with whose quintet Bolton recorded *The Fox*, has since become one of the elder statesmen of modern jazz. A few weeks before his seventy-second birthday, he had just returned to Los Angeles from a week's residency in a New York club when I telephoned and asked for his earliest memories of Dupree Bolton. He didn't know Bolton was dead, but he wasn't surprised to hear it. He told me he remembered hearing him play for the first time and later inviting him to join the band that was about to record *The Fox*. 'I was impressed, that's for sure, and I sounded him out about a record date,' Land said. 'As I recall, he was strung out, but it can't have been as badly as at other periods in his life. The way he was playing, he can't have been at the utmost point [of his addiction]. Preparing for it, rehearsing with us, might have slowed him down a little.'

Land had grown up during the boom years of Central Avenue, the old main stem of black Los Angeles. He had toured the US with the great drummer Max Roach and the trumpet prodigy Clifford Brown, until Brown was killed at the age of twenty-five in 1956. At that point Land could have opted for a comfortable life within the Hollywood studio orchestras. Instead he chose the less secure but more creative path of modern jazz. When he heard Dupree Bolton, he found a perfect musical partner.

The Fox contained a mere thirty-six minutes of music, but those thirty-six minutes were played by men operating at the maximum of invention and intensity. Yet even Land didn't fully appreciate its quality at the time. 'I knew it was special, but maybe I didn't realize how special,' he said. 'People still talk to me about it today. Sometimes I even get asked to play some of the tunes.'

Of the five musicians on the session, three were lifetime junkies. Elmo Hope, a brilliant pianist and composer, had sent the manuscripts of the scores to Land from a California prison, where he was completing a sentence for possession. But it was Frank Butler, the most gifted drummer on the West Coast, whom Land remembered as being close to Dupree Bolton. They were 'on the same page in regard to their extra-curricular activity'.

Land himself had already been dabbling in heroin—'dipping', in the vernacular term for occasional usage—as was almost inescapable for a Los Angeles jazz musician in those years. Some of the older musicians, he said, tried to discourage him. Butler had been among them, his advice imparted in a big-brotherly way but also out of self-interest—less for someone else meant more for himself. But Land was lucky enough to have a wife and a son who also tried, eventually with success, to divert him away from narcotics.

The cost of recording *The Fox* was borne by a young producer named David Axelrod, who borrowed the money to pay the musicians and the studio. The musicians were paid at the union's standard rate, a total of ninety-six dollars each for six hours' work. As the leader, Land received double, plus the promise of royalties. Axelrod supervised the session, and then arranged for the album to be released by a small Los Angeles label, Hi Fi Jazz.

Today Axelrod is enjoying an unexpected burst of belated celebrity thanks to the fondness of the acid jazz crowd for his Sixties recordings with Cannonball Adderley, Lou Rawls, the Electric Prunes and others. He needed no encouragement to talk about Dupree Bolton, and his first memories were of the trumpeter's talent. 'When Harold found Dupree, he found a beauty. I loved him as soon as I heard him. An incredible player. But he could be a very mean guy. He'd served a lot of time and it wasn't for doing nice things. He was a junkie and he needed money. He'd do armed robbery without batting an eyelid.' Axelrod also remembered a particular incident that disrupted the recording of *The Fox*. 'Dupree was unhappy about the amount of solo space he was getting, and he offered to fight Harold and me over it. He wanted to go on to the sidewalk outside the studio to sort it out. We tried to tell him that it was Harold's album and that Elmo had written most of the tunes, but he wouldn't listen to us. Eventually he cooled himself out. Maybe Elmo said something. Like, "What is all this nonsense about violence?" That's how Elmo was. I think Dupree had a lot of respect for him.'

After the recording was completed, Land found it hard to keep track of Bolton. 'He was getting busted all the time.' He knew nothing about Bolton's family, either. He was 'kind of hush-hush about that'. And the trumpeter was always on the move. 'We only had time to talk about music, and then he was off into the other areas of his life. Being strung out is a very time-consuming business.'

There is no firm evidence to tell us how Bolton spent the next three years. This may have been when he served time in San Quentin, where California incarcerates its most violent criminals, but the prison's records of that era have been purged. So the next evidence of his activities was the review by John Tynan in *Down Beat* of Curtis Amy's gig at the It Club.

Curtis Amy was saddened, although not surprised, to learn about Bolton's death. 'I kind of assumed he'd died many years ago,' he said. He remembered first meeting Bolton around the time he was signed to Pacific Jazz. 'I liked Dupree an awful lot,' he said. 'You've got to like a guy who has that much talent.' But by the time they came to record *Katanga!* he realized Bolton was in trouble. 'We were all trying to calm Dupree down,' Amy said. 'If he could have gotten himself together, he would have done marvellous things.' Amy had also met Bolton's younger brother Dodge, who worked as a pianist, though he wasn't a musician of the same quality as his brother. The two were on good terms, Amy said, but for some reason Dupree was always rebelling.

'For one thing, having been incarcerated the amount of time he was, I think he was very bitter. And it seems as though he thought he should have been in a better position than he was. That was a part of himself that he couldn't escape. He talked a lot about what he wanted to do, and how much he thought he should be recognized. Some of it was jive, but a lot of it was sincere. If he could just have sustained it. If you caught him in a nice groove, he was cool. But he was always very highly strung, and very...' Amy paused, and remained silent. I tried a few suggestions. Unreliable, awkward, truculent, some of those things? 'All of those things. But when we got in the studio, he was just a perfect and very outstanding musician.'

As part of his attempt to make his latest acquisition feel comfortable and confident, Richard Bock, the owner of Pacific Jazz, gave Bolton a new beige Ford Thunderbird. Amy got one, too, in black. 'Dick also bought Dupree a new horn,' Amy said, 'and then another one after the first one went missing. And we got him some beautiful clothes. There was a store here called Ziedler and Ziedler on Venice Boulevard and Western Avenue—Zee and Zee, I called it— where I turned him over to a friend who always took care of me. We were trying to accommodate him because he was a special young man. I'm sure Dick gave him money, too. Dick loved him. What Dick was trying to do was get the best music. If the young man had a problem but he could play, Dick would embrace him. Dick really cared about Dupree.'

Curtis Amy didn't remember appearing on the *Frankly Jazz* film. But he did remember something else. Along with the car, the trumpets and the suits, Dupree Bolton had also acquired a new girlfriend. 'You need to talk to Dahle Scott,' he told me, and gave me her number.

D ahle Scott had assumed Dupree Bolton long dead. She hadn't seen him in thirty years. When I told her the circumstances of his death, and described how he had been buried, there was a silence over the telephone before she spoke again. 'Had I known,' she said, 'that would not have happened to Dupree.'

They had met in 1962. She was working as a singer in Los Angeles nightclubs and Dodge Bolton was her accompanist. When Dupree came out of prison, Dodge introduced them. At the time she was taking a vacation from a thirty-year marriage to a well-known jazz organist, Jack McDuff, with whom she had moved to California from Chicago in 1959. She was—still is—a singer, a show business publicist, a nightclub consultant and a gossip columnist, and when she and Dupree got together they set up home in a bungalow on Smiley Drive in west Los Angeles, on the north side of Baldwin Hills.

She had liked him straight away. 'He was thin and good-looking, and he loved to dress,' she said. 'Really a neat person. The girls were always after him. He was just a little dude, really. No more than a hundred and fifty pounds, maybe five-six or seven. He was very into his music, very creative, but he was used to being institutionalized. He was very conditioned by that, more comfortable in that environment. He had a phobia against crowds, a phobia against going

246

into a grocery store with crowded aisles, a phobia against driving down a freeway and finding a big truck drawing up beside him. He had to get away from that truck.'

A few weeks later I arranged to meet Dahle Scott at the Cat and Fiddle, an English pub on Sunset Boulevard, where she sometimes sings on Sunday nights. She cut a startlingly soignée figure as she entered the courtyard, where tables are arranged around a small bandstand. The bronze curls, the dark brown fur jacket, the neat black boots, the artful make-up and the beautifully manicured nails were impressive on a woman of seventy. At thirty, when she and Dupree Bolton were together, she must have been a sensation.

I asked her to take me on a ride through black Los Angeles, back into the history of the Forties and Fifties, to the city in which Bolton grew up as a musician. We drove out of Hollywood, through the downtown and Skid Row until we turned south into Central Avenue, and on down to a nondescript apartment block at the corner of Forty-fifth Street. Once known as the Hotel Dunbar, this was the city's finest black hotel, and is virtually the only surviving relic of Central's heyday, during the late Thirties and, particularly, the early Forties, when the wartime industries virtually wiped out black unemployment and there was money to spend on the sort of recreation that also attracted whites downtown. The Dunbar was where the stars were bivouacked, including those, such as Duke Ellington and Louis Armstrong, who played the Club Alabam next door, where Mae West, John Barrymore, Lana Turner or Orson Welles might be in the audience. Jack Johnson, the first black world heavyweight boxing champion, had a nightclub in the Dunbar. Along the street were the Memo, the Last Word, the Downbeat Room, owned by the gangster Mickey Cohen, and Jack's Basket Room, where there were jam sessions every night. By the end of the Forties, the souring economy had combined with the LAPD's distaste for race-mixing to turn the once-glittering strip into a trashed ghetto thoroughfare. Today nothing of them remains except the Dunbar, alone amid the heavily shuttered convenience stores and vacant lots.

We turned right along Vernon Avenue, where the open doors of the storefront churches revealed their seated congregations, some of them with choirs, their white surplices gleaming in the dusk, and into

South Central. It was a warm Sunday night in late autumn, and on the darkened side-streets there were yard parties taking place outside a few of the frame houses. At Leimert Park we stopped in front of the World Stage, a little club where a regular Sunday-night jam session was in progress. Dahle talked to a couple of musicians standing outside, one of whom had played the drums in her ex-husband's band. She had been a drummer once herself, she said. Then she showed me the post office that had once been the Parisian Room, the best jazz club in Los Angeles throughout the Seventies, to which she was a consultant. When we returned to the Cat and Fiddle at the end of the evening, she took the microphone on the patio and sang Ellington's 'Take the A Train' with impressive vigour to a crowd of a couple of dozen drinkers and diners. Afterwards she got her old silver Lincoln Continental out of the valet parking and set off to hear another band at another club and, in all probability, to sing some more. Pleading exhaustion, I declined to join her. 'You can't *hang*, Richard,' she said, scorn and amusement in her voice.

She had promised that when we met she'd have something special for me. It turned out to be a packet containing snapshots from her time together with Bolton. A couple of them were taken at his thirty-fourth birthday party, and show him turning to smile at the camera as he cuts a cake, watched by his brother Dodge, and Dodge's first wife. In another, Dupree stands in the Los Angeles sunshine outside their house, his right hand resting on the window ledge of her white Cadillac convertible. The sun is high, and the shadow abbreviated. He's wearing a grey silk suit with the top button done up, a grey shirt, black loafers and black-framed shades. There's a cigarette in his left hand. He looks sharp and confident, and only slightly self-conscious.

Dahle and Dupree were together almost two years, during which she occasionally accompanied him on visits to his parents' house. 'It was a good family,' she said. 'His mother was a Christian woman.' But Dahle Scott's experience of the jazz world had taught her about its darker side, and there were things she was not prepared to endure. 'There was a man coming to the house, acting like he was Dupree's doctor. Sometimes you don't question things. But I just accidentally caught what was happening. He was giving Dupree his little shots. And when I found out he was going to be a junkie again, I couldn't deal with it. When I was younger I used to travel around with Charlie Parker, and I'd seen what happens. Dupree was one of those good players who felt that everybody else was getting high and got caught up in it. I understood that he was not going to give up the habit. So I called Curtis Amy and told him to come and get him.'

'Dahle Scott was an amazing young lady,' Curtis Amy said. 'She was trying to help Dupree, too. She tried everything. But it did no good.' And eventually Bolton's temperament began to destroy the band. 'Dupree could be a difficult person,' Amy continued. 'We had a guitarist, Ray Crawford, and he and Dupree never got along. It was a musical thing. Dupree didn't want Ray to play behind him.' Nor did he want Amy to play the fashionable soprano saxophone instead of his usual tenor instrument, as he was doing on several tunes. 'Dupree felt the soprano was in the same range as his trumpet, and he had the idea it would be competition for him. He was wrong, of course.'

The group, so full of promise, finally disintegrated one Tuesday night in the summer of 1963, during an engagement at a Hollywood club called Shelly's Manne-Hole, owned by the drummer Shelly Manne. Amy remembered how the music had been on fire, which made it seem even more of a waste. 'The band sounded so good, and Dupree was extraordinary. But after the second set we took an intermission and he just didn't come back.' After trying to keep the band together in the face of growing indifference from club owners who could make more money from providing music for people to dance the Twist, Amy found failure hard to accept. 'It was such a good group. You hit the right ingredients, and when it falls apart it's disappointing. It all seemed to peter out at the same time. There had to have been something that was negative in Dupree's life. I knew he wanted to live good and play good. But something defeated that.'

Yet again, Bolton went missing. Curtis Amy saw him only once more, at a benefit gig. 'We played a set and it was marvellous. Then he just went off again.' In 1967 Bolton returned to the It Club for a brief reunion with Harold Land. Dahle Scott saw him from time to time before she left Los Angeles to spend several years in Europe. 'We stayed friends,' she said, 'like me and all my ex-boyfriends.'

Among a batch of documents from the Alameda County coroner's department was a record of the dead man's next of kin. It listed three brothers, two of whom had predeceased him, and a sister, who was said to be living at an address in South Central Los Angeles. The report also gave a telephone number. It was six years old, but I tried it anyway.

After a dozen or so rings, someone answered. The woman's voice at the other end sounded a long way away, and not welcoming. Yes, she said, with some reluctance, her name was Mary Hendrix. And had she been related to the late Dupree Bolton? No, she said, there must be some confusion. But her name and address had been on the coroner's report. Well, that must be a mistake. Understandably, it was taking the sixty-five-year-old retired telephone company employee some time to accustom herself to the idea that she was being called out of the blue by a man with an English accent asking questions about her dead brother. At first she thought it could only mean more trouble, something coming back from Dupree's past. But gradually she came round. Yes, maybe that was her name and address on the coroner's form. And maybe she did once have a brother called Dupree who had been a musician and left home early. But she hadn't really known him at all.

When I explained what I was trying to do, she didn't sound very convinced that it was a story anyone would really be interested in. I mentioned Dahle Scott, and asked if she remembered her. She wasn't sure. I said I'd leave it a week, and call her back when she'd had a chance to think about it. Then I phoned Dahle, who remembered doing Dupree's sister's hair on a visit to his family thirty-five years earlier. They hadn't seen each other since then, but it turned out that they were living only four blocks apart. Dahle said she'd call Mary, and try to arrange a visit. And a week later, when I spoke to Mary again, she agreed to fill in some of her family's story.

Her memories were sketchy. They'd lived in Oklahoma City, at 423 East First Street, the house where Dupree had been born. He was the oldest child, named after his father, Dupree Bolton Sr, who was working as a mechanic. Dupree Sr and his wife, Juanita, had four sons—Dupree, then Douglas, who died in infancy, Dodge and Frederick. Mary was their only daughter, five years younger than

Dupree. There was also an older half-sister, Iris, the child of Dupree Sr's relationship with another woman before his marriage.

In 1941, like many Oklahoma families, black and white, the Boltons moved west, making the 1,200-mile journey to Los Angeles. 'My father went out to California by himself to find work,' Mary told me. 'He got a job with a family in Los Angeles and then he sent for us. I went with my mother and Dodge on the train. Dupree wasn't with us. I guess he'd already gone.'

It was Dupree Sr who had been responsible for the music in the house. He played the piano, and Mary thought he might have given a few lessons to neighbours. She also remembered him singing, accompanying himself on the guitar and banjo. Dupree Jr had taken up the trumpet early, and Dodge, who was four years younger, studied the trombone before switching to the piano. Mary, too, played a little piano, 'enough to pick out a tune'.

The next time she saw her oldest brother she was in junior high school. 'I must have been thirteen or fourteen. He'd been travelling, or maybe he'd been to jail. He stayed maybe a couple of months, until he found a place of his own or went back on the road, I don't know.'

Bolton also spent some time back in Oklahoma City, where his half-sister Iris and his mother's brother, George Dobbin, were still living. Mary thought he lodged with them, both then and at a later period in his life. But on 6 April 1956, according to the files of the Oklahoma State Bureau of Investigation, he was arrested on a charge of forging a cheque, and on 19 October he was given a three-year sentence. After his release, he headed back to Los Angeles and picked up his old way of life.

The only time Mary saw him play was when Dahle took her to the It Club in 1963. And that was just about the last time she ever saw him. Her father died in 1965 and her mother in 1972. Of her other brothers, Dodge, the quiet pianist whom everyone liked, was treated for cancer before dying in his sleep in 1993, a few months before Dupree's death. Fred, she believes, is still living somewhere in Los Angeles, although she doesn't know where. Mary herself worked as a nurse in the early Sixties, and then spent seventeen years at the Pacific Bell telephone company until her retirement. She has a daughter, who lives with her. She owns none of Dupree's recordings.

'I never knew him well enough to get fond of him,' she said. 'I just accepted him as a brother.'

On 25 August 1978, Bolton was arrested by the Oklahoma City police on suspicion of forgery, but released due to insufficient evidence. Six months later he was less fortunate. He and an accomplice, William F. Jones, were arrested and charged with attempting, on 15 February 1979, to obtain forty-eight four-milligram tablets of the morphine-based painkiller Dilaudid from Vernon Nash, a pharmacist on Arlington Street in Chickasha, Oklahoma, by presenting a prescription ostensibly made out by Dr Leonard W. Rozin MD of Oklahoma City in the name of Martha Sharp. A couple of days later Bolton was also charged with possessing heroin and cocaine, and freed on bail in the sum of $1,000, secured by the signature of his uncle, George Dobbin. On 15 March the charge of possessing cocaine was 'dismissed to best meet the ends of justice', in the words of the official motion, on the grounds of misidentification. Bail on the other charges was set at $2,500 but when Dupree missed the preliminary hearing on 3 May, and failed to surrender himself to the court within five days, a warrant was issued for his arrest. The case was eventually heard on 10 January 1980 at Grady County district court, where he pleaded guilty both to the original charge and to a second one of jumping bail. The district judge handed down sentences of three years in prison on the first count and one year on the second, to run consecutively, with one year suspended. On 24 January Sheriff Ron Taylor and Deputy Buddy Boggess delivered Dupree Bolton to the warden of the state penitentiary at McAlester, Oklahoma, where he was registered as prisoner number 105369. Three months later he was transferred to the Joseph Harp Correctional Center in Lexington, Oklahoma.

While I was searching for leads, I was sent a cassette tape containing three tunes recorded in 1980 by a band made up of inmates of the Joseph Harp Center. Each piece features a solo by Bolton, making it clear that his range, tone and ability to construct a line were still intact. So, too, was something of that remarkable intensity, even in these humdrum surroundings. Every time he plays, the music crackles into life. The recording was strictly for private circulation, and was sent to me by a discographer in Wales who had acquired it from a jazz historian in New England, who had been sent it by a musician in Oklahoma. When you hear it, this last recorded performance, you can't help thinking about all the notes he played that were never recorded, and all the music that may have been inside him that somehow never got made at all.

That year, too, Dupree played his last public concert. I heard about it from Kent Kidwell, a music professor at the University of Central Oklahoma. Among his former pupils was a man called Paul Brewer, who specialized in working with prisoners and had acted as musical director of the Joseph Harp Center band. One evening in 1980, Brewer took the band to the university to play for Kidwell's students. In a large cafeteria on the campus, in front of an audience of three or four hundred young people, Dupree Bolton played in a formal setting for the last time, with armed guards on either side of the stage.

Eventually he was released, although there are records of a dispute, starting in 1981, in which he petitioned the US District Court of West Oklahoma in an attempt to win relief from the loss of 105 days of 'earned credits' after being found in possession of 'home brew, suspected of containing alcohol'—cans of vegetable juice and fruit juice, according to the charge, which he must have been accused of trying to ferment, probably by mixing it with sugar and letting it stand. Bolton seems to have taken pains over his appeal, filling in the documents in a careful hand. In March 1982, after being moved to the McLeod Correctional Center in Farris, Oklahoma, he wrote to the same court complaining that some of his legal documents, along with a box of clothing and other personal items, had been 'either lost or misplaced by the correctional officers assigned the duty of packing my belongings'. Nevertheless the court turned down his request to restore the lost days of remission.

In the early Eighties there were sightings of him jamming at jazz clubs in Oklahoma City, once sitting in with the great tenor saxophonist Dexter Gordon and apparently playing with his old brilliance. But before long he was in San Francisco, busking on the streets while receiving methadone treatment for his addiction. Those who came across him said that some of the characteristic qualities of his playing were still apparent. By chance they included David

Axelrod, who had produced *The Fox*.

'I was in San Francisco, walking through Ghirardelli Square,' Axelrod told me. 'And I saw this guy who looked familiar to me. He was very raggedy, and he was playing a trumpet, and he had a hat for people to throw money in. He was wearing a pair of old slacks, and an old shirt, and some kind of topcoat, kind of old and pretty funky, but he looked clean. He had a kind of beard—not stubble, but not a full beard, either. He looked like a man in his middle-to-late fifties, who'd seen a lot in his life. And I heard that sound. It was, how can I say it, a semblance of the sound he used to have. He'd never sounded like Miles Davis, which was what most young trumpeters were after, and he didn't sound like Dizzy Gillespie, either. He always sounded like himself.'

Axelrod approached him. 'I said, "Are you Dupree Bolton?" He said yes, and I told him who I was. He grabbed me and hugged me, which was a surprise. I didn't really know him that well. His attitude was very different. He was very friendly, and in the days when I knew him before he had not been the friendliest of people. That was his character. I always thought that even if he hadn't been a junkie, he'd have been just the same. But he must have changed. The belligerence had gone. We talked about *The Fox*. What else did we have to talk about? We talked about Harold and Frank and Elmo. And then we said goodbye. He gave me another hug.'

The nickels and dimes that Dupree Bolton earned from busking were certainly never supplemented by an income from the recordings he left behind, although the two albums which preserve his brilliance for posterity are available all over the world. The reputation of *The Fox* continues to grow, and although its ownership passed through various hands it has never been out of print. *Katanga!* was reissued in 1999 as part of a series called *West Coast Classics*.

What did he think of his gift for music, and of his life in this world? In all his sixty-four years it seems that no one, not his girlfriend or his bandleaders or even his sister, learned to know him well enough to be able to draw conclusions. Just like me, who never met him, they were left to make assumptions. People knew one facet of him—the trumpeter, the junkie, the sharp-dressed man, the criminal, the lover, the paranoiac—or maybe sometimes two, but the whole man remained a secret, perhaps also to himself.

Although Curtis Amy described Bolton as 'embedded in music', it seems probable that his talent was never going to prevail over the other imperatives that controlled his life. Many of his contemporaries had their careers dislocated or even destroyed by heroin, but music usually retained its priority to them. It was how they defined themselves, first and foremost. Charlie Parker and Chet Baker were still playing right up to the time they died. With Dupree Bolton, however, there hardly seemed to be a contest between the elements of his character. He had the talent, and he let it go.

Perhaps, as Curtis Amy suggested, he knew his own worth as a musician. He cannot possibly have imagined how great the reach of his music would turn out to be. The imbalance between what his listeners received for their small investment in his music and what he received for it in terms of remuneration—a matter of a few hundred dollars, a T-bird, some suits and a couple of trumpets—may not be our fault, but it must always be a source of unease.

He may or may not have been a very nice man. His weaknesses may have damaged whatever goodness was in him. The precision with which his story conforms to the myth of the foredoomed jazz genius can make it uncomfortable to press his claim too forcefully. He wouldn't have changed the course of jazz, even if fate had arranged his life differently. But I can't persuade myself that I was wrong to feel so strongly about him. Listening once again to the few minutes of music that he left behind almost forty years ago makes me think that, for all the sadness and confusion and waste in this story, for all the disappearances and disappointments, for all the holes he made in his own life and those of the people who knew him, the fact that Dupree Bolton found his self-expression in the language of jazz turned out, in the end, to be not just my good luck but his, too. □

NOTES ON CONTRIBUTORS

Diana Athill was one of the most respected editors in British publishing during her fifty-year career. 'Editing Vidia' is taken from her forthcoming memoir, *Stet*, which will be published by Granta Books in August this year. Granta Books is also republishing her documentary novel *After a Funeral*. She lives in London.

Kent Klich is a Swedish photographer and former psychologist. He joined Magnum Photos in 1998. His previous photography projects include *The Book of Beth* (Aperture), about the life of a drug addict and prostitute; and *El Niño* (Syracuse University Press), about street children in Mexico City. He is currently photographing children with HIV/Aids in Romania with the help of a grant from the Hasselblad Foundation.

Hanif Kureishi's 'The Umbrella' appeared in *Granta* 65. His new collection of short stories, *Midnight All Day*, has recently been published by Faber. He is working on a new novel, *Gabriel's Gift*.

Keith Ridgway was born, lives and works in Dublin. His first novel, *The Long Falling*, was published by Faber in Britain and Houghton Mifflin in the United States. A collection of short stories, *Standard Time*, will be published later this year.

Graham Swift's memoir of Ted Hughes, 'Fishing, Writing and Ted', appeared in *Granta* 65. His most recent novel, *Last Orders* (Picador/Vintage), won the 1996 Booker Prize.

Paul Theroux's 'Unspeakable Rituals' appeared in *Granta* 61. His most recent book was *Sir Vidia's Shadow: A Friendship across Five Continents* (Hamish Hamilton/Houghton Mifflin). A compilation of his travel-writing, *Fresh-Air Fiend* (Penguin/Houghton Mifflin), is published this year.

Henk van Woerden is a novelist and painter. He lives in Amsterdam. 'The Assassin' is taken from *A Mouthful of Glass* which will be published by Granta Books this summer. **Dan Jacobson** has written fiction and non-fiction on many subjects. 'Arguing with the Dead', an extract from his most recent book *Heshel's Kingdom* (Hamish Hamilton/Northwestern University Press), appeared in *Granta* 60.

Richard Williams has written books on Miles Davis, Bob Dylan, and the racing driver Ayrton Senna. A collection of his music pieces, *Long Distance Call*, is published later this year by Aurum Press. He is chief sports writer for the *Independent* in London.